Strategic Help Seeking
Implications for Learning and Teaching

◆ ❖ ◆

Strategic Help Seeking
Implications for Learning and Teaching
◆❖◆

Edited by

Stuart A. Karabenick
Eastern Michigan University

LEA LAWRENCE ERLBAUM ASSOCIATES, PUBLISHERS
1998 Mahwah, New Jersey   London

Lawrence Erlbaum Associates, Inc., Publishers
10 Industrial Avenue
Mahwah, NJ 07430
Cover design by Kathryn Houghtaling Lacey

Library of Congress Cataloging-in-Publication Data

Strategic help seeking : implications for learning and teaching / edited by Stuart A. Karabenick
      p. cm

    Includes bibliographical references and index.
    ISBN 0-8058-2384-0 (cloth : alk. Paper). --ISBN 0-
8058-2385-9
    (pbk. : alk. Paper)
    1. Teaching. 2. Learning. 3. Help-seeking behavior. 4.
Social interaction in children. 5. Motivation in education.
    6. Questioning. I. Karabenick, Stuart A.
    LB1027.S853 1998   98-11402
                                    CIP

Printed in the United States of America
10 9 8 7 6 5 4 3 2 1

for my parents, Florence and George Karabenick,
with love and appreciation

Contents

Preface

Following a seminal article by Sharon Nelson-Le Gall (1981), extensive research has examined the person and situation variables that affect learners' use of help seeking to accomplish academic tasks such as solving problems or completing writing assignments. Once identified with dependency, substantial evidence now indicates that seeking assistance from others is a valuable self-regulating, proactive learning strategy that can provide the foundation for autonomous achievement. Help seeking differs from other strategies because it is inherently social and thus susceptible to numerous cultural and interpersonal influences. In addition to whether or not help is needed, such culture-related traits as independence, respect for authority and competence, and norms of reciprocity and equity can determine whether or not learners will use others as learning resources. Asking a teacher or a friend for the answer to a math problem is, therefore, often more complex than, for example, deciding to organize one's notes or to rehearse a speech. Imagine the following self-examination by someone who is considering asking for help: Am I bothering them? Will they consider me incompetent? Is obtaining help really necessary? How can I pay them back? Maybe I'm not so smart after all. Others have asked questions, why not me? Issues raised by these and other questions have been the focus of considerable empirical research and theoretical development. For example, studies have examined the relationships between help seeking and self-esteem, ability, achievement goal orientation, and extent of need. And theoretical work has integrated help seeking within contemporary frameworks such as self-regulated learning and achievement goal theory.

It is a propitious time to capture the current state of knowledge, implications for teaching and learning, and future directions for research on help seeking. The last comparable work, DePaulo, Nadler & Fisher, *New Directions in Helping: Vol. 2. Help Seeking*, was published in 1983. A more recent edited book, Spacapam and Oskamp (1992), *Helping and Being Helped*, includes chapters on help seeking, but it focuses on nonacademic domains (e.g., seeking others for social support and psychological services) with less direct relevance for instructional settings. Chapters on help seeking and knowledge acquisition have been included in edited volumes on, for example, student perceptions in the classroom and self-regulated learning, but there is no collection that is specifically devoted to the implications of help seeking for learning and teaching.

In this volume we present work by the major contemporary contributors to the help-seeking literature. Authors were free to determine chapter content, including whether to present theoretical or empirical work. They were, however, asked to include implications for learning and teaching, which are stated throughout their work or in separate sections. The book is not explicitly divided into sections but is grouped by topic. After an introductory chapter that provides a conceptual overview and briefly summarizes the contributions, three chapters examine help seeking from complementary theoretical perspectives and make important distinctions between forms of help seeking. Two chapters then focus on how learners' achievement and social goals affect classroom help seeking. In addition to discussions of culture in several chapters, one is specifically devoted to cross-cultural comparisons of help seeking in Western cultures with that in Japan. Two chapters then focus on the most frequent manifestation of help seeking, that of question asking. The final chapter explores the implications for help seeking of the dramatic changes in access to information and communications technology, and raises the issue of social versus artificial agency in the help-seeking process.

The book is intended for educational researchers and for educational practitioners (e.g., teachers, school administrators, instructional designers) whose focus is on creating more effective learning environments. Critical to that goal is understanding social influences on learning in general and the help-seeking process in particular. Because teachers, especially, are often the target of requests for assistance, how they respond can have enormous impact on their students. Teachers are more likely to know when and how to respond to such requests if they understand the person and situation variables that prompted them. Just as important is understanding the conditions that promote passivity despite students' obvious need for assistance.

ACKNOWLEDGMENTS

Numerous individuals contributed directly or indirectly to this work. My colleague, John Knapp, has for many years provided wise counsel as either research collaborator or inveterate reader of manuscripts. Paul Pintrich and Bill McKeachie furnished a rich intellectual climate and considerable logistical support through the National Center for Research to Improve Post-Secondary Teaching and Learning at the University of Michigan. The inclusion of help seeking as a dimension of the Motivated Strategies for Learning Questionnaire, which emerged from that program, added to our understanding of how seeking help relates to students' use of other learning strategies and motivational tendencies. Collaboration with Rajeev Sharma, a visiting scholar from India, led to studies of student questioning and a scale to assess teachers' support of student questions. Considerable support for these and other studies was provided by the Graduate School at Eastern Michigan University (EMU), and the Research Excellence Fund, which for several years funded EMU's Research on Teaching and Learning Program. Discussions with my colleague, Richard Newman, in addition to his many insightful studies and theoretical work, contributed immensely to the creation of this volume.

The following EMU colleagues created a supportive and stimulating intellectual environment for this and other scholarly pursuits and are gratefully acknowledged: Morell Boone, Barbara Brackney, Jeffrey Dansky, Jan Collins-Eaglin, Robert Ferrett, Barry Fish, Monroe Friedman, Raouf Hanna, Michael Harris, George Klein, Julie Klein, Robert Kraft, Jennie McCafferty, Paul McKelvey, Mansoor Moaddel, Joseph Rankin, Charles Roth, Kenneth Rusiniak, Keith Stanger, Sylvia von Kluge, and Zakhour Youssef. Special thanks, as always, to Marsha Kolar for her expertise in manuscript preparation and editing, and to LEA editor, Naomi Silverman. Finally, deep appreciation to Julie, Robin, Scott, Rachel, and Leah for the many opportunities to personally experience what it means to give and to receive help.

—Stuart A. Karabenick

REFERENCES

DePaulo, B. M., Nadler, A., & Fisher, J. D. (Eds.). (1983). *New directions in helping: Vol. 2. Help seeking.* New York: Academic Press.

Nelson Le-Gall, S. (1981). Help-seeking: An understudied problem-solving skill in children. *Developmental Review, 1*, 224–246.

Spacapan, S., & Oskamp, S. (Eds.). (1992). *Helping and being helped.* Newbury Park, CA: Sage.

1

Help Seeking as a Strategic Resource

Stuart A. Karabenick
Eastern Michigan University

When learners are unable to solve problems, comprehend text materials, or understand their teacher's explanations, their options include not only continued persistence or abandoning tasks (Feather, 1961, 1963) but also obtaining assistance from a variety of sources, such as friends, classmates, teachers, and colleagues. The importance of social processes in knowledge acquisition has long been proposed (Vygotsky, 1978), but until recently, seeking assistance was considered to have little significance for learning. The predominant view, reflected in the early achievement motivation literature (e.g., Atkinson, 1964), stressed independence. Those who sought help were denigrated as dependent, and the act of relying on others was considered the antithesis of what it means to strive for excellence (e.g., Winterbottom, 1958). That view has changed dramatically, however, with the recognition of help seeking's strategic value in the learning process.

In addition to an edited series that laid the groundwork for subsequent research (DePaulo, Nadler, & Fisher, 1983), much of the credit for this change is attributable to Nelson-Le Gall's (1981) influential work that described help seeking as an important developmental skill. Focusing on the motives of those seeking help rather than the ostensible act, her analysis differentiated executive and instrumental goals, a distinction that is made repeatedly by contributors to the present volume. In many ways similar to the typical view of help seeking, executive help seeking employs others to reduce the cost of achievement, for example, by obtaining direct solutions to problems. This may constitute a short-term solution, but it does not decrease a learner's dependence on others when subsequently faced with similar problems. By contrast, instrumental help seeking is designed to increase mastery and competence by procuring only the assistance necessary to accomplish tasks independently. In this manner, instrumental help seeking has long-term strategic value.

Several other conceptual approaches also emphasize the value of help seeking. Ames (1983), for example, conceptualized help seeking within attribution theory—as a strategic achievement behavior. In action control theory (Heckhausen & Kuhl, 1985; Kuhl, 1985) help seeking is considered a way of acquiring volitional control over the environment in the pursuit of learning goals. Similarly, Rohrkemper and Corno (1988) regarded seeking assistance from others as an adaptation to difficulty or unfamiliarity, and Aberbach (now Arbreton) and her colleagues (Aberbach, Harold, & Eccles, 1990; Aberbach & Lynch, 1991) linked appropriate help seeking to autonomous learning behavior (Fennema & Peterson, 1985). And, in what is perhaps the most comprehensive explication, Newman (1991, 1994) identified adaptive help seeking as a strategy of self-regulated learners who efficiently seek necessary assistance in response to perceived lack of comprehension (Schunk & Zimmerman, 1994; Zimmerman & Martinez-Pons, 1986).

Considerable evidence supports this view of help seeking. That is, more active, engaged, and self-regulating learners who are more motivated to achieve are more likely to seek assistance when necessary (Karabenick & Sharma, 1994). For example, children who prefer challenge and independent mastery are more likely to seek such help (Arbreton, chap. 5, this volume; Arbreton & Wood, 1992; Nelson-Le Gall & Jones, 1990; Newman, 1990), and high school students who use other self-regulating strategies also seek help from peers, teachers, and adults. In response to poor performance, college students with achievement-oriented, help-relevant beliefs (Ames, 1983) and those who use a variety of cognitive, metacognitive, and self-regulating learning strategies (Karabenick & Knapp, 1991) will also seek help more frequently.

Studies have focused on the conditions that affect help seeking in learning settings, complemented by work in the areas of health and social support (e.g., Spacapan & Oskamp, 1992; Veroff, Kulka, & Douvan, 1981; Wills, 1990). These include the conditions that prompt help-seeking episodes (Graesser, Person, & Huber, 1993; van der Meij, 1990); magnitude of need (Karabenick & Knapp, 1988; Nelson-Le Gall, 1987; Nelson-Le Gall & Glor-Scheib, 1985; Nelson-Le Gall et al., 1990;

van der Meij, 1990); psychological deterrents to seeking help, such as indebtedness to the provider of assistance (Greenberg & Wescott, 1983); individualistic cultural norms (van der Meij, 1986); embarrassment (Shapiro, 1983); self-esteem threat (Karabenick & Knapp, 1991; Fisher, Nadler, & Whitcher-Alagna, 1982); and characteristics of the source of assistance, such as the degree of formality (Knapp & Karabenick, 1988; Newman & Goldin, 1990) and communal versus exchange relationship status (Clark, 1983).

A considerable amount is known, therefore, about the basic determinants of help seeking and the help-seeking process. Contributions to this volume expand our understanding not only by reporting additional empirical studies but also by the more extensive integration of help seeking within major contemporary theoretical approaches: achievement goal theory (e.g., C. Ames, 1992; Dweck & Leggett, 1988; Meece, 1991; Nicholls, 1979, 1984) and self-regulated learning (e.g., Schunk & Zimmerman, 1994). What emerges is further support for the importance of help seeking as a strategic resource, which learners should employ and teachers should support, under conditions that would maximize its benefits. Furthermore, help seeking takes on greater significance within a social-interactionist framework that views it as an essential social-interactional process of learning in addition to its status as a self-regulatory strategy (Resnick & Nelson-Le Gall, 1996; Vygotsky, 1978). Its status as a learning strategy renders even more important the present contributions, which examine classroom, cultural, and technological factors that affect help seeking's adaptive use, with implications for the design of promotive learning environments.

OVERVIEW OF CHAPTERS

The volume begins with three chapters that consider help seeking within these theoretical approaches. In chapter 2, Richard Newman elaborates his model of adaptive help seeking, which is based on principles of self-regulated learning, by focusing on the social-interactive processes of students' help seeking in classrooms. Adaptive help seeking consists of a sequence of cognitive, metacognitive, and interpersonal events that maximize the efficiency and effectiveness of assistance for task mastery and subsequent autonomous learning. Optimally self-regulating learners effectively calibrate task difficulty, determine that help is necessary, formulate a request for assistance, select and approach a target person, and process the information obtained from the interaction. Although it is readily apparent that social-interactive factors are involved when selecting and approaching the help giver, Newman's analysis describes how social factors also impact motivational and affective determinants of cognition and metacognition at other stages of the help-seeking process. These influences begin in early childhood when self-regulated learning emerges from interactions with parents (or other caregivers) from whom children acquire the strategic skills related to seeking help and the value of these skills. He considers early affective experiences especially critical, suggesting that adaptive help seeking in classrooms would result from similar quality nurturance and support for autonomy. Studies indicate that personal relationships with teachers—based on friendship or instructional assistance—predict help-seeking intentions. Although instructional assistance becomes more important with age, teacher support and personal involvement remain critical. Classroom environment, such as the degree of autonomy and opportunities for collaborative learning, achievement goals, and self-perceptions of ability also determine whether, and from whom, students seek help. As Newman concludes (and which is documented amply in this volume, help seeking, determined by a complex interaction of many cognitive and motivational factors, is a social-interactional process influenced by academic and social goals, affective states, and contextual characteristics that can either facilitate or hinder its strategic role in the learning process.

Sharon Nelson-Le Gall and Lauren Resnick (chap. 3) define intelligence as "a set of social practices attuned to a sociocultural milieu ... a conception of skill acquisition that is tied at least as much to social competence as to cognitive development." From this perspective, seeking help is "not merely a self-regulatory learning strategy in the individual students' repertoire, [but also] a part of the social-interactional process of learning." Nelson-Le Gall and Resnick review how cultural values and features of the classroom influence achievement goals, beliefs, attitudes, values, and personal theories of intelligence (entity vs. incremental), and how these intervening variables affect help seeking. They contend that culture also affects help seeking by influencing how learners construe the rights, responsibilities, and roles that are rooted in intersubjectively negotiated experiences and community-valued practices. U.S. educational practices, which stress individual performance goals and discourage help seeking, are contrasted with more communally oriented non-Western cultures (e.g., Japan—see chap. 7). The authors discuss the relative emphasis placed on individualistic and community-oriented values in racial groups within the United States. They contend that African-American children's socialization is more likely to involve multigenerational networks, interpersonal relatedness, and collective responsibility, which results in greater value accorded interdependence and cooperative learning. This places African-American children at a disadvantage in the ubiquitous individualistic-oriented school environments that they typically encounter. Under those conditions, these students would be unable to use the cooperative strategies, including seeking and giving help, that are central to their socialization. They recommend that instructional settings become more cooperative and relation-oriented—communities of learners that would encourage help seeking, and other socially oriented learning practices and experiences.

In chapter 4, Arie Nadler elaborates the distinction between autonomous and dependent help seeking as a way of understanding the dilemma of asserting one's individuality versus depending on others. Autonomous help seeking, similar to Nelson-Le Gall's instrumental and Newman's adaptive constructs, is a means to achieving goals, an active social orientation, and a primary, mature, problem-focused (and thus more effective) coping strategy. Dependent help seeking, analogous to Nelson-Le Gall's executive help seeking, is associated with learners' over- or underutililization of assistance, relying on others to solve problems for them, or resigning themselves to accept their inability to accomplish their goals, respectively. With this distinction, Nadler is able to resolve inconsistencies in empirical studies of person-helper relationships, self-esteem, and cognitive processes in achievement settings. For example, in descriptive (epidemiological and field) studies, those in need prefer help from friends and family rather than from strangers, whereas the reverse occurs in experimental settings. The findings are reconciled by observing that epidemiological studies involve long-term relationships that permit considerable flexibility over when and how assistance is requested (e.g., disguising it as advice sought for somebody else). This allows people to maintain their autonomy in a way that is unavailable in short-term experiments, which offer only a dichotomous choice between failure and dependency-promoting assistance.

According to Nadler, autonomous help seeking is more likely in learning environments that promote mastery goals, high self-esteem, incremental beliefs about intelligence, the potential for reciprocity and environments that reduce performance goals, task ego-centrality, and entity beliefs about intelligence. Degree of perceived control and whether help seeking serves developmental (i.e., long-term) or task-specific goals emerge as especially critical for determining whether individuals seek autonomous or dependent help. High perceived control and a developmental perspective facilitate autonomous help seeking. In contrast, low levels of perceived control and the accompanying helplessness engender either dependent help seeking or unproductive task persistence that underutilize available assistance.

In chapter 5, Arbreton describes how elementary school students' help-seeking tendencies are a function of their personal goal orientations in the (mathematics) classroom context. In addition to students' intentions to avoid seeking help, she assessed independently their tendency to seek both instrumental and executive help from teachers or classmates. Results are consistent with the predicted relationships. Specifically, learning-focused goals predict instrumental help seeking, indicative of a concern with problem-solving and deeper processing. By contrast, relative ability and extrinsic goals, indicative of a more superficial approach to learning, are higher for students who either avoid help or report seeking executive help. Arbreton's findings emphasize the importance of differentiating between types of help seeking rather than treating it as a unitary dimension. Her results also suggest quite clearly that more adaptive, self-regulating forms of help seeking will emerge when teachers promote learning goals.

Allison Ryan and Paul Pintrich (chap. 6) expand the role of classroom goals to include the effects of students' concerns about social relationships and social status. Social relationship goals focus on establishing and maintaining close personal friendships, whereas social status goals reflect a concern with popularity and prestige within a group. Social goals parallel achievement goals in important ways. Relationship and task-focused goals are similar by virtue of their common focus on process—building relationships and learning new skills, respectively. Status and relative ability goals are similar, insofar as they both involve social comparisons and evaluation. There are additional parallels between achievement and social goals' influences on help seeking, and the interaction of goals with students' perceived cognitive and social competence. For example, just as students concerned with maintaining high ability relative to others are more likely to avoid seeking help (especially those with low task-related self-efficacy), avoidance is higher among students who worry that asking for help will negatively impact their social status, more so for students who view themselves as less socially competent. In addition to personal achievement goals, Ryan and Pintrich discuss how dimensions of learning environments (e.g., task structure, authority, evaluation, time; see Ames, 1992) and teacher social support affect student goals and help seeking. They advocate changes in instructional practices (e.g., Anderman & Maehr, 1994; Maehr & Midgley, 1996) that are likely to facilitate students' asking for help when necessary.

In chapter 7, David Shwalb and Seisoh Sukemune present a cross-cultural analysis that contrasts Western individualism with Japan's non-Western, collectivist values, where help seeking and help giving should emerge quite readily given such national characteristics as dependency, empathy, group effort, and cooperation. In Japan, cooperation is especially valued and, although its form changes and study skills and information acquisition become more individualistic in the higher grades, prosocial behavior is stressed throughout childhood and adolescence. However, help seeking in school does not occur as frequently as expected. One explanation is that teacher control and presentational-style teaching in Japanese primary, secondary, and college classes promote student passivity, which counters the sociocultural conditions that are conducive to help seeking. Japanese students also view their teachers as ultimate sources of knowledge (sensei), who are not to be questioned, even though students may attribute this reluctance to person (e.g., shyness, embarrassment) rather than situation factors (classroom structure, teacher omnipotence). Shwalb and Sukemune review research on help seeking by Japanese college students and find that it is generally consistent with results from studies of American students. More prevalent among Japanese students, however, is their heightened sensitivity to disturbing or confronting teachers and peers. The authors complement their analysis with personal reflections that illuminate the classroom dynamics that influence help seeking in Japanese schools. Calling for greater attention to cultural differences, they also recommend educational practices designed to promote help seeking by both Japanese and Western students.

We next focus on the most ubiquitous form of help seeking in learning settings—student questioning. In chapter 8, James Dillon examines the process, practice, and benefits of questioning for learning and development. The process begins with the experience of *perplexity*, a necessary condition without which questioning and learning cannot occur. Perplexity is the perception of an event that is inconsistent with existing knowledge (e.g., cognitive conflict, unachieved goals, and gaps). Perplexity is followed by an interrogative mood and the selection, formulation, and utterance of a question. The answer to questions is conjoined with existing beliefs, which can lead to a resolution of the initiating perplexity or to additional perplexity.

Given this process, Dillon proposes a scheme of practice, a set of interrelated activities designed to maximize the benefits of questioning for student learning, organized around instructional moments (assignments, discussions, exams), and five levels of questioning that vary in how questions are formulated and answers incorporated into existing structures. At the first level, for example, students are assigned the task of studying a preformulated question, developing the answer in discussion with others, and answering the question combined with its evaluation. By contrast, the fifth level requires that students formulate the question, enter into discussions to benefit from others' deliberations, and construct answers, which may lead to further questions and question–answer relationships. Dillon stresses the iterative nature of formulating, questioning, answering, evaluating and reformulating. Most important, he advocates that responsibility for the question–answer interaction lies with students, and not with teachers whose role should be to listen and facilitate rather than to direct.

As with help seeking in general, Dillon cites the cognitive, affective, and behavioral benefits of questioning. With respect to cognition, questions increase knowledge and are (a) essential for interacting with the world and the construal of meaning (e.g., King, 1991), which is a significant component of intelligence (Sternberg, 1987); (b) related to creativity (divergent thinking); and (c) important for problem solving and, of course, learning. Affective features of questioning refer to its active form of engagement, including motives, attitudes, beliefs, and interests. Behavioral features involve action (search behavior that enhances coping and mastery), interaction that includes social competence and interpersonal participation, and language, which provides the ability for active expression.

In chapter 9, Hans van der Meij presents a three-stage model of student questioning that includes stages for the onset of questioning, question development, and the search for, and processing of, an answer. As with Dillon, the onset of questioning is assumed to be characterized by perplexity, a condition precipitated by surprising or conflicting facts external to or presented by the person. Perplexity involves presuppositions, that is, assumptions present in questions, and presumptions regarding the motives and beliefs of the questioner, the most important of which is the validity of the question's presuppositions. Learners find the second stage, question development, most difficult because it involves both framing a question and determining its contents. Van der Meij observes that teachers often exert too much control at this stage, and he suggests reflective discourse and guided cooperative questioning (King, 1994) as likely to result in more productive questions. In addition to socially induced inhibition, the formation of questions and their expression is difficult for learners, which may account for why so many go unasked. Answering and answers, at Stage 3, focus on the search processes and the adequacy of information obtained given the question. There are also suggestions for promotive responses to student questions proposed by Dillon (1988). These include the avoidance of evaluative feedback by teachers and suggestions that teachers model the higher level questions they want their students to ask.

In the final chapter, Jane Keefer and I examine the implications for help seeking of changes in information and computer-mediated communication (CMC). The rapid increase in available information, the development of sophisticated tools to manage and retrieve it, and changes in the interaction between learners and sources of assistance raise several issues, such as: (a) How will new technologies affect the likelihood of help seeking? (b) What role will traditional information providers, such as library personnel, play, given that learners have more direct access to information resources? and (c) Are the features of CMC likely to facilitate or create barriers to those seeking assistance? We note similarities between models of the information search process, developed in the context of library and information sciences, and models of the help-seeking process, but question the proposed equivalence of seeking both help and information (e.g., Kuhlthau, 1993). We suggest that features of CMC, such as increased perceived anonymity and psychological distance and the minimization of social status cues, should facilitate help seeking, which has considerable importance for information seekers and providers (e.g., library reference personnel). Both CMC and information technology in general are altering the role of teachers from that of seer to that of guide in the learning process. Understanding the changes in their relationship to information can sensitize teachers to how they can best facilitate strategic help seeking.

We also speculate that seeking help may take on different meaning as assistance from artificial sources becomes increasingly sophisticated and assumes more human characteristics, such as the use of natural language interactions and speech (e.g., HAL in Arthur C. Clarke's 2001). For example, rather than opting for artificial assistance automatically signaling that one has engaged in self-help, such actions may increasingly be construed as help seeking to the extent that the source is responded to as a social agent. Whereas features that promote viewing them as social agents could result in facilitating their effective use, we caution that the reverse is also possible if what we now understand about the deterrents of help seeking are not taken into consideration.

REFERENCES

Aberbach (Arbreton), A. J., & Lynch, S. (1991, April). *When getting help is helpful: Age and gender differences in children's autonomous help-seeking.* Paper presented at the biennial meeting of the Society for Research in Child Development, Seattle, WA.

Aberbach (Arbreton), A. J., Harold, R., & Eccles, J. S. (1990, April). *Parental helping behaviors and children's autonomous help-seeking.* Paper presented at the annual meeting of the American Educational Research Association, Boston, MA.

Ames, C. (1992). Classrooms: Goals, structures, and student motivation. *Journal of Educational Psychology, 84,* 261–271.

Ames, R. (1983). Help-seeking and achievement orientation: Perspectives from attribution theory. In B. M. DePaulo, A. Nadler, & J. D. Fisher (Eds.), *New directions in helping: Vol. 2. Help seeking* (pp. 165–186). New York: Academic Press.

Anderman, E., & Maehr, M. L. (1994). Motivation and schooling in the middle grades. *Review of Educational Research, 64,* 287–309.

Arbreton, A. J., & Wood, S. (1992, March). *Help-seeking behaviors and children's learning preferences in the middle school years.* Paper presented at the biennial meeting of the Society for Research on Adolescence, Washington, DC.

Atkinson, J. W. (1964). *An introduction to motivation.* Princeton, NJ: Van Nostrand.

Clark, M. S. (1983). Reactions to aid in communal and exchange relationships. In B. M. DePaulo, A. Nadler, & J. D. Fisher (Eds.), *New directions in helping: Vol. 2. Help seeking* (pp. 205–229). New York: Academic Press.

DePaulo, B. M., Nadler, A., & Fisher, J. D. (Eds.). (1983). *New directions in helping: Vol. 2. Help seeking.* New York: Academic Press.

Dillon, J. T. (1988). *Questioning and teaching: A manual of practice.* New York: Teachers College.

Dweck, C., & Leggett, E. L. (1988). A social-cognitive approach to motivation and personality. *Psychological Review, 95,* 256–273.

Feather, N. T. (1961). The relationship of persistence at a task to expectations for success and achievement-related motives. *Journal of Abnormal and Social Psychology, 63,* 552–561.

Feather, N. T. (1963). Persistence at a difficult task with an alternative task of intermediate difficulty. *Journal of Abnormal and Social Psychology, 66,* 604–609.

Fennema, E. H., & Peterson, P. L. (1985). Autonomous learning behavior: A possible explanation of gender-related differences in mathematics. In L. C. Wilkinson & C. B. Marrett (Eds.), *Gender influences in classroom interaction* (pp. 17–35). New York: Academic Press.

Fisher, J. D., Nadler, A., & Whitcher-Alagna, S. (1982). Recipient reactions to aid. *Psychological Bulletin, 91,* 27–54.

Graesser, A. C., Person, N., & Huber, J. (1993). Mechanisms that generate questions. In T. W. Lauer, E. Peacock, & A. C. Graesser (Eds.), *Questions and information systems* (pp. 167–187). Hillsdale, NJ: Lawrence Erlbaum Associates.

Greenberg, M. S., & Westcott, D. R. (1983). Indebtedness as a mediator of reaction to aid. In J. D. Fisher, A. Nadler, & B. M. DePaulo (Eds.), *New directions in helping: Vol. 1. Recipient reactions to aid* (pp. 85–112). New York: Academic Press.

Heckhausen, H., & Kuhl, J. (1985). From wishes to action: The dead ends and short cuts on the long way to action. In M. Frese & J. Sabini (Eds.), *Goal directed behavior: The concept of action in psychology* (pp. 134–160). Hillsdale, NJ: Lawrence Erlbaum Associates.

Karabenick, S. A., & Knapp, J. R. (1988). Help seeking and the need for academic assistance. *Journal of Educational Psychology, 80,* 406–408.

Karabenick, S. A., & Knapp, J. R. (1991). Relationship of academic help seeking to the use of learning strategies and other instrumental achievement behavior in college students. *Journal of Educational Psychology, 83,* 221–230.

Karabenick, S. A., & Sharma, R. (1994). Seeking academic assistance as a strategic learning resource. In P. Pintrich, D. Brown, & C. E. Weinstein (Eds.), *Student motivation, cognition, and learning: Essays in honor of Wilbert J. McKeachie* (pp. 189–211). Hillsdale, NJ: Lawrence Erlbaum Associates.

King, A. (1991). Effects of training in strategic questioning on children's problem-solving performance. *Journal of Educational Psychology, 83,* 307–317.

King, A. (1994). Autonomy and question asking: the role of personal control in guided student generated questioning. *Learning and Individual Differences, 6,* 163–185.

Knapp, J. R., & Karabenick, S. A. (1988). Incidence of formal and informal help-seeking in higher education. *Journal of College Student Development, 29,* 223–227.

Kuhl, J. (1985). Volitional mediators of cognition-behavior consistency: Self-regulatory processes and action versus state orientation. In J. Kuhl & J. Beckmann (Eds.), *Action control: From cognition to behavior* (pp. 101–128). New York: Springer-Verlag.

Kuhlthau, C. C. (1993). *Seeking meaning: A process approach to library and information services.* Norwood, NJ: Ablex.

Maehr, M. L., & Midgley, C. (1996). *Transforming school culture.* Boulder, CO: Westview Press.

Meece, J. (1991). The classroom context and students' motivational goals. In M. Maehr

& P. Pintrich (Eds.), *Advances in motivation and achievement*, (Vol. 7, pp. 261–285). Greenwich, CT: JAI.

Nelson-Le Gall, S. (1981). Help-seeking: An understudied problem-solving skill in children. *Developmental Review, 1*, 224–246.

Nelson-Le Gall, S. (1987). Necessary and unnecessary help-seeking in children. *Journal of Genetic Psychology, 148*, 53–62.

Nelson-Le Gall, S., & Glor-Scheib, S. (1985). Academic help-seeking and peer relations in school. *Contemporary Educational Psychology, 11*, 187–193

Nelson-Le Gall, S., & Jones, E. (1990). Cognitive-motivational influences on children's help-seeking. *Child Development, 61*, 581–589.

Nelson-Le Gall, S., Kratzer, L., DeCooke, P., & Jones, E. (1990). Children's self-assessment of performance and task-related help seeking. *Journal of Experimental Child Psychology, 49*, 245–263.

Newman, R. S. (1990). Children's help-seeking in the classroom: The role of motivational factors and attitudes. *Journal of Educational Psychology, 82*, 71–80.

Newman, R. S. (1991). Goals and self-regulated learning: What motivates children to seek academic help? In M. L. Maehr & P. R. Pintrich (Eds.), *Advances in motivation and achievement* (Vol. 7, pp. 151–183). Greenwich, CT: JAI.

Newman, R. S. (1994). Adaptive help seeking: A strategy of self-regulated learning. In D. H. Schunk & B. J. Zimmerman (Eds.), *Self-regulation of learning and performance: Issues and educational applications* (pp. 283–301). Hillsdale, NJ: Lawrence Erlbaum Associates.

Newman, R. S., & Goldin, L. (1990). Children's reluctance to seek help with schoolwork. *Journal of Educational Psychology, 82*, 92–100.

Nicholls, J. (1979). Quality and equality in intellectual development: The role of motivation in education. *American Psychologist, 34*, 1071–1084.

Nicholls, J. (1984). Achievement motivation: Conceptions of ability, subjective experience, task choice, and performance. *Psychological Review, 91*, 328–346.

Resnick, L., & Nelson-Le Gall, S. (1996, April). *Socializing intelligence*. Paper presented at the meeting of the Piaget-Vygotsky 1996 Centenary Conference, Brighton, England.

Rohrkemper, M., & Corno, L. (1988). Success and failure on classroom tasks: Adaptive learning and classroom teaching. *The Elementary School Journal, 88*, 297–312.

Schunk, D. H., & Zimmerman, B. J. (Eds.). (1994). *Self-regulation of learning and performance: Issues and educational applications*. Hillsdale, NJ: Lawrence Erlbaum Associates.

Shapiro, E. G. (1983). Embarrassment and help-seeking. In B. M. DePaulo, A. Nadler, & J. D. Fisher (Eds.), *New directions in helping: Vol. 2. Help seeking* (pp. 143–163). New York: Academic Press.

Spacapan, S., & Oskamp, S. (Eds.). (1992). *Helping and being helped*. Newbury Park, CA: Sage.

Sternberg, R. (1987). Questioning and intelligence. *Questioning Exchange, 1*, 11–14.

van der Meij, H. (1986). *Questioning: A study on the questioning behavior of elementary school children*. The Hague, The Netherlands.

van der Meij, H. (1990). Question asking: To know that you don't know is not enough. *Journal of Educational Psychology, 82*, 505–512.

Veroff, J. B., Kulka, R. A., & Douvan, E. (1981). *Mental health in America: Patterns of help-seeking 1957–1976*. New York: Basic Books.

Vygotsky, L. S. (1978). *Mind in society: The development of higher psychological processes* (M. Cole, V. John-Steiner, S. Scribner, & E. Saberman, Eds.). Cambridge, MA: Harvard University Press.

Wills, T. A. (1990). Social support and the family. In E. Blechman & M. McEnroe (Eds.), *Emotions and the family* (pp. 75–98). Hillsdale, NJ: Lawrence Erlbaum Associates.

Winterbottom, M. (1958). The relation of need for achievement to learning experiences in independence and mastery. In J. Atkinson (Ed.), *Motives in fantasy, action, and society* (pp. 453–478). Princeton, NJ: Van Nostrand.

Zimmerman, B. J., & Martinez-Pons, M. (1986). Development of a structured interview for assessing student use of self-regulated learning strategies. *American Educational Research Journal, 23*, 614–628.

Adaptive Help Seeking: A Role of Social Interaction in Self-Regulated Learning

Richard S. Newman
University of California at Riverside

Students often do not take an active role in their own learning. For one thing, they tend not to seek help from their teacher or classmates when they encounter academic difficulties. Despite awareness of difficulties they may have, and despite availability of assistance, many students tend to persist unsuccessfully on their own, give up prematurely, or sit passively, waiting for the teacher to come to them. Recent research aimed at understanding why this is the case and what can be done to help students become more active and successful learners is based on the assumption that help seeking can be viewed as an adaptive strategy of self-regulated learning (see Schunk & Zimmerman, 1994). Self-regulated learners are characterized by their purposeful control over academic outcomes. Their activity is combined with goals of learning and beliefs of efficacy; they monitor their performance and apply cognitive and environmental resources as tasks demand. As such, self-regulated learners are aware of occasional difficulty and have the wherewithal, self-determination, and sometimes even a sense of challenge, to remedy that difficulty.

This view of adaptive help seeking contrasts sharply with an older, more traditional view, whereby seeking help indicates a student's incompetence, immaturity, and dependence on others. Since the early 1980s, research has followed the lead of Nelson-Le Gall (1981, 1985) in differentiating between help seeking that indicates overdependence and help seeking that indicates a striving for mastery and academic independence. It has become clear that when fused with one set of goals, intentions, and knowledge, raising one's hand and asking for help are behaviors that may maintain a student's dependence on others. When fused with a different set of goals, intentions, and knowledge, the same behaviors function as a means for overcoming difficulty in learning and, in the long run, achieving mastery and autonomy.

The goal of this chapter is to further understanding of adaptive help seeking in the classroom. In order to pursue the goal, it is necessary to consider help seeking from both a cognitive-strategy perspective and a social-interactional process. Students who adaptively seek help are aware of their difficulty and needs, and they link this awareness to an action in order to address the difficulty. In this sense, seeking assistance is a volitional strategy for maintaining task involvement, averting possible failure, and optimizing the chance for mastery (Corno, 1989; Kuhl, 1985). Help seeking is also a classroom social-interactional process that is initiated by the learner. At first glance, "ideal" self-regulated learners might appear to be self-sufficient; however, they frequently must regulate cognitive activity through interaction with teachers and classmates. Adaptive help seeking is qualitatively different from other strategies of self-regulated learning that the child carries out alone or perhaps with the assistance of notes, reference books, or a computer: It necessarily involves another person.

I begin the chapter by briefly discussing adaptive help seeking from these two perspectives (a cognitive strategy and a social-interactional process). In previous work, I focused on the first perspective (see Newman, 1991, 1994). Here, I focus on the second by addressing affective and motivational factors in the social-interactional process of help seeking and examining developmental aspects of this process.

ADAPTIVENESS OF HELP SEEKING
IN THE CLASSROOM

Expanding Nelson-Le Gall's (1985) sequence of actions and decisions in instrumental help seeking, Newman (1991, 1994) proposed that adaptive help seeking in the classroom involves the student

1. being aware of task difficulty;
2. considering all available information (e.g., regarding task demands, personal resources, and costs and benefits) in deciding (a) the necessity of the request: Is it necessary that I ask another person for help? or, alternatively, Can I persevere?, or Can I try a new strategy, or Can I take an educated guess?, or Can I wait for help?, or Do I give up?; (b) the content or form of the request: What should I ask? or How shall I formulate the particular question?; (c) the target of the request: Whom

should I ask? (i.e., the teacher or a classmate);
3. expressing the request for help in a way that is most suitable to the particular circumstance; and
4. processing the help that is received in such a way that the probability of success in subsequent help-seeking attempts is optimized.

To what degree are students aware and consciously in control of these help-seeking actions and decisions? An important assumption of the present view of adaptive help seeking, and of self-regulated learning in general, is that learners reflect on their mental activity, especially at times of difficulty. Because of its self-reflective nature, adaptive help seeking can be considered a metacognitive strategy. A number of the individual actions and decisions making up the help-seeking process can be described as cognitive or metacognitive. These are briefly discussed next.

First, being aware of task difficulty is a function of students' metacognitive monitoring or awareness of their current knowledge state. Awareness of task difficulty, a feeling of knowing, and calibration of comprehension exemplify a major metacognitive function (e.g., Flavell, 1979; Markman, 1981; Pressley, Levin, Ghatala, & Ahmad, 1987). W

Second, requests for help that are necessary are restricted, presumably to occasions when students recognize that their knowledge or comprehension is lacking and they cannot independently resolve the difficulty. Opportunities for mastery are maximized when students are challenged by difficulty, but only to a point; beyond that point, further independent work would be frustrating and counterproductive (Covington, 1992). Determining the necessity of asking for help rather than choosing an alternative strategy is a function of students' reflecting on their sense of task difficulty in relation to (a) their knowledge and beliefs about alternative strategies (Paris & Newman, 1990; Pressley, Borkowski, & Schneider, 1987), and (b) their beliefs and feelings about themselves, for example, perceived competence (Harter, 1983), self-efficacy and self-confidence (Schunk, 1989), and achievement goals (Dweck, 1986; Nicholls, 1979).

Third, determining how the request should be worded to match the specific task demands is a function of students' knowledge and skills of discourse (C. R. Cooper, Marquis, & Ayers-Lopez, 1982; Wilkinson & Calculator, 1982). In theory, adaptive help seekers explicitly address their difficulty, both averting short-term failure and optimizing the chance for long-term mastery (e.g., by not asking for unnecessary help). Requests for explanations, clarification of information, confirmation of uncertain answers, and justifications tend to be relatively frequent among self-regulated learners (Karabenick & Knapp, 1991; Newman & Schwager, 1995; Zimmerman & Martinez-Pons, 1986).

Important in operationalizing adaptiveness is the degree to which the request meets task demands. A match depends on, at least partially, how much task-specific knowledge students already have as well as their motivational goals. So, for example, when considering a choice among different types of requests for clarification (e.g., a hint vs. a direct request for the correct answer), one can imagine that hints are most appropriate when students have partial knowledge as well as a desire for challenge. Yet, directly asking for the correct answer might also be adaptive at times, for example, when students have no knowledge in a particular task domain and they can use the answer for debugging and self-correcting previously unsuccessful solutions (Newman & Schwager, 1995).

Fourth, students' processing the help that they receive is certainly cognitive. Although the definition of adaptive help seeking does not require that requests necessarily lead to, for example, successfully solving a math problem, understanding a paragraph of text, or completing a reading assignment, adaptive help seeking does presume that students are goal-directed and purposefully striving for long-term success. Hence, adaptive help seekers profit from good communication and information processing skills of listening, integrating incoming information, and evaluating the quality of the response. These skills are important in deciding whether further help is needed. If it is, students will build on, and benefit from, answers to earlier requests for information.

The remaining components of the help-seeking process, that is, choosing an appropriate target and expressing the request to that person, can best be examined from a social-interactional perspective. Initiating the social interaction necessary to get assistance is when many students abort their help-seeking efforts. Affective and motivational factors strongly come into play at the time of choosing and approaching a particular individual for assistance. The critical role of an affective and motivational filter through which the cognitive processing involved in help seeking presumably occurs (Newman, 1994) is evident when one considers students who do not bother to reflect on or take control of their own learning, in spite of necessary cognitive capabilities to do so. Students have personal feelings about their capabilities and about school that they bring to the classroom. Affective histories as well as current feelings about themselves, teachers, and classmates determine the degree to which students are comfortable in revealing that they need help. Students have academic goals, expectancies, and values that they also bring to the classroom. A desire to learn and be challenged, a desire not to look "dumb" in front of others, and a desire to finish an assignment as quickly as possible must influence, in very different ways, students' decisions and actions regarding help seeking.

It should be noted that the order in which the components of the help-seeking process are presented here is not meant to imply a fixed sequence of decision making in the student's mind. Presumably, there is a nonsequential and interactive nature to the processing (Graesser & McMahen, 1993). So, for example, a student who feels anxious and does not want to look dumb in class might rethink or edit certain decisions and conclude that a request for help was not really necessary after all.

SOCIAL INTERACTION AND HELP SEEKING

Affective factors (e.g., emotions, feeling states, and attitudes) and cognitive-motivational factors (e.g., self-perceptions of ability, perceptions of control, causal attributions, expectancies for success and failure, and achievement goals) are integrally involved in the social-interactional process of help seeking. The relation between the two sets of factors is not well understood, however. In the following discussion, I separate affect and motivation for organizational reasons rather than any specific theoretical reason.

Affective Factors in Help Seeking

How do students feel about seeking assistance in the classroom? How is it that students come to feel comfortable or uncomfortable, going up to the teacher or a classmate to ask for help? We can learn about the role of affect in the social interaction of help seeking by examining: (a) early formation of children's self-regulatory functions, (b) students' feelings about different helpers, and (c) students' feelings about different environmental supports for learning.

Social and Affective Origins of Self-Regulation.   How students approach difficulties in the classroom must, to some extent, reflect their earlier experiences in dealing with the many facets (e.g., novelty, frustration, and challenge) of normal developmental tasks. Can we trace the beginnings of self-regulated learning, and more specifically, adaptive help seeking, to the home? Further, does an understanding of the social and affective origins of the child's capacity for self-regulation help in understanding and facilitating adaptive help seeking in the classroom?

The term, self-regulation, has been used prominently in the contexts of sociocultural views of human development (e.g., Vygotsky, 1978; Wertsch, 1985) and research on mother–child interaction and affect regulation (e.g., Garber & Dodge, 1991; Kopp, 1991; Stern, 1985).

According to Vygotsky (1978), a child's cognitive development is necessarily linked to social influences. The child is not just a recipient of knowledge from more skilled individuals. Rather, the child is an active participant in social interaction with an adult caregiver—usually a parent. Tasks, such as reading stories, categorizing objects, and assembling puzzles, are worked on intersubjectively, that is, with shared understanding of the task and goals (e.g., Wertsch, 1979; Wood, Bruner, & Ross, 1976). Assistance, or coaching, is provided in the form of scaffolding, whereby the adult carefully monitors how the child is doing and what the child needs so that just the right amount of help—not too little and not too much—can be given. The adult provides needed assistance and responsiveness, weans the child from unneeded assistance, and shares a sense of goal-directedness. Executive functioning becomes internalized. In time, the child has not simply internalized the adult's directives, but has taken over the adult's regulating role and goals (for further discussion, see Diaz, Neal, & Amaya-Williams, 1990; Wertsch, 1985).

It is important to note that this transition from other-regulation to self-regulation, or processing at an interpsychological to intrapsychological plane of functioning, is not a simple, linear progression. Cognitive and social development are intimately and dynamically intertwined. What seems to be overlooked, or perhaps just understood implicitly, in accounts of Vygotsky's theory is the individual's ongoing, lifelong need to return to an interpsychological plane of functioning. When children are on their own, at times of task difficulty, they may have to seek assistance from someone else. When goals require volitional protection and maintenance, self-regulation may require help seeking. An integral part of self-regulation then is knowing when it is desirable, or indeed necessary, to fall back to other-regulation.

How do children come to know that help seeking has such an important instrumental value and that question asking, in particular, can serve that instrumental function? Although the function of other-regulation can be provided at times by peers (Azmitia, 1988; Tudge & Rogoff, 1989; Verba, 1994), teachers and mentors (Lave, 1988; Palincsar & Brown, 1984), and even interactive computer tools (Salomon, Globerson, & Guterman, 1989), it is the parent-child relationship that is the most natural context for the child's transformation from interpsychological to intrapsychological functioning (Rogoff & Gardner, 1984). I believe it is the *affective experiences* inherent in the early intersubjectivity between parent and child that are so critical for children's learning about the adaptiveness of help seeking.

Social origins of self-regulation can be traced to early parent–child interaction and the development of children's ability to regulate their affect. Attachment theory stresses the adaptive function, for the infant's survival, of physical and emotional closeness (Bowlby, 1969). Secure attachment between mother and her young infant is regulated by the mother through actions such as cuddling, holding, touching, and looking into each other's eyes. Within a context of social responsiveness and nurturance, the infant engages in a sharing of experiences about events and things and feels comfortable in exploring and seeking information from the environment (Ainsworth, Blehar, Waters, & Wall, 1978). By the time the infant is 7 to 9 months old, mother and infant share the focus of attention by joint pointing and gesturing, smiling, and vocalizing; and they share subjective feeling states such as happiness, fear, and uncertainty. It is important that all these experiences involve an attunement of mother's and infant's affect (Stern, 1985).

With the emergence of language and conversational communication, sharing also involves words (Bus & van IJzendoorn, 1988; Wertsch, 1979). From age 2 on, during joint problem solving with adults, children use speech when encountering difficulty. They communicate their frustration and ask for help. Young children's ability to talk about their feelings allows them to enlist the help of others in alleviating physical as well as emotional discomfort (Dunn & Brown, 1991). Especially in securely attached dyads, when children ask for help or advice, parents respond meaningfully, for example, by giving advice or instructions (van der Veer & van IJzendoorn, 1988). Ideally, children come to understand that verbally asking for help is an instrumental means both to solve difficult problems and to regulate their own affect.

Through social interaction at home, numerous opportunities exist for communication lessons that serve as parents' scaffolding for their children's help seeking. When children have difficulty with a task, adults may introduce additional assistance and encourage and instruct the children to actively seek needed assistance on their own (Radziszewska & Rogoff, 1988). Parents share and practice with their children the value of asking questions and the knowledge of when, how, and to whom to ask questions. This conditional knowledge of strategy use (cf. Paris, Lipson, & Wixson, 1983) helps prepare children for the important decisions (i.e., necessity, content, and target of the request) that define adaptiveness of help seeking. Furthermore, children observe how their parents ask questions of them and of each other. They observe how their parents solve problems and deal with adversity. No doubt, all these lessons are a natural part of "successful" parents' scaffolding, and unfortunately, may be missing from the homes of children who become non-self-regulated learners.

Intersubjectivity, affective attunement, joint problem solving, and shared goals are most likely to be experienced in families that provide security, nurturance, optimal challenges, and support for autonomy. It is presumed that children who have these experiences benefit both cognitively and emotionally. They are likely to develop instrumental competence (i.e., achievement orientation, social responsibility, and autonomy) as well as "mental muscle" for coping with frustration and difficulty, both intellectual and interpersonal (cf. Main, Kaplan, & Cassidy, 1985; Ryan & Stiller, 1991; Winnicott, 1965). The question at hand is whether the sorts of affective experience that characterize good parent–child relationships can be extrapolated to educational settings and used as a model for good teacher–student and peer relationships, in particular, with the aim of supporting students' academic help seeking.

Students' Feelings About Helpers.　A second way that we can learn about the role of affect in the social interaction of academic help seeking is by directly examining students' feelings about potential helpers. How do students perceive their relationships in the classroom with their teachers and classmates? Are there particular features of good teacher–student and peer relationships that support students' help seeking? A good place to start with answers to these questions is by examining what students say that they get out of help seeking, that is, their perceived costs and benefits of seeking assistance from teachers and classmates.

Mediating between a student having the ability to use a particular strategy and spontaneously using it is the student's consideration of costs and benefits (Paris & Newman, 1990). In theory, self-regulated learners believe that the potential benefits of using an effective strategy (e.g., the value of task success) outweigh the potential costs (e.g., the amount of effort required or the time taken away from competing activities). For adults, seeking help in job- and health-related situations typically evokes a threat to their self-esteem due to perceived personal inadequacy. Typical benefits are the resultant success and task mastery (Rosen, 1983; Shapiro, 1983).

For children as young as 8 years old, perceived costs and benefits of help seeking are similar to those of adults. Students associate low ability with unsolicited help from the teacher (Graham & Barker, 1990). They commonly fear negative reactions from their teacher, especially if there is an expectation that they should not require additional assistance. They fear embarrassment in the eyes of their classmates. In addition, students commonly report that teachers and classmates are unavailable or unwilling to help (Newman & Goldin, 1990; van der Meij, 1988). On a more positive note, however, students are also aware of the benefits of seeking help. In fact, elementary and middle-school students think the benefits of seeking help (e.g., "I think that asking questions helps me learn math," or "I feel smart when I ask a question during math") outweigh the costs (e.g., "I think the teacher might think I'm dumb when I ask a question," or "I feel like it's just too much of a bother to ask questions"; Newman, 1990). Over time, there is a growing recognition that asking for help has important academic benefits. Newman and Schwager (1993) asked students to choose a label for children who ask the teacher questions: third graders strongly identified them as the dumb kids rather than the smart kids, fifth graders were evenly split, and seventh graders strongly identified them as the smart kids.

Children's attitudes about individual helpers change significantly over the school years. For example, children become increasingly aware of numerous characteristics that distinguish effective helpers from ineffective helpers (Barnett, Darcie, Holland, & Kobasigawa, 1982). Whereas kindergartners seem concerned with personal aspects of helpers (e.g., niceness and kindness), children in middle-elementary and upper-elementary grades seem more concerned with academic aspects (e.g., competence and willingness to help). Similarly, Nelson-Le Gall and Gumerman (1984) showed that, with age, elementary-school children increasingly reason about helpers by focusing on traditional academic and social roles (e.g., "I ask the teacher for help because that's the teacher's job"). For adolescents, rationales for choosing a helper become more complex. Decisions are based on the helper's competence, expected guidance, and familiarity, as well as confidentiality and skill at communicating (Wintre, Hicks, McVey, & Fox, 1988).

These different attitudes about teachers and classmates are clearly reflected in students' actual choice of helpers. Elementary-school students generally prefer to go to teachers more than classmates when they need help with academic problems (Nelson-Le Gall & Gumerman, 1984). They believe that asking for help from teachers (vs. classmates) is more likely to result in learning and less likely to result in the helper thinking they are dumb (Newman & Goldin, 1990). Obviously, the structure of the classroom (e.g., whole-class vs. small-group), in particular the accessibility to the teacher and opportunities for working collaboratively with peers (see discussion later), helps determine students' experiences and attitudes about teachers and classmates. Regardless of the classroom structure implemented by teachers, however, it is fair to say that teachers have a tremendous influence on whether a student feels comfortable seeking assistance from either a teacher or classmates.

Throughout the elementary and middle-school grades, students' beliefs about the benefits of seeking help from the teacher (e.g., learning, feeling smart) have a positive, encouraging influence on the students' stated intentions of requesting academic help. At middle school, beliefs about potential costs (e.g., fear of looking dumb) also enter the picture and have a competing, that is, an inhibiting, influence on help seeking. This is not to say that younger children are not aware of potential costs; they are. With age and transition to middle school, however, thoughts and fears about potential costs take on a more prominent, causal role in students' decisions of whether to seek help (Newman, 1990; Newman & Schwager, 1993).

The personal relationships that teachers maintain with their students influence the general climate of the classroom and sense of belongingness, and hence set a facilitative or inhibitory tone for students' self expression (Goodenow, 1993; Moos, 1979). The importance of classroom climate, then, parallels the importance in infants' and young children's lives of parental sensitivity and responsiveness (van der Veer & van IJzendoorn, 1988). Teachers can establish a facilitative climate for help seeking in different ways. Newman and Schwager (1993) asked elementary and middle-school students about two different roles played by their teacher: (a) a person with whom there is mutual liking and friendship and (b) a person who directly encourages and answers task-related questions. We found that third graders more than fifth or seventh graders perceived their teacher as a source of personal friendship, whereas children in the upper two grades perceived their teacher as directly encouraging and responsive to questions. We asked the same students how likely they were to seek help from their teacher if they did not understand something in math class. Whereas perceptions of friendship were predictive of students' help seeking at all three grades, perceptions of teacher encouragement were also predictive, over and above the influence of perceptions of friendship, at Grades 5 and 7. Thus, although older students may be more attuned than younger ones to the academic side of helpers, the importance of the personal side of a helper–helpee relationship does not disappear.

Throughout the elementary and middle-school grades, teachers' personal involvement is clearly communicated to students. Teachers' involvement, operationalized as affection for their students (e.g., liking, appreciating, and enjoying), dedication of resources (e.g., aid, time, and energy), dependability (e.g., availability in case of need), and attunement (e.g., understanding, sympathy, and knowledge about the student), influences the degree to which students feel involved and respected in the classroom and comfortable with the classroom structure (e.g., regarding expectations and the availability of help and support; Skinner & Belmont, 1993). In turn, students' feelings influence their emotional engagement (happiness and interest), behavioral engagement (e.g., effort, attention, and help seeking), and actual achievement (Skinner, Wellborn, & Connell, 1990). Unfortunately, many teachers are not involved with their students and do not encourage them to seek help, or, worse yet, they stifle students' inquisitiveness and inhibit self-expression. It is not surprising that, when they do not feel involved or respected but instead experience a sense of personal failure, inadequacy, and low self-esteem, students show little behavioral or emotional engagement in the classroom (C.Ames & Archer, 1988; Covington, 1992).

In summary, students' feelings play a crucial role in task engagement. As students go through elementary school, their decisions and actions regarding help seeking are influenced by diverse feelings, attitudes, and perceptions regarding their teachers and classmates. As students transition to middle school, influences on help seeking become increasingly complex.

Students' Feelings About the Classroom. The structure or organization of classroom activity is an important feature around which teachers organize rules of feedback, student–teacher interaction, and communication among students. Different types of activity (e.g., whole-class, small-group, and individual) are associated with particular social-interactional norms, achievement goals, and, as a result, patterns of help-seeking attitudes and behavior (C. Ames, 1992).

During whole-class activity, there generally is less help seeking than during either of the other two types of classroom activity (Nelson-Le Gall & Glor-Scheib, 1985). It is important to note that students engaged in small-group activity, in comparison to students in whole-class activity, are relatively likely to seek help, not just from other students, but from the teacher as well (Meece, Blumenfeld, & Puro, 1989). Collaborative small-group activity is explicitly designed to promote children's interacting with one another in terms of both giving and receiving help, and often these interactions are positively related to achievement (C. R. Cooper, Marquis, & Ayers-Lopez, 1982; Rogoff & Gardner, 1984; Slavin, 1983; Webb, 1982). Collaborative activity facilitates students' help seeking for several reasons.

First, working in groups may facilitate students' initiative and task engagement because of a lack of normative comparison and competitiveness. It can be argued that the most salient feature of the upper-elementary, middle, and high school grades that inhibits students' willingness to seek help is the degree of normative comparison in the classroom. A classroom environment based on normative comparison typically promotes competitiveness and increases the opportunities for students to judge themselves negatively (Rosenholtz & Simpson, 1984). As a result, students, especially those with low achievement, attempt to maintain their sense of self-worth by not revealing that they have difficulty (Covington, 1992). Under these conditions, students invariably are reluctant to seek assistance.

Second, working in groups may facilitate task engagement because of students' accompanying sense of control over their own academic outcomes. Students' perception of having control is partially a function of teachers' expectations of students. Teachers have different expectations of, and exhibit different behavior toward, students with high and low achievement (H. M. Cooper, 1979; Eccles & Wigfield, 1985). Teachers view students with low achievement as less controllable than students with high achievement, and accordingly, attempt to control the timing, duration, and initiation of interactions with them. It is important that within-classroom differences in teachers' expectations and control-related behavior do not go unnoticed by the students (Weinstein, 1983). In fact, it is likely that the degree to which students perceive control to be in the hands of their teacher is inversely related to the degree to which students exert control over their own learning, for example, by seeking help. Students with high achievement, who generally are given autonomy and chances for self-direction, perceive an absence of teacher control and learn to initiate interactions with the teacher and classmates. Students with low achievement, on the other hand, generally perceive that they are being controlled and learn not to volunteer questions and answers; instead, they learn to be passive. It is likely that small-group activity gives students, especially students with low achievement, more of a sense of control over their own learning.

The importance of collaborative small-group activity for help seeking is illustrated in a study by Newman and Gauvain (1996). Sixth graders were observed as they worked in small groups during math class for ten weeks. At the end of the tenth week, students were given a questionnaire asking about their attitudes and goals and the strategies in which they had engaged. Several items measured how often students had sought help from their teacher (who was present, and walking around the room throughout the class) and from group members. Girls reported, more often than boys, that they asked for help from both the teacher and classmates when they did not understand something. Contrasting with this finding is Newman and Goldin's (1990) report of second-, fourth-, and sixth-graders' attitudes about help seeking. In that study, several items referred to students' concerns about negative reactions from the teacher and classmates when they asked questions in front of the whole class. Girls reported greater concern than did boys that the teacher might think they were dumb when they asked questions. The gender difference was significant in the context of math class, but not reading class.

In addition to illustrating how help seeking in elementary school can be facilitated with collaborative activity, the findings of these two studies point to an important implication regarding the gender differences in math achievement that are often reported in junior- and senior-high school students (Meece, Parsons, Kaczala, Goff, & Futterman, 1982). It is not uncommon for students to perceive math, compared to reading and language arts, to be more difficult and more contingent on help from the teacher (Licht & Dweck, 1984; Newman & Stevenson, 1990). Girls' reluctance to seek help from their teacher in math class in the elementary grades may be at least partially responsible for their not getting adequate help, and therefore, not performing as well as boys in later years. Clearly, there is a greater sense of vulnerability and reluctance for children—perhaps especially girls because of gender stereotyping of math—to raise their hand and ask for help in front of the whole math class. Findings from Newman and Gauvain (1996) and Newman and Goldin (1990), taken together, suggest that collaborative, small-group activity can be an important instructional tool to facilitate help seeking and learning among any group of students who may be at risk of poor performance (see also Slavin, 1983; Tharp & Gallimore, 1988; Webb, 1982).

Finally, in their study of 6th-graders working on collaborative math activities, Newman and Gauvain (1996) reported several correlational findings on students' choice of helper. The more important it was for students to do well, the more they reported seeking help from the teacher. The more students were engaged within their collaborative groups and the stronger their goals of social affiliation, the more students reported seeking help from group members. Findings support previous research, which shows that students have differential motivations for approaching different people for help; sometimes, the preference is for the teacher and, at other times, peers (Nelson-Le Gall & Gumerman, 1984). In the context of small-group activity, teachers may be sought by students who find it especially important to be successful and feel they sometimes have to go to the "source" for help when peers cannot meet their needs. On the other hand, peers may be sought by students who have a high need for social affiliation and perceive relatively few potential costs of embarrassment in interacting with their fellow group members.

In summary, students' feelings about help seeking reflect developmental processes, personal characteristics, and characteristics of the home and school. Prominent environmental features of the classroom that affect whether students feel comfortable seeking help include the availability of potential helpers, structure of activity, degree of normative comparison, and degree of shared control.

Motivational Factors in Help Seeking

The behavior of raising one's hand to ask a question can serve multiple functions and may be motivated by very different purposes. Theories linking achievement motivation to task engagement have emphasized a large number of cognitive constructs, for example, self-perceptions, perceived control, causal attributions, expectancies, task value, and goals. In the following section, I discuss two constructs, goals and self-perceptions of ability, that have been shown most clearly to influence students' academic help seeking.

Goals. Achievement-related goals have a positive effect on adults' and children's task engagement and performance (e.g., Diener & Dweck, 1978; Graham & Golan, 1991), and so it makes sense that goals would be important in explaining students' academic help seeking. Goals can be discussed both as situational characteristics of the classroom and as personal characteristics of the learner (Maehr & Pintrich, 1991).

Research focusing on achievement goals as a situational rather than a personal characteristic has distinguished between (a) learning and performance goals (Dweck, 1986), (b) mastery and performance goals (C. Ames & Archer, 1988), and (c) task-involved and ego-involved goals (Nicholls, 1979). Different goals in the classroom are associated with different achievement-related behaviors, such as attention, persistence, effort, and use of task-relevant strategies (C. Ames, 1992). For example, in classrooms that emphasize learning goals (or alternatively, mastery or task-involved goals), children are socialized to seek long-term mastery; success is seen as dependent on effort; and performance feedback stresses each individual's intellectual and social development. In classrooms that emphasize performance goals (or alternatively, ego-involved goals), children are socialized to get good grades and be judged able; success is seen as dependent on ability; and performance feedback stresses social comparison with classmates.

R. Ames (1983) argues that classroom goals have associated with them distinctive student attitudes and behaviors regarding help seeking. Classrooms that emphasize learning goals are presumed to encourage all students to deal with academic difficulty as a challenge, that is, with positive affect, increased persistence, and seeking of assistance when needed. Classrooms emphasizing performance goals, on the other hand, are presumed to lead to a wide dispersion of help-seeking attitudes and responses within the classroom. This is because of the salience of public evaluation and social comparison that generally accompanies performance goals. Although some students in such a classroom are likely to engage in adaptive help seeking, others are likely to deal with academic difficulty with maladaptive self-attributions, by exhibiting negative affect, and by giving up.

Experimental research in which students' goals have been manipulated to simulate classroom conditions shows how help seeking is perceived differently, depending on goals. According to Butler and Neuman (1995), second and sixth graders working on difficult puzzles under goals of task involvement explained that they occasionally avoided seeking help because they were striving for independent mastery. In contrast, under goals of ego involvement, students explained avoidance of help seeking as a way of masking low ability. Overall, students were more likely to ask for help, especially for hints (vs. answers), in the task-involved condition than in the ego-involved condition. Similarly, Newman and Schwager (1995) showed that third and sixth graders working under a condition of learning goals, in comparison with students given performance goals, were more likely to request confirmation of an answer on math problem-solving tasks. The presumption was that requesting a confirmation was indicative of self-regulated learning; that is, students were acquiring information to help them debug faulty solutions. Students given performance goals, on the other hand, were more likely than those given learning goals to show maladaptive, noninquisitive patterns of questioning (e.g., immediately asking for the correct answer without first attempting to do the problem on their own).

Research focusing on achievement goals as a personal rather than a situational characteristic has distinguished between intrinsic and extrinsic orientations (Harter, 1981) and has provided clear support for the importance of goals in self-regulated learning (Dweck & Leggett, 1988; Maehr & Pintrich, 1991). According to Harter (1981), children with an intrinsic orientation to learning are thought to strive toward independent mastery, to prefer academic challenge, and to show curiosity and interest in their work. In contrast, children with an extrinsic orientation are overly dependent on others, prefer relatively easy assignments, and do their schoolwork to satisfy the teacher and get good grades. Intrinsic (vs. extrinsic) orientation is strongly predictive of children's cognitive engagement, in general (Meece, Blumenfeld, & Hoyle, 1988), and of help seeking, in particular. Nelson-Le Gall and Jones (1990), for example, showed that the type of help 3rd- and

5th-grade students sought during task performance varied according to their goals. Students with an intrinsic orientation (i.e., striving for independent mastery) were more likely to seek help by asking for hints than by directly asking for answers on a vocabulary task, whereas students characterized as having an extrinsic orientation were just as likely to ask for hints and answers.

Newman (1990) showed a more complex relation between intrinsic orientation and help seeking, that is, one that involved different grade levels and different subscales of intrinsic orientation (i.e., striving for independent mastery and preference for challenge; Harter, 1981). Across Grades 3, 5, and 7, students who strongly preferred challenge were likely to seek help when they encountered difficulties in math class. A second subscale of intrinsic orientation, that is, striving for independent mastery, was related to help seeking differentially according to grade level. That is, at the two elementary grades, relatively weak striving for independent mastery was associated with help seeking, and at middle school, relatively strong striving for independent mastery was associated with help seeking. For younger children, then, two seemingly divergent purposes (challenge and dependency on the teacher) predicted help seeking; for older children, two seemingly convergent purposes (challenge and independent mastery) were predictive.

These findings remind us that motivational goals are personally constructed. Goals can be expected to have different meanings for different individuals and take on different meanings at different ages and grade levels (e.g., Eccles, Midgely, & Adler, 1984; Nicholls, 1979). So, young children may seek help for very different reasons than would older children. Indeed, early elementary-age students may seek help in order to maintain a certain degree of dependence on their teacher, and this may be quite appropriate if they feel unsure of themselves in their work and feel a need to "stay close to home." With development, and most important, successful learning and social-interactional experiences with adults, students' help seeking is more likely to be motivated by a desire to gain independent mastery and long-term autonomy.

Finally, it should be pointed out that this discussion focuses on achievement goals. Social goals, as well, need to be taken into account in understanding students' classroom motivation (Dodge, Asher, & Parkhurst, 1989; Urdan & Maehr, 1995; Wentzel, 1991). Although little research on social goals and help seeking has been reported, one can imagine possible relations. For example, goals of social status (e.g., gaining peer approval, being popular), social affiliation (e.g., making friends, having fun with friends), and social responsibility (e.g., being dependable, helping others) can be expected to affect students' help seeking in different ways. Students trying to gain social status probably will be encouraged to seek help if their peers value academic success. If, on the other hand, their peers reject behaviors that typically lead to school success, students probably will be inhibited from seeking help (see Berndt & Keefe, 1992; Ogbu, 1987). Goals of social affiliation are expected to facilitate help seeking, especially during classroom activities that involve small-group collaboration (Newman & Gauvain, 1996). When students' goals stress social responsibility, help seeking probably will be inhibited if being dependable and helping others preclude students from taking care of their own needs. On the other hand, help seeking might be facilitated if helping others actually frees students from social obligations so they can then take care of their own needs (Dodge et al., 1989).

In sum, when students do not have to worry about normative evaluation and are encouraged to work for the sake of mastery and intrinsic enjoyment, they are much more likely to ask for assistance when they face difficult tasks. The assistance that students seek under conditions of learning, or task-involved, goals is most likely to be adaptive for long-term mastery and success. Further research that takes into account the fact that students simultaneously pursue multiple achievement, as well as social, goals is expected to demonstrate complex motivational influences on help seeking in the classroom.

Self-perceptions of ability. A second motivational factor that influences students' help seeking is self-perceptions of ability. Self-perceptions of ability are considered part of the child's self-schema (i.e., a conglomerate of self-concept of ability, perceived academic competence, perceived self-efficacy, and self-esteem; see Markus & Nurius, 1986). There is consistent evidence of a strong, positive relation between students' self-perceptions of ability and their actual academic performance and achievement. Students who do relatively well have relatively good self-perceptions of ability (Harter, 1983; Harter & Connell, 1984; Newman, 1984; Schunk, 1989; Shavelson & Bolus, 1982). The relation between self-perceptions and task engagement is also positive. Students who perceive themselves as relatively capable and efficacious are relatively strategic and self-regulated in their learning (Schunk, 1989; Schunk & Zimmerman, 1994). Regarding the specific strategy of help seeking, however, the relation is more complex.

Students with high self-perceptions of ability (and concomitantly, high achievement) typically do not need much help (Karabenick & Knapp, 1988). However, if the need does arise, they are expected to be ready and willing to seek assistance from others. A vulnerability hypothesis predicts that students with low self-perceptions of ability are most reluctant to seek help because they feel they have the most to lose from others knowing that they are having academic difficulty (Karabenick & Knapp, 1991). An alternative consistency hypothesis predicts just the opposite. That is, students with high self-perceptions of ability are thought to be most reluctant to seek help because having, and letting others know about, academic difficulty is inconsistent with their existing self-perceptions (Nadler, 1983). Research shows that the resolution of these two competing hypotheses depends on students' achievement goals. In other words, self-perceptions of ability and achievement goals show an interactive effect on help seeking.

Under conditions of task-involvement, that is, when one's motivational goal is to learn and master a lesson without concern for performing better than others, failure generally is perceived as a natural part of the learning process and not indicative of global inadequacy (Nicholls, 1979). Under these conditions, individuals are relatively likely to interpret help seeking as an adaptive means of resolving problem difficulty and eventually mastering the material; so, reluctance to seek help should be minimal. If need for assistance is threatening to anyone under conditions of task involvement, it is expected to be students who already have low self-perceptions of ability (i.e., support for the vulnerability hypothesis).

Under conditions of ego involvement, that is, when one's motivational goal is to get good grades and be judged by others to be smart, failure is more likely to be perceived as indicative of global inadequacy (Nicholls, 1979). Under these conditions, a curvilinear relation between self-perceptions of ability and help seeking is expected. That is, help seeking is perceived as more threatening at both low and high levels than at intermediate levels of perceived ability. Working under ego-involved conditions, students with low self-perceptions are likely to perceive the need for help as confirming their inadequacy and hence are unlikely to seek help (i.e., further support for the vulnerability hypothesis). However, even students with high self-perceptions may be adversely affected by conditions that promote the belief that failure is due to global inadequacy and that compel them to constantly demonstrate superior performance. Under these conditions, failure is inconsistent with students' favorable self-perceptions so that even those with high self-esteem are unlikely to seek help (i.e., support for the consistency hypothesis).

Support for these predictions comes from correlational findings in elementary and middle school math classrooms that students with lower self-perceptions of ability and achievement tend to have greater concern about personal costs associated with seeking help (Newman,

1990; Newman & Goldin, 1990). The implication, in support of the vulnerability hypothesis, is that students who perceive themselves as academically weak tend to be afraid of looking dumb and thus are relatively unlikely to seek needed assistance from others. Experimental findings by Butler and Neuman (1995) showed that, under conditions of ego-involvement, elementary school students' skill level on a puzzle task moderated help seeking. Students' requests for help were more frequent at an intermediate level of skill than at both low (and presumed low self-perception of ability) and high (and presumed high self-perception of ability in addition to low need for help) levels of skill. Under conditions of task involvement, help seeking did not vary with skill level, but rather, was more frequent overall than in the ego-involved condition. The findings of Butler and Neuman are consistent with other research showing that self-perceptions of ability moderate the impact of performance, but not learning, goals on task persistence (Elliott & Dweck, 1988). Further research, such as studies that take into account developmental factors, is needed to specify more precisely how self-perceptions of ability and goals may interact.

In summary, students' thoughts and feelings about their capabilities, in interaction with goal conditions in the classroom, influence students' willingness to reveal a need for help. Help seeking necessarily involves others, and so students are especially in the spotlight at a time of requiring assistance. Students who are thought to need help the most (i.e., students with low achievement who also have low self-perceptions of ability and low self-esteem) are the most reluctant to seek help. The degree to which supportive classrooms, with task-involved goal conditions, might help these students is not clear. It is clear, however, that ego-involved goals inhibit the classroom engagement of all students. Under ego-involved conditions, even students with high achievement, who feel they must maintain consistently high perceptions in the eyes of their classmates, are reluctant to seek assistance when it is needed.

CONCLUSIONS

There is no doubt that seeking needed help is an essential part of learning in the classroom, and more generally, in people's everyday lives. It is taken for granted that individuals will ask for help when they do not understand something that is important to them, for example, in the workplace, the clinic, and the classroom. Yet managers, doctors, and teachers routinely report a paucity of questions in such situations, either questions directed from client to expert, among the clients, or even among themselves as the experts (Dillon, 1990). Help seeking is a difficult construct to research because of its infrequency, but in its very infrequency lies the importance of educators understanding and helping—individuals who are reluctant to seek needed assistance.

Self-regulated learners have a variety of ways of affecting the learning process and learning outcomes. This chapter has focused on one specific way in which self-regulated learners can, and often do, exert control of features in the classroom environment to help them learn. I have focused on affective and motivational factors involved in the social-interactional process of help seeking. Self-regulated learners do not simply possess a bag of tricks or techniques to help them learn. They typically do have the requisite cognitive strategies and behavioral routines to deal with academic problems, but, more important, they also have the will and the means to deal with situations in which skills and knowledge are absent. They possess and employ an executive processing system that allows them to improvise and fall back, if necessary, to a position of dependence on others.

Feeling states contribute to the filtering or construction of our memories, thoughts, and actions. In the particular case of help seeking, important decisions—regarding whether to ask, what to ask, and whom to ask—are controlled to a large extent by our feelings and personal beliefs. Students have personal beliefs about their capabilities and about schooling, in general, which they bring to the classroom. Affective histories as well as dynamic, moment-to-moment feelings evoked in interactions with teachers and classmates influence the degree to which students are comfortable asking questions in class. Variations in the teacher–learner relationship account significantly for students' capacities to regulate their affect and cope in difficult academic situations. Variations in the early parent–child attachment relationship no doubt play an important role in the development of these capacities.

Goals that students bring from home as well as goals that are infused in the classroom significantly influence the academic help-seeking process. Students have both achievement and social goals motivating them in the classroom. Those who desire and value challenge and mastery of material rather than simply getting a good grade tend to be self-regulated in how they go about seeking assistance. They ask for hints rather than answers. They are likely to try to confirm whether or not their work is right, presumably so they can use that feedback for future mastery attempts. They show evidence of not giving up after failure; they persevere and try to get back on track. Reluctance to seek help is expected in situations where failure is perceived as indicative of an injured ego. When students' egos are not perceived to be in jeopardy, reluctance to seek help is minimized.

The chapter has examined help seeking from a social-interactional perspective. If help seeking could be viewed solely from a "cold" cognitive perspective, understanding developmental and individual differences in its functioning would be less complicated. But raising one's hand, admitting difficulty or failure, and asking for help is a social-interactional exchange between people. It is also a very personal event that evokes anxiety in most individuals at one time or another. Students make cognitive decisions about requesting help in the context of many different affective and motivational, as well as environmental, factors. Recognizing the "hot" nature of self-regulated learning in general, and of help seeking in particular, is essential for a better understanding of how to help students take a more active role in their own learning in the classroom.

REFERENCES

Ainsworth, M. S. D., Blehar, M. C., Waters, E., & Wall, S. (1978). *Patterns of attachment: A psychological study of the strange situation.* Hillsdale, NJ: Lawrence Erlbaum Associates.

Ames, C. (1992). Classrooms: Goals, structures, and student motivation. *Journal of Educational Psychology, 84,* 261–271.

Ames, C., & Archer, J. (1988). Achievement goals in the classroom: Students' learning strategies and motivation processes. *Journal of Educational Psychology, 80,* 260–267.

Ames, R. (1983). Help-seeking and achievement orientation: Perspectives from attribution theory. In B. M. DePaulo, A. Nadler, & J. D. Fisher (Eds.), *New directions in helping: Vol. 2. Help seeking,* (pp. 165–186). New York: Academic Press.

Azmitia, M. (1988). Peer interaction and problem solving: When are two heads better than one? *Child Development, 59,* 87–96.

Barnett, K., Darcie, G., Holland, C. J., & Kobasigawa, A. (1982). Children's cognitions about effective helping. *Developmental Psychology, 18,* 267–277.

Berndt, T. J., & Keefe, K. (1992). Friends' influence on adolescents' perceptions of themselves at school. In D. Schunk & J. Meece (Eds.), *Student perceptions in the classroom* (pp. 51–73). Hillsdale, NJ: Lawrence Erlbaum Associates.

Bowlby, J. (1969). *Attachment and loss: Vol. 1. Attachment.* New York: Basic Books.

Bus, A. G., & van IJzendoorn, M. H. (1988). Mother–child interactions, attachment, and emergent literacy: A cross-sectional study. *Child Development, 59,* 1262–1272.

Butler, R., & Neuman, O. (1995). Effects of task and ego achievement goals on help-seeking behaviors and attitudes. *Journal of Educational Psychology, 87,* 261–271.

Cooper, C. R., Marquis, A., & Ayers-Lopez, S. (1982). Peer learning in the classroom: Tracing developmental patterns and consequences of children's spontaneous interactions. In L. C. Wilkinson (Ed.), *Communicating in the classroom* (pp. 69–84). New York: Academic Press.

Cooper, H. M. (1979). Pygmalion grows up: A model for teacher expectation communication and performance influence. *Review of Educational Research, 49*(3), 398–410.

Corno, L. (1989). Self-regulated learning: A volitional analysis. In B. J. Zimmerman & D. H. Schunk (Eds.), *Self-regulated learning and academic achievement: Theory, research, and practice* (pp. 111–141). New York: Springer-Verlag.

Covington, M. (1992). *Making the grade: A self-worth perspective on motivation and school reform.* New York: Cambridge University Press.

Diaz, R. M., Neal, C. J., & Amaya-Williams, M. (1990). The social origins of self-regulation. In L. C. Moll (Ed.), *Vygotsky and education: Instructional implications and applications of socio-historical psychology* (pp. 127–154). New York: Cambridge University Press.

Diener, C. & Dweck, C. (1978). An analysis of learned helplessness: Continuous changes in performance, strategy, and achievement cognitions following failure. *Journal of Personality and Social Psychology, 36*, 451–462.

Dillon, J. T. (1990). *The practice of questioning.* New York: Routledge.

Dodge, K. A., Asher, S. R., & Parkhurst, J. T. (1989). Social life as a goal-coordination task. In C. Ames & R. Ames (Eds.), *Research on motivation in education: Goals and cognitions* (pp. 107–135). New York: Academic Press.

Dunn, J., & Brown, J. (1991). Relationships, talk about feelings, and the development of affect regulation in early childhood. In J. Garber & K. A. Dodge (Eds.), *The development of emotion regulation and dysregulation* (pp. 89–108). Cambridge, England: Cambridge University Press.

Dweck, C. (1986). Motivational processes affecting learning. *American Psychologist, 41*, 1040–1048.

Dweck, C. & Leggett, E. L. (1988). A social-cognitive approach to motivation and personality. *Psychological Review, 95*, 256–273.

Eccles, J., Midgley, C., & Adler, T. F. (1984). Grade-related changes in the school environment: Effects on achievement motivation. In J. Nicholls (Ed.), *Advances in motivation and achievement* (Vol. 3, pp. 283–331). Greenwich, CT: JAI.

Eccles, J., & Wigfield, A. (1985). Teacher expectations and student motivation. In J. Dusek (Ed.), *Teacher expectancies* (pp. 185–226). Hillsdale, NJ: Lawrence Erlbaum Associates.

Elliott, E. S., & Dweck, C. (1988). Goals: An approach to motivation and achievement. *Journal of Personality and Social Psychology, 54*, 5–12.

Flavell, J. H. (1979). Metacognition and cognitive monitoring: A new area of cognitive developmental inquiry. *American Psychologist, 34*, 906–911.

Garber, J., & Dodge, K. A. (Eds.). (1991). *The development of emotion regulation and dysregulation.* Cambridge, England: Cambridge University Press.

Goodenow, C. (1993). Classroom belonging among early adolescent students: Relationships to motivation and achievement. *Journal of Early Adolescence, 13*, 21–43.

Graesser, A. C., & McMahen, C. L. (1993). Anomalous information triggers questions when adults solve quantitative problems and comprehend stories. *Journal of Educational Psychology, 85*, 136–151.

Graham, S., & Barker, G. P. (1990). The down side of help: An attributional-developmental analysis of helping behavior as a low-ability cue. *Journal of Educational Psychology, 82*, 7–14.

Graham, S., & Golan, S. (1991). Motivational influences on cognition: Task involvement, ego involvement, and depth of information processing. *Journal of Educational Psychology, 83*, 187–194.

Harter, S. (1981). A new self-report scale of intrinsic versus extrinsic orientation in the classroom: Motivational and informational components. *Developmental Psychology, 17*, 300–312.

Harter, S. (1983). Developmental perspectives on the self-system. In P. Mussen (Ed.), *Handbook of child psychology: Vol. 4. Socialization, personality, and social development,* (pp. 275–385). New York: Wiley.

Harter, S., & Connell, J. P. (1984). A model of children's achievement and related self-perceptions of competence, control, and motivational orientation. In J. Nicholls (Ed.), *Advances in motivation and achievement* (Vol. 3, pp. 219–250). Greenwich, CT: JAI.

Karabenick, S. A., & Knapp, J. R. (1988). Help seeking and the need for academic assistance. *Journal of Educational Psychology, 80*, 406–408.

Karabenick, S. A., & Knapp, J. R. (1991). Relationship of academic help seeking to the use of learning strategies and other instrumental achievement behavior in college students. *Journal of Educational Psychology, 83*, 221–230.

Kopp, C. B. (1991). Young children's progression to self-regulation. In M. Bullock (Ed.), *The development of international action: Cognitive, motivtional, and interactive processes* (pp. 38–54). Basel, Switzerland: Karger.

Kuhl, J. (1985). Volitional mediators of cognition-behavior consistency: Self-regulatory processes and action versus state orientation. In J. Kuhl & J. Beckmann (Eds.), *Action control: From cognition to behavior* (pp. 101–128). Berlin, Germany: Springer-Verlag.

Lave, J. (1988). *Cognition in practice.* Cambridge, England: Cambridge University Press.

Licht, B. G., & Dweck, C. S. (1984). Determinant of academic achievement: The interaction of children's achievement orientations with skill area. *Developmental Psychology, 20,* 628–636.

Maehr, M. L., & Pintrich, P. R. (Eds.). (1991). *Advances in motivation and achievement* (Vol. 7). Greenwich, CT: JAI.

Main, M., Kaplan, N., & Cassidy, J. (1985). Security in infancy, childhood, and adulthood: A move to the level of representation. In I. Bretherton & E. Waters (Eds.), *Growing points of attachment theory and research* (pp. 66–104). *Monographs of the Society for Research in Child Development, 50* (1-2, Serial No. 209).

Markman, E. M. (1981). Comprehension monitoring. In P. Dickson (Ed.), *Children's oral communication skills* (pp. 61–84). New York: Academic Press.

Markus, H., & Nurius, P. (1986). Possible selves. *American Psychologist, 41,* 954–969.

Meece, J. L., Blumenfeld, P. C., & Hoyle, R. H. (1988). Students' goal orientations and cognitive engagement in classroom activities. *Journal of Educational Psychology, 80,* 514–523.

Meece, J. L., Blumenfeld, P. C., & Puro, P. (1989, January). *A motivational analysis of elementary science learning environments.* Paper presented at the annual meeting of the American Association for the Advancement of Science, San Francisco.

Meece, J. L., Parsons, J. E., Kaczala, C. M., Goff, S. B., & Futterman, R. (1982). Sex differences in math achievement: Toward a model of academic choice. *Psychological Bulletin, 91,* 324–348.

Moos, R. H. (1979). *Evaluating educational environments.* San Francisco: Jossey-Bass.

Nadler, A. (1983). Personal characteristics and help-seeking. In B. M. DePaulo, A. Nadler, & J. D. Fisher (Eds.), *New directions in helping: Vol. 2. Help seeking* (pp. 303–340). New York: Academic Press.

Nelson-Le Gall, S. (1981). Help-seeking: An understudied problem-solving skill in children. *Developmental Review, 1,* 224–246.

Nelson-Le Gall, S. (1985). Help-seeking behavior in learning. In W. Gordon (Ed.), *Review of research in education* (Vol. 12, pp. 55–90). Washington, DC: American Educational Research Association.

Nelson-Le Gall, S., & Glor-Scheib, S. (1985). Help seeking in elementary classrooms: An observational study. *Contemporary Educational Psychology, 10,* 58–71.

Nelson-Le Gall, S., & Gumerman, R. A. (1984). Children's perceptions of helpers and helper motivation. *Journal of Applied Developmental Psychology, 5,* 1–12.

Nelson-Le Gall, S. & Jones, E. (1990). Cognitive-motivational influences on the task-related help-seeking behavior of Black children. *Child Development, 61,* 581–589.

Newman, R. S. (1984). Children's achievement and self-evaluations in mathematics: A longitudinal study. *Journal of Educational Psychology, 76,* 857–873.

Newman, R. S. (1990). Children's help-seeking in the classroom: The role of motivational factors and attitudes. *Journal of Educational Psychology, 82,* 71–80.

Newman, R. S. (1991). Goals and self-regulated learning: What motivates children to seek academic help? In M. L. Maehr & P. R. Pintrich (Eds.), *Advances in motivation and achievement* (Vol. 7. pp. 151–183). Greenwich, CT: JAI.

Newman, R. S. (1994). Adaptive help seeking: A strategy of self-regulated learning. In D. H. Schunk & B. J. Zimmerman (Eds.), *Self-regulation of learning and performance: Issues and educational applications* (pp. 283–301). Hillsdale, NJ: Lawrence Erlbaum Associates.

Newman, R. S., & Gauvain, M. (1996, April). *Mathematical communication and thinking: The role of peer collaboration in the classroom.* Paper presented at the annual meeting of the American Educational Research Association, New York.

Newman, R. S., & Goldin, L. (1990). Children's reluctance to seek help with schoolwork. *Journal of Educational Psychology, 82,* 92–100.

Newman, R. S., & Schwager, M. T. (1993). Student perceptions of the teacher and classmates in relation to reported help seeking in math class. *Elementary School Journal, 94,* 3–17.

Newman, R. S., & Schwager, M. T. (1995). Students' help seeking during problem solving: Effects of grade, goal, and prior achievement. *American Educational Research Journal, 32,* 352–376.

Newman, R. S., & Stevenson, H. W. (1990). Children's achievement and causal attributions in mathematics and reading. *Journal of Experimental Education, 58,* 197–212.

Nicholls, J. G. (1979). Quality and equality in intellectual development: The role of motivation in education. *American Psychologist, 34,* 1071–1084.

Ogbu, J. (1987). Variability in minority school performance: A problem in search of an explanation. *Anthropology and Education Quarterly, 18,* 312–334.

Palincsar, A., & Brown, A. L. (1984). Reciprocal teaching of comprehension-fostering and comprehension-monitoring activities. *Cognition and Instruction, 1,* 117–175.

Paris, S. G., Lipson, M. Y., & Wixson, K. K. (1983). Becoming a strategic reader. *Contemporary Educational Psychology, 8,* 293–316.

Paris, S. G., & Newman, R. S. (1990). Developmental aspects of self-regulated learning. *Educational Psychologist, 25,* 87–102.

Pressley, M., Borkowski, J. G., & Schneider, W. (1987). Cognitive strategies: Good strategy users coordinate metacognition and knowledge. In R. Vasta & G. Whitehurst (Eds.), *Annals of child development* (Vol. 4, pp. 89–129). Greenwich, CT: JAI.

Pressley, M., Levin, J. R., Ghatala, E. S., & Ahmad, M. (1987). Test monitoring in young grade school children. *Journal of Experimental Child Psychology, 43,* 96–111.

Radziszewska, B. & Rogoff, B. (1988). Influence of adult and peer collaborators on children's planning skills. *Developmental Psychology, 24,* 840–848.

Rogoff, B., & Gardner, W. (1984). Adult guidance of cognitive development. In B. Rogoff & J. Lave (Eds.), *Everyday cognition: Its development in social context* (pp. 95–116). Cambridge, MA: Harvard University Press.

Rosen, S. (1983). Perceived inadequacy and help-seeking. In B. M. DePaulo, A. Nadler, & J. D. Fisher (Eds.), *New directions in helping: Vol. 2. Help seeking* (pp. 73–107). New York: Academic Press.

Rosenholtz, S. J., & Simpson, C. (1984). The formation of ability conceptions: Developmental trend or social construction? *Review of Educational Research, 54,* 31–63.

Ryan, R. M., & Stiller, J. (1991). The social contexts of internalization: Parent and teacher influences on autonomy, motivation, and learning. In M. L. Maehr & P. R. Pintrich (Eds.), *Advances in motivation and achievement* (Vol. 7, pp. 115–149). Greenwich, CT: JAI.

Salomon, G., Globerson, T., & Guterman, E. (1989). The computer as a zone of proximal development: Internalizing reading-related metacognitions from a reading partner. *Journal of Educational Psychology, 81,* 620–627.

Schunk, D. H. (1989). Self-efficacy and cognitive skill learning. In C. Ames & R. Ames (Eds.), *Research on motivation in education* (Vol. 3, pp. 13–44). New York: Academic Press.

Schunk, D. H., & Zimmerman, B. J. (1994). (Eds.), *Self-regulation of learning and performance: Issues and educational applications.* Hillsdale, NJ: Lawrence Erlbaum Associates.

Shapiro, E. G. (1983). Embarrassment and help-seeking. In B. M. DePaulo, A. Nadler, & J. D. Fisher (Eds.), *New directions in helping: Vol. 2. Help seeking* (pp. 143–163). New York: Academic Press.

Shavelson, R. J., & Bolus, R. (1982). Self-concept: The interplay of theory and methods. *Journal of Educational Psychology, 74,* 3–17.

Skinner, E. A., & Belmont, M. J. (1993). Motivation in the classroom: Reciprocal effects of teacher behavior and student engagement across the school year. *Journal of Educational Psychology, 85,* 571–581.

Skinner, E. A., Wellborn, J. G., & Connell, J. P. (1990). What it takes to do well in school and whether I've got it: A process model of perceived control and children's engagement and achievement in school. *Journal of Educational Psychology, 82,* 22–32.

Slavin, R. (1983). *Cooperative learning.* New York: Longman.

Stern, D. N. (1985). *The interpersonal world of the infant: A view from psychoanalysis and developmental psychology.* New York: Basic Books.

Tharp, R. G., & Gallimore, R. (1988). *Rousing minds to life: Teaching, learning, and schooling in social context.* New York: Cambridge University Press.

Tudge, J., & Rogoff, B. (1989). Peer influences on cognitive development: Piagetian and Vygotskian perspectives. In M. Bornstein & J. Bruner (Eds.), *Interaction in cognitive development* (pp. 17–40). Hillsdale, NJ: Lawrence Erlbaum Associates.

Urdan, T. C., & Maehr, M. L. (1995). Beyond a two-goal theory of motivation and achievement: A case for social goals. *Review of Educational Research, 65,* 213–243.

van der Meij, H. (1988). Constraints on question asking in classrooms. *Journal of Educational Psychology, 80,* 401–405.

van der Veer, R., & van IJzendoorn, M. H. (1988). Early childhood attachment and later problem solving: A Vygotskian perspective. In J. Valsiner (Ed.), *Child development within culturally structured environments: Parental cognition and adult–child interaction* (Vol. 1. pp. 215–246). Norwood, NJ: Ablex.

Verba, M. (1994). The beginnings of collaboration in peer interaction. *Human Development, 37,* 125–139.

Vygotsky, L. S. (1978). *Mind in society: The development of higher psychological processes* (M. Cole, V. John-Steiner, S. Scribner, & E. Souberman, Eds.). Cambridge, MA: Harvard University Press.

Webb, N. M. (1982). Student interaction and learning in small groups. *Review of Educational Research, 52,* 421–445.

Weinstein, R. (1983). Student perceptions of schooling. *Elementary School Journal, 83*(4), 287–312.

Wentzel, K. R. (1991). Social and academic goals at school: Motivation and achievement in context. In M. L. Maehr & P. R. Pintrich (Eds.), *Advances in motivation and achievement* (Vol. 7. pp. 185–212). Greenwich, CT: JAI .

Wertsch, J. V. (1979). From social interaction to higher psychological processes. *Human Development, 22,* 1–22.

Wertsch, J. V. (1985). *Vygotsky and the social formation of mind.* Cambridge, MA: Harvard University Press.

Wilkinson, L., & Calculator, S. (1982). Effective speakers: Students' use of language to request and obtain information and action in the classroom. In L. Wilkinson (Ed.), *Communicating in the classroom* (pp. 85–99). New York: Academic Press.

Winnicott, D. W. (1965). *The maturational processes and the facilitating environment.* London: Hogarth Press.

Wintre, M. G., Hicks, R., McVey, G., & Fox, J. (1988). Age and sex differences in choice of consultant for various types of problems. *Child Development, 59,* 1046-1055.

Wood, D., Bruner, J., & Ross, G. (1976). The role of tutoring in problem solving. *Journal of Child Psychology and Psychiatry, 17,* 89–100.

Zimmerman, B. J., & Martinez-Pons, M. (1986). Development of a structured interview for assessing student use of self-regulated learning strategies. *American Educational Research Journal, 23,* 614–628.

3

Help Seeking, Achievement Motivation, and the Social Practice of Intelligence in School

Sharon Nelson-Le Gall
University of Pittsburgh

Lauren Resnick
University of Pittsburgh

Increasingly, our society expects schools to produce students who possess sound knowledge and basic skills, as well as high level, embedded symbolic thinking and problem-solving skills. Our schools also are expected to produce students who value the process of learning and the improvement of their skills, who willingly try to develop and apply their skills and knowledge, and who have a long-term commitment to learning. Educational systems that do not increase the value that learners hold for hard work and persistent effort are unlikely to improve and sustain long-term achievement.

In this chapter, we suggest that a social constructivist approach to human cognition and motivation can enrich our understanding of children's skill acquisition and school achievement. Following a discussion of help seeking as a crucial achievement-related strategy, we advocate a view of help seeking as a constituent of adaptive, intelligent practice in learning settings. This view of help seeking is supported by the interpretation of intelligence as social practice (Resnick & Nelson-Le Gall, 1997). We explore a conception of skill acquisition that closely unites social competence and cognitive development. This conception also springs from our efforts to contribute to the development of educational programs aimed at raising the overall academic achievement of the least advantaged children in the educational system. We also discuss how help seeking as a social practice of intelligence reflects motivational orientation and important individual differences in achievement-related beliefs. The most important of these beliefs concerns the relation between effort and ability, that is, whether people believe that effort can create abilities or only manifest the limits of ability. We examine the social construction of attitudes, beliefs, and values that motivate and channel the use of help seeking as a problem-solving strategy in skill acquisition. This discussion highlights not only how help seeking reflects individual differences in motivation and goals but also how it can be conditioned by cultural values and classroom features. Finally, we ask how schools, as institutions charged with promoting human development, might nurture help seeking as part of a social practice of intelligence.

HELP SEEKING AND LEARNING

The ideology of individualism characterizes Western models of human learning and performance. Individualism portrays human beings as essentially isolated from their environments, standing apart from other persons and things, and relying on their own internal resources to deal with the demands of the self and the outside world. This view of human learning, however, does not ring true to the actual experiences of individuals learning throughout their lives. Most learning is rarely an asocial enterprise. The acquisition of knowledge and skill occurs in a socioculturally organized environment. Learners are influenced directly and indirectly by social constraints and cultural norms, which contribute greatly to the what, when, where, why, and how of learning. Learning under these environmental realities requires help and encouragement from others. Thus, an individual learner not only must be open to receiving help from more knowledgeable and experienced persons in the learning context but also must be willing and able to seek help from more expert individuals.

Help seeking is a general problem-solving strategy that allows learners to cope with academic challenges by keeping them actively involved in learning tasks. The student who seeks and obtains help when needed has engaged in intelligent practice. Help seeking not only holds the potential for working through an immediate academic difficulty but also contributes to the acquisition of skills and knowledge that can be used later to help one's self or others. Help seeking can be a mature and even sophisticated strategy for coping with difficult tasks. As a self-initiated, task-oriented behavior, help seeking is regarded (Nelson-Le Gall, 1981) as a manifestation of achievement motivation, in that the child seeking help is actively using available human resources to increase success. Use of help seeking as a learning strategy is appropriate when the help requested is focused on acquiring the processes of problem solution. Learners with effective instrumental help-seeking skills will refuse help when they are able to perform a task by themselves but will seek help when needed. From this perspective, help seeking represents effective classroom coping behavior. Whether as a less skilled novice in an interaction or as an equally competent collaborator, learners seeking mastery-oriented help mediate their learning and problem solving by taking the initiative to question, suggest, observe, and imitate.

HELP SEEKING AS A CONSTITUENT
OF INTELLIGENCE AS SOCIOCULTURAL PRATICE

Resnick and Nelson-Le Gall (1997) argued for a view of intelligence as a set of social practices by which individuals adapt and tune their behavior to immediate contexts of performance. Such a view necessitates expanding the definition of intelligence to include more than just individual mental capacity or an individual, biologically founded construction. The definition must also include a cluster of social acts such as asking questions and seeking help in problem solving. Furthermore, one's likelihood of engaging in these social practices of intelligence is as much a matter of how one construes his or her rights, responsibilities, and role as it is a matter of purely cognitive capacities. Stated simply, the argument is that if you believe it to be the right, responsibility, and role of someone like you to ask questions and learn new things all the time, you will ask lots of questions and strive to keep learning.

This view of intelligence, as a set of social practices attuned to a sociocultural milieu, is inspired by sociocultural perspectives on mental development. For example, Vygotsky proposed that the development of human mental functioning "presupposes a certain social nature and a process by which children grow into the intellectual life of those around them" (1978, p. 88). In each sociocultural context, children participate in both formal and informal instructional exchanges that bring about their adaptive functioning within those contexts. Through reciprocal processes of social interaction, children develop a system of cognitive representations as interpretive frameworks and make a commitment to the common value system and sets of behavioral norms promoted in their sociocultural context. This process of socialization thus incorporates the acquisition and use of knowledge, ways of representing that knowledge, and ways of thinking and reasoning with that knowledge.

In our earlier chapter (Resnick & Nelson-Le Gall, 1997), we suggested that, if we as a nation want to see our children develop a general value for and facility in acquiring and using knowledge, we need to attend to these robust habits of mind and how they are nurtured as much as to the specifics of thinking processes or knowledge structures. In our working definition, the constituents of intelligence include a full and continually developing repertoire of specific cognitive skills and problem-solving strategies. The constituents also include, however, beliefs and attitudes about one's competence and about one's action in the world. Several of these constituents are discussed briefly in the following sections.

A Tool Kit of Problem-Analysis Tools and Good Intuitions About When to Use Them

These might be metacognitive skills, analogical reasoning skills, quantitative analysis skills, or a host of other specific, learnable capabilities usually recognized as cognitive in nature. This tool kit would also include social and social-cognitive skills such as knowing how to ask questions, seek help, and get enough information to solve problems (Nelson-Le Gall, 1981). In this definition of intelligence, making use of the social environment is an integral part of the understanding process. Moreover, help seeking exemplifies the critical role of social influences on learning and cognitive development. Help seeking is not merely a self-regulatory learning strategy in the individual student's repertoire but also a part of the social-interactional processes of learning.

The Habits of Mind That Lead One Actively to Use the Tool Kit of Analysis Skills and Various Strategies for Acquiring Information

The habits of mind are socialized in a community of learners that value such behavior. This community will also enculturate correlated beliefs and attitudes, such as the belief that one has a right (and an obligation) to understand things and make things work and the belief in one's self-efficacy to analyze problems successfully to yield solutions.

Goodenow (1990) observed that we do not merely acquire knowledge, cognitive skills, and strategies or learn to apply that knowledge and skill in problem solving, but we also learn that we are expected to acquire some pieces or forms of knowledge and skill and that some knowledge or skill areas belong more to some people than to others. By fostering the belief that acquisition of knowledge and new skills is every individual's responsibility, opportunities to develop mentally and to grow into the intellectual life of the society are extended to all.

To seek help is to recognize the limitations of one's own current knowledge or skill vis-à-vis some task demand and to find this state of affairs unsatisfactory. In particular, to seek help is to see addressing this undesirable state as one's right and obligation. Seeking help also admits to another's superior knowledge or skills relative to oneself. By seeking help from more knowledgeable or expert persons, the learner is recognizing and utilizing the social affordances in the task setting. When these more experienced individuals respond to the help seeker's bid for help, they validate the help seeker's claim to possession of the necessary ability, permission, and responsibility to acquire the more advanced knowledge and skills of the helper.

The belief in one's efficacy in using knowledge and skills to solve problems leads individuals to persist in working on challenging tasks and to recruit various cognitive and social-cognitive strategies to aid in this work. This belief in the value of persistent thoughtful activity can be socialized through the tacit messages embedded in the routines of daily practices.

Achievement Goals, Effort, and Help Seeking

The routine inclination to use one's tool kit of analysis skills and one's strategies for gathering information raises the issue of motivation. Evidence of children's basic ability and motivation to use their tool kits for learning can be found in any of several settings at a given point in time. Hence, the more meaningful questions for informing educational practice and policy must address students' functional abilities, adaptive skills, cognitive strategies, and social competencies, and how they fit with the context of classroom learning. It is critical then to examine the goals that direct learners' effort and attention in school-task settings and the active use of information-gathering strategies, such as help seeking.

Several classes of achievement goals that are associated with different conceptions of success and failure and with different beliefs and attitudes about the self, learning tasks, and task outcomes have been identified (Ames, 1984; Dweck & Leggett, 1988). Among these goals, two major types have been labeled, contrasted, and given the most attention: ego-involved versus task-involved (Nicholls, 1979, 1984) or performance-oriented versus learning-oriented (Dweck & Elliott, 1983). These goals appear to be closely related to the amount and, above all, to the kinds (e.g., help seeking) of effort they exert in situations of learning or problem solving. For the purposes of this discussion, these achievement goal orientations are referred to as performance and learning goals.

People with performance goals strive to obtain positive evaluations of their ability and to avoid giving evidence of inadequate ability relative to others. Performance goals are associated with the view of ability as an unchangeable, global entity that is displayed in task performance as adequate or inadequate. This view of aptitude has been called an entity theory of intelligence (Dweck & Leggett, 1988). In contrast, people with learning goals try to develop their ability by taking an active stance toward learning and mastery opportunities. Learning goals are associated with the view of ability as a repertoire of skills continuously expandable through one's efforts. Accordingly, this view of aptitude has been labeled an incremental theory of intelligence (Dweck & Leggett, 1988). How individuals view ability becomes especially significant for their immediate achievement motivation and behavior when they perceive their ability to be low and they encounter difficulty at a task.

Dweck and her colleagues have shown that individuals who believe in an entity theory of ability tend to invest energy in achievement settings to obtain positive judgments of their competence and to avoid negative ones. In other words, those who assume ability is a fixed, inborn entity tend to be oriented toward performance goals. When faced with task difficulties, these individuals are likely to focus on their perceived lack of ability or on the difficulty of the task, to engage in simplistic and inflexible reasoning, and to resort to ineffectual strategies. They show decreasing effort or even a complete lack of task-related effort, such as abandoning the task (Miller, 1986).

In contrast, individuals who believe in an incremental theory, which holds that ability can be enhanced and increased through effort, tend to invest their energy to learn something new or to increase their understanding and mastery of tasks. These individuals tend to adopt learning goals; thus, when they encounter task difficulties, they are likely to apply self-regulatory metacognitive skills, to focus on analyzing the task before them, and to attempt to generate and plan the execution of alternative strategies. In general, these individuals display continued high levels of task-related effort in response to difficulty. Such effort may include strategically seeking help from more expert others. Thus, performance goals place the greater effort necessary for mastering challenging tasks in conflict with the need to be regarded as already competent, whereas learning goals lead to adaptive motivational patterns that can produce a quality of task engagement and commitment to learning that fosters high levels of achievement over time.

The achievement goals that individuals pursue also appear to influence the inference rules used to process information about the contribution of personal effort to success or failure at a task. Performance goals appear to be associated with the inference that effort and ability are negatively related in determining achievement outcomes so that high effort leading to success or failure is taken as a sign of low ability. Learning goals are associated with the inference that effort and ability are positively related so that greater effort creates and makes evident more ability (Dweck & Leggett, 1988).

Learners pursuing learning goals are likely to garner resources for problem solving, both from their internal repertoire of cognitive strategies and by strategically seeking help from others (Dweck, 1988; Nelson-Le Gall & Jones, 1990; Nelson-Le Gall, Kratzer, DeCooke, & Jones 1990). This distinction between blind personal exertion or arbitrary effort and productive, goal-directed effort has been drawn clearly by John Dewey (1966), who wrote, "The really important matter in the experience of effort concerns its connection with thought. The question is not the amount of sheer strain involved, but the way in which the thought of an end persists in spite of difficulties and induces a person to reflect upon the nature of the obstacles and the available resources by which they may be dealt with." (p. 171)

Dewey's emphasis on evaluating and garnering available resources suggests an alternative and potentially adaptive strategy that could be used to master a task that is beyond a student's current level of competence: namely, to seek help from others. As a self-initiated behavior, help seeking has been conceptualized as strategic effort when the individual seeking help is actively using available resources external to the self to increase the probability of achieving some goal (e.g., Nelson-Le Gall, 1981). This conceptualization distinguishes between help seeking as a substitute for active involvement in the learning process and help seeking to support active involvement in the learning process. Help seeking can be used opportunistically to maintain task engagement. Furthermore, when help seeking is used strategically, we would expect to see individuals in a learning group move in and out of this role during the course of work on a task so that donors of help become recipients and vice versa.

This body of research on achievement goal orientation shows that these beliefs and the habits of mind that we have defined as the practices of intelligence are indeed associated. Moreover, it shows that there are individual differences in beliefs about the nature of intelligence and, therefore, its associated practices. How are these beliefs acquired and nurtured? How are the habits of practice acquired? We address these questions in the next section.

THE SOCIAL CONSTRUCTION
OF MOTIVATION FOR LEARNING

Persistent habits and deeply held beliefs about the self and human nature in general are acquired through processes that developmentalists usually call *socialization* (Grusec & Lytton, 1988). Socialization refers to the incorporation of the individual as a member of a community. Socialization proceeds not so much through direct formal instruction of the young or novice individual, although there are instances in which direct instruction or tutoring occurs; rather, it proceeds primarily via social interaction: through observation and modeling, cooperative and guided participation, and scaffolding. It depends, furthermore, on the negotiation of mutual expectations, that is, intersubjectivity. As soon as a child is born, adults and other knowledgeable individuals begin to contribute to the child's socialization by arranging the environment and the tasks the child encounters in it, and by guiding the child's attention to and participation in the community's valued practices.

Individual differences in beliefs about effort and ability are, we assume, socialized within the context of different patterns of family beliefs and practice. But there are also broad societal differences reported in these beliefs. In the United States, most adults hold the view that effort and ability are distinct, negatively related causes of achievement outcomes. Most also tend to recognize ability as an inherently stable characteristic of individuals, one that is unequally distributed among the human population and not subject to being increased by personal or environmental influence (Nicholls, 1984). These assumptions about ability and effort are shared throughout our society and promoted by our societal institutions (Nicholls, 1979), so it is not surprising to see them clearly manifested in most traditionally structured school settings.

Unfortunately, most standard U.S. educational practice provides contexts and environments that orient students to performance goals rather than to learning goals. Early in the 1900s, the United States committed to an education system built around the assumptions that aptitude is paramount in learning and is an unalterable personal quality that can be shown but not grown. The system was oriented toward distinguishing the naturally able from the less able and providing students with programs thought suitable to their talents (Resnick, 1995).

In classrooms that operate under this model, direct comparisons of one student's work and learning outcomes to another's occur frequently and often in public ways. Teachers and students find it normal that some students do not learn what is taught and do not achieve as well as others. When the emphasis in the classroom or school is on relative ability and performance outcomes and on competition for grades and rewards, and when instructional policies and practices seek to sort students by aptitude, then students and teachers alike are likely to focus more on performance goals than on learning goals (Nicholls, 1979).

In other cultures, however, effort and ability are not viewed as independent dimensions. It has been reported, for example, that in several Asian cultures (i.e., Chinese and Japanese) people are typically socialized to espouse and act on the belief that high effort and perseverance are the key to successful performance; indeed, working hard is even a moral obligation. The positive orientation that Japanese people are socialized to adopt toward hard work and effort conveys a shared belief that ability can be changed and that its change through hard work and persistence refines and enhances the self (Holloway, 1988; Peak, 1993; Stevenson & Lee, 1990). People in such cultures behave in ways consonant with learning goals. This alternative view about the relation of effort and ability is likewise reflected in these societies' educational philosophies, and is promoted by their educational institutions.

As an example of the differences in how beliefs about the relation among effort, ability, and achievement manifest themselves in U.S. classrooms versus classrooms in China, consider the implications of teacher responses to student mistakes or errors. When U.S. teachers see student mistakes and call them to public attention in the classroom, the act will be seen as punitive to the student because of the negative relation perceived to exist between ability and effort in the American ethos. In Asian classrooms, it is commonplace for student mistakes to be shared publicly with the class to demonstrate misconceptions and to use them as learning opportunities for all students. This event is not viewed as punitive because mistakes are not an implication of low ability but simply a part of the learning process (Li, 1997).

In their extensive comparative studies of U.S., Japanese, and Chinese education systems, Stevenson and Stigler (1992) described in substantial detail a very different pattern of beliefs and practices in Chinese and Japanese schools compared with those in the United States. Differences in organization, expectation, and practice can be detected between U.S. educational systems and Chinese and Japanese systems as early as the preschool period (Peak, 1986, 1993; Tobin, Wu, & Davidson, 1989). These differences in motivational orientations and their associated institutional support may have much to do with the generally higher academic performance of students from those countries.

Typically, schooling in the United States tends to reflect and promote notions about the desirability of autonomous functioning and individual problem solving, even though the classrooms in which this schooling is delivered are intensely social in both form and function. The critical role that the social context can play in enculturating desirable habits of mind is often overlooked or undervalued.

In contrast, in Japan, folk beliefs place more emphasis on social competence as a component of intelligence than is true of lay wisdom in the United States (Holloway, 1988). Being an effective speaker and listener, being good at getting along with others, and taking another person's point of view are all aspects of social competence that tend to be viewed as controllable by the individual and as essential in the cultivation of intelligence. This emphasis on the quality of interactions and relations between individuals and their social environment reinforces the development of a sense of connectedness and collective identity. Failure in performance becomes a failure for others as well as the individual learner, and this belief appears to sustain the kind of hard work and persistence that minimizes the chances of failure.

This discussion suggests that, rather than viewing the individual as the locus of all action and motivational outcomes as products solely of the individual, we may view motivation as a social construction. By viewing motivation as a socially negotiated process, we can examine the influence of contextual and cultural issues on motivation. We can also examine the interpersonal relations that influence, shape, and maintain motivation and motivated behaviors (Sivan, 1986).

The learning that occurs in classrooms is not merely an individual accomplishment supported by the social context; it is also the result of a continuous and dynamic negotiation between the student and the social environment provided by the adults and other children present. Although help seeking has been characterized as personal effort subordinated to the goal of extending one's knowledge and skill, it still depends on the negotiated and coordinated participation of others in pursuing that goal. Accordingly, it is also important for children who would seek help with problem solving to know and to act on the knowledge that the help seeker and the helper may need to renegotiate their ways of viewing the task and the interaction before helping can proceed effectively. Children seem to be aware that the extent to which the help seeker and the helper hold a shared definition of the problem and of their roles in the helping exchange can facilitate or impede their attempts to use their peers as resources (e.g., DeCooke & Nelson-Le Gall, 1989; Ladd & Oden, 1979). Ladd and Oden (1979) found that among elementary school children, knowledge about peer norms for giving and seeking help were positively associated with status in the peer group. Similarly, DeCooke and Nelson-Le Gall (1989) found that the familiarity of help seekers to their targeted helpers influenced both the help seekers' success and their social status in the classroom. Increased familiarity with peer norms concerning help exchanges seems to be the reason for this success.

Thus, just as higher mental processes in individuals can be seen to emerge from reciprocal processes of social interaction (Vygotsky, 1978), so can the emergent capacity for self-direction be seen as located in the socioculturally organized environments of instruction that the child experiences. From this perspective, the development of motivation is seen as the internalization of values and goals and the command of strategies to commit to and alter them. This development necessarily means being a member of a learning community and transforming that community while being transformed by it. Let us consider as an example the socialization that occurs for children around one of the important social practices of intelligence that we have identified: help seeking in problem solving.

Socializing Strategic Effort: The Case of Help Seeking

The analysis of help-seeking behavior that we have outlined thus far highlights the role of interpersonal relations and social interaction in shaping and maintaining motivational competence. Although we view seeking help from others as an important social practice of intelligence for all learners, we have found it to be of particular interest in the case of low income, racial and ethnic minority children whose achievement behavior has often been characterized as deviant and deficient (see Nelson-Le Gall & Jones, 1991). In fact, a common lament we hear from teachers of low income, underserved African-American children concerning the issue of achievement motivation is, "They just aren't interested in learning." In other words, these teachers represent the children as being unmotivated and, consequently, showing little or no effort and interest to learn in school. Yet, there is compelling evidence to suggest that displays of interest and effort in school learning may not be shown by African-American children because the social affordances to which these displays are attuned may not be present in the school settings and that, even when children are motivated, their behavior may not be recognized by their teachers as motivated behavior (e.g., Allen & Boykin, 1991, 1992).

The African-American socialization patterns and the traditional family and community learning contexts that children experience present social affordances to shape their help-seeking behaviors in ways that could be, but are not generally, routinely and successfully exploited in the traditional schooling environment. Indeed, in classrooms and task structures where the home–school cultural discontinuities are minimized by organizing academic tasks so that they afford a more active, participatory approach from the child, motivation and task performance were found to be improved (Allen & Boykin, 1991; Tharp, 1989). We turn now to a brief discussion of some of the relevant, salient features cultivated in African-American homes and proximal environments and those features typically afforded in traditionally organized U.S. educational systems.

Socialization in the Cultural Context of Family.   An examination of the cultural patterns of socialization that many African-American children experience in their families reveals how strategic motivation and the practice of help seeking emerge in these social and informal instructional experiences. For example, many African Americans participate in a kinship network that is a multigenerational network of relatives (e.g., Harrison, Wilson, Pine, Chan, & Buriel, 1990). As members of this network, children are socialized to orient toward interpersonal relatedness, to respond to the authority of a dominant family member, and to recognize collective responsibility. Combined with the emphasis on giving and receiving support within the network, the caregiver–child relationship within African-American families encourages the child to seek help while moving toward independence (Aschenbrenner, 1973; Tolson & Wilson, 1990).

An orientation toward interdependent and cooperative functioning entails individuals assuming particular responsibilities but functioning as a collective unit in efforts to meet task demands. Reflecting their group-oriented culture, African Americans (Rotheram & Phinney, 1987) tend to value collective efforts more than competition as viable strategies in goal-oriented situations (Boykin, 1986; Ogbu, 1982; Tolson & Wilson, 1990). Therefore, it seems reasonable, on conceptual grounds, to expect that seeking and accepting help when necessary would be an adaptive strategy employed in achievement-oriented situations by African-American children.

This striving for individual accomplishment within the context of social support and active coping with difficulty is evident in children's academic help-seeking behaviors (e.g., Nelson-Le Gall & Glor-Scheib, 1986). We should point out, however, that individual differences in motivation can also be found among African-American children. For example, Nelson-Le Gall and Jones (1990) examined the type of help sought by third and fifth grade African-American students during a vocabulary task. A measure of students' intrinsic orientation to mastery and learning in academic achievement settings was independently obtained for each child observed. Students characterized by high intrinsic orientation to mastery showed a clear preference for help that allowed them to figure out solutions for themselves as opposed to help that directly supplied a ready-made solution. In contrast, students characterized by low intrinsic orientation to mastery showed no clear preference for one type of help over the other. Note that these differences in motivational orientation were evident only in cases where the students thought they had given incorrect initial answers to the problems presented in the task. This finding suggests that the adoption of mastery goals in the face of perceived failure underlies the tendency to prefer instrumental, or knowledge-extending, help.

A substantial body of literature associates positive achievement outcomes with African-American socialization patterns (Shade, 1978). Researchers have found that high achieving African-American children have parents who are responsive to their help seeking and encourage an active coping style (Garmezy, 1983; Holliday, 1985; Shade, 1978). An active coping style involves initiating change and manipulating the environment to produce resources that can help overcome obstacles in achieving personal goals and desired outcomes. Children with an active coping style in problem-solving situations tend to initiate solutions to problems rather than waiting for intervention.

Socialization in the Cultural Context of School. What messages do children in school receive about their right, responsibility, and role in actively striving to learn new things all the time? How are they socialized into the roles they assume in the learning community of the classroom and school? There is ready acknowledgment of the socialization process and its function and products in informal, everyday out-of-school settings such as the family. But, with few exceptions (e.g., Brown & Palincsar, 1989), researchers often fail to recognize its role in intellectual functioning in more formally organized contexts such as schools. Instead of learning and performing in the context of mutual and ongoing social relationships, regarded as desirable in many out-of-school settings, children must often work independently from others and even without any social communication (Nelson-Le Gall, 1992). To understand how information gathering strategies such as help seeking, which are a part of one's tool kit, fit into school learning settings, we must recognize the socialization that occurs in the social context of school.

In schools, achievement motivation develops through social interaction into recognizable and socially acceptable motivated behaviors. In discussing motivation in the classroom, we act as if there is general consensus about what it is and how it is shown. What leads us to say that a person is or is not motivated, or is not putting forth effort? Although we cannot say exactly what trying is in absolute terms, we act as if we know very well when a person is trying hard or not trying very much at all. If we think about it, however, there is no straightforward way to assess effort devoted to school tasks. We know little about the specific signs of effort in the classroom that are valued jointly by students and teachers.

The concept of effort may be more globally defined for younger children than for older ones. For young students, good conduct (i.e., not fooling around, working quietly) is synonymous with effort or trying hard (Blumenfeld, Pintrich, Meece, & Wessels, 1982). Young children do not appear to consider explicitly the nature or quality of effort displayed (e.g., persisting, applying alternative strategies on their own, or seeking the help of others). For example, Nelson-Le Gall and Scott-Jones (1985) reported that children's judgments of what constitutes adequate persistence in the face of task difficulty may depend on their perception of the appropriateness of producing different manifestations of effort. Such perceptions of appropriate and desirable learning behavior are defined through social contact in the classroom and through experience in the school culture over time, so that teachers' and students' views of appropriate work behaviors begin to overlap (Nelson-Le Gall & Scott-Jones, 1985).

In some classrooms, other students, a readily available source of help, may be ignored by a student seeking help because of explicit or implicit classroom norms (supported by teachers and students alike) that discourage cooperative work by associating it with cheating. Consider the social norms for students' behavior in traditional classrooms in general and how these norms support or detract from appropriate task-related help seeking. Relatively few children attend schools that regularly encourage peer interaction as a major means of learning in the classroom. Moreover, as grade level in school increases, children are likely to encounter classroom learning situations in which competition and independent performance are increasingly common (Eccles, Midgley, & Adler, 1984). It is also likely that, unless children begin elementary school in classrooms that emphasize the social sharing of cognitive learning activities, children may come to cooperative learning groups thinking that collaborating with and assisting peers in classroom learning activities are not normal behaviors for students.

If, however, classroom norms support and encourage active and interactive learning by students as part of the routine practices of learning, such as can occur in the context of cooperative and helping exchanges among peers, then the perceived costs of help seeking may be lessened. For example, Hertz-Lazarowitz (1992) reported that as the central role of the teacher in the classroom instructional process decreases and the legitimization of peer interaction in learning increases, a corresponding dramatic increase in cooperation, help-giving, and help-seeking behaviors occurs among students.

Although many racial minority children may experience learning environments outside school that are very cooperatively structured, and attempt to apply help-seeking strategies to the classroom learning environment, grade-related changes in the classroom environment may determine the effectiveness of help seeking as an achievement strategy. The socially interactive style many African-American children bring to school is somewhat compatible with the task environment typically encountered in the first few years of formal schooling (i.e., kindergarten through Grade 2) because of the teacher's concern with the child's socialization into the student role (Nelson-Le Gall & Scott-Jones, 1985). Around Grade 3, however, the dynamics of teacher–child interactions change, and the teachers in typical elementary classrooms function less as parent substitutes. Student–teacher relationships are less personalized, and standards for classroom performance are redefined with more emphasis being placed on individual achievement and competition among students (Eccles, Midgley, & Adler, 1984).

Note that this change in U.S. classroom environment coincides with the beginning of a frequently observed, marked divergence of African-American students' achievement levels from those of their White counterparts. In many classrooms serving low income, urban minority children, classroom norms emphasizing passivity, quietness, and individual achievement through competition become increasingly salient with advancing grade level. Yet, African-American students' behavior in the classroom group continues to reflect a preference for an active and socially interactive style of learning (Allen & Boykin, 1992). Comparisons of African-American and White eighth grade students' behavior while actively engaged in classroom tasks indicate that African-American students were more likely to seek out classmates and teachers for discussion, clarification, elaboration, and aid. When allowed, African-American students were also more likely to prefer working in small groups (Morgan, 1990).

Asking students to accept without question an individualistic interpretation of motivation and learning, when their own experience has been based on interpersonal relations and social interaction within the context of the family unit or ethnic or racial community, can lead to cognitive dissonance. They may interpret functioning as an individual alone not as empowering, but rather as isolating and punishing. We want to push the argument further, however, by underscoring the important role that social participation and support in learning activity play in developing and sustaining the motivation and learning. Social participation in and support from a group whose existence is based on learning and teaching contributes to a social identity as a learner. Not only do individuals become socialized into the group, accepting the groups' values for actively and collaboratively expanding their knowledge and skills, but also they develop a sense of belonging or being valued by the group, establishing a social identity based on membership in a learning community. That sense of belonging can also motivate the individual to cultivate the social practices valued by the learning community.

EDUCATIONAL DESIGNS THAT NURTURE SOCIAL PRACTICES OF INTELLIGENCE

In our theoretical conception, motivation cannot be understood as just a motor for mental activity, unconnected to the content and processes of learning. We emphasize, instead, the notion that the organization of instruction embodies and can nurture differing conceptions of intelligence and of the broader purposes of school learning, which in turn motivate varying forms of cognitive activity. The motivational patterns most productive of extended effort also evoke the very strategic modes of learning in which the individual becomes an intentional agent in crafting his or her own knowledge and understanding. In the final section of our chapter, we consider how schools might be organized to deliberately nurture social practices of intelligence in all children. Our attention focuses on U.S. schools, the only ones that we know well and the ones where we have an opportunity to explore ideas offered here.

The possibility that effort actually creates ability, that people can become smart by working hard as a member of a learning community at the right kinds of learning tasks, has never been taken seriously in the U.S. Resnick and Nelson-Le Gall, 1997) observed that certain educational initiatives and programs (e.g., Edmonds, 1979; Escalante & Dirmann, 1990) appeared to operate on the implicit assumption that well-directed effort could create ability, rather than only reveal its limits. Although the organizers of these programs did not speak explicitly to theories of motivation, they all implicitly depended on changes in the mediating motivational characteristics of students and their schooling environments. That is, the increased investment of effort in courses that were initially difficult for them and the subsequent high levels of learning and achievement that they showed were, it is presumed, partly a function of changes in their motivational orientations. In addition, these programs created a sense of community within the learning environment. Moreover, the programs created social identities for the participants whose interpersonal and personal responsibility for creating and sharing knowledge and skill was not only valued but also demanded from all participants. However, each of these programs and others like them have had to work against beliefs widely held in U.S. society and influential in its educational institutions: namely, that what individuals can learn and what schools can teach is largely determined by ability, and that ability is largely unalterable by effort or environmentally offered opportunities. Thus, we must take seriously the idea that learning and performance goals do not merely emerge full-blown from individual intrapsychological processes but that they can be elicited and made differentially salient by situational or instructional demands (e.g., Ames, 1992; Jagacinski & Nicholls, 1984).

Several structures of the classroom environment have an impact on student motivation and are largely controlled by teachers (Rosenholtz & Simpson, 1984). Included among these are the design of academic tasks and activities, the evaluation practices employed, and the distribution of authority and responsibility in the classroom. For example, the climate and structure of a schooling environment can have the effect of fostering in students an identification with the aims of schooling, a sense of belonging within a learning community, and a commitment—even a sense of responsibility—to participate actively in all learning activities. Alternatively, the climate can have the effect of focusing students on the adequacy of their present ability as the only valued capital in the setting. This alternative is costly both to students and to society, because preoccupation with determining individuals' ability or potential in the classroom can create conditions that reduce the chances of fulfilling that very potential.

Learning goals that focus students on developing competence should be salient to students when they are involved in making real choices and decisions concerning authentic learning tasks, when grouping is based on interests and needs, when there are opportunities for peer interaction and cooperation around meaningful academic tasks so that social goals directed to achieving a sense of belongingness are not devalued, and when success is defined in terms of effort, improvement, and progress toward clear and high standards of achievement (Ames & Archer, 1988; Nelson-Le Gall, 1992, 1993; Resnick, 1995). We suggest here that, in classrooms in which learning goals are salient, motivation would not be seen as something existing solely in students, that they bring to the classroom and academic tasks, but rather as an outcome of meaningful participation in the classroom and the social practices that accomplish its everyday practical activities.

Many educators and laypeople intuitively believe that institutional demands and rewards can change psychological belief structures. The effects of such institutional features on individual motivational orientations have not been directly examined, however. Similarly, although research has shown that certain motivational orientations raise performance on particular tasks, it has not shown that these orientations raise overall academic achievement. We have undertaken such a research program in collaboration with the educators in a small number of schools that have decided to implement an overall school program promoting learning goal orientations and treating effort, rather than aptitude, as the primary determinant of learning results.

SUMMARY AND CONCLUSIONS

A broader conceptualization of learning and skill acquisition that construes learning capability as a set of habits for questioning, for seeking help, and for exerting other forms of deliberate effort to expand skills and understanding has been presented. This conceptualization actively links strategy learning with motivation. Moreover, it holds promise for engendering research on how to create environments for learning that will promote the habits of active mental elaboration and self-management associated with effective learning (see Collins, Greeno, & Resnick, 1994).

In this chapter, we have argued that motivation is not only an outcome of individual differences but also the product of the social conditions at the time of learning. It is constrained by the social context, the goals, wishes, and desires of both the student and the teacher. As a cultural norm, motivation is used to define what is appropriate and what is desirable. Understanding this norm helps the student display appropriate motivated behaviors and achieve competent membership and social acceptance by teachers and peers. To illustrate, we have discussed a particular manifestation of student effort that is also an aspect of intelligence: namely, help-seeking behavior. By attempting to study and account for this type of active, help-seeking behavior that is concerned with extending knowledge and understanding, attention is drawn to the reality that learners actively construct and practice academic as well as social knowledge in the contexts of learning. Attention is also drawn to the very fundamental way in which the cognitive and affective support provided by others in learning situations can keep children involved in optimally challenging tasks working within their range of competence, and to the way in which such support provides the opportunity to learn, through observation, discussion, and feedback, the successful means to solving the task and maintaining cognitive and affective engagement.

When help seeking occurs as a manifestation of strategic effort in the activity of a learning group, social and cognitive processes are interdigitated. Social competence, as an aspect of the individual learner, and as a characteristic of the group of classroom peers, may constrain the acquisition and display of knowledge mediated by help seeking. Academic competence, as a feature of the individual learner and as a characteristic of peer and teacher resources in a classroom, may moderate the effectiveness of the help seeking and help giving that occurs and may consequently affect the acquisition and mastery of new knowledge and skill. Effectiveness in using peers as resources for learning is a result of being aware that it is important to seek out explanations, justifications, and demonstrations. Finally, effectiveness in using others as resources in learning groups is influenced by the prevalent norms in the learning context that support and encourage willingness to collaborate, help, and question rather than to attack, compete, interfere, or isolate. Cultivation of adaptive help-seeking skills occurs in a sociocultural community that values such skills, provides opportunities for their acquisition and practice, and re-sponds encouragingly to their expression.

We believe the approach to motivation and skill acquisition that we espouse is central also to any concern for finding ways to bridge the equity gap in U.S. education. Without special attention to developing students' dispositions for strategic learning as well as their skills, educators will, however unintentionally, perpetuate a situation in which those already rich in knowledge and in school-valued learning strategies are most likely to benefit from the new opportunities for learning offered in school. Emphasis on motivation as a socially constructed process in a specific cultural context of practice means also that we must ask questions about what types of interactions result in motivated behavior in various learning settings. What types of motivated behaviors do different populations value and how do different social norms inhibit or facilitate the creation, form, and maintenance of motivation in the classroom?

One task for educational practitioners, administrators, re-searchers, and policymakers concerned with understanding and en-hancing children's motivation to learn and achieve involves finding ways to build and support a community of learners in the classroom setting. This must be a community in which students feel legitimate despite their ethnic origins or family background. It must be a commu-nity that encourages both the appropriation of values and goals and the strategic motivation and competence to commit to or change them; this includes the responsibility to cultivate social supports to achieve aca-demically. Classrooms can then be communities of learners wherein more experienced members of the community are sought out to guide the less experienced in accomplishing culturally meaningful tasks. Accordingly, the rewards for such accomplishment must be equally accessible to all who participate actively in the community's work.

REFERENCES

Allen, B., & Boykin, A. W. (1991). The influence of contextual factors on Afro-American and Euro-American children's performance: Effects of movement opportunity and music. *International Journal of Psychology, 26*, 373–387.

Allen, B., & Boykin, A. W. (1992). African American children and the educational process: Alleviating cultural discontinuity through prescriptive pedagogy. *School Psychology Review, 21*, 586–593.

Ames, C. (1984). Competitive, cooperative, and individualistic goal structures: A cognitive-motivational analysis. In R. Ames & C. Ames (Eds.), *Research on motivation in education* (Vol. 1, pp. 177–207). San Diego, CA: Academic Press.

Ames, C. (1992). Classrooms: Goals, structures, and student motivation. *Journal of Educational Psychology, 84*, 261–271.

Ames, C., & Archer, J. (1988). Achievement goals in the classroom: Students' learning strategies and motivation processes. *Journal of Educational Psychology, 80*, 260–267.

Aschenbrenner, J. (1973). Extended families among Black Americans. *Journal of Comparative Family Studies, 3*, 257–268.

Blumenfeld, P., Pintrich, P., Meece, J., & Wessels, K. (1982). The formation and role of self perceptions of ability in elementary classrooms. *Elementary School Journal, 82*, 401–420.

Boykin, A. W. (1986). The triple quandary and the schooling of Afro-American children. In U. Neisser (Ed.), *The school achievement of minority children* (pp. 57–92). Hillsdale, NJ: Lawrence Erlbaum Associates.

Brown, A., & Palincsar, A. (1989). Guided, cooperative learning and individual knowledge acquisition. In L. Resnick (Ed.), *Knowing, learning, and instruction: Essays in honor of Robert Glaser* (pp. 393–451). Hillsdale, NJ: Lawrence Erlbaum Associates.

Collins, A., Greeno, J., & Resnick, L. (1994). Learning environments. In T. Husén & T. Postelthwaite (Eds.), *International encyclopedia of education* (2nd ed., Vol. 6, pp. 3297–3302). Oxford: Pergamon.

DeCooke, P., & Nelson-Le Gall, S. (1989). The effects of familiarity on the success of children's help seeking. *Journal of Applied Developmental Psychology, 10*, 195–208.

Dewey, J. (1966). Effort, thinking, and motivation. In F. W. Garforth (Ed.), *John Dewey: Selected educational writings* (pp. 168–180). London: Heinemann Educational Books.

Dweck, C. (1988). Motivation. In R. Glaser & A. Lesgold (Eds.), *Handbook of psychology and education* (pp. 187–239). Hillsdale, NJ: Lawrence Erlbaum Associates.

Dweck, C., & Elliott, E. (1983). Achievement motivation. In P. H. Mussen (Series Ed.) & E. M. Heatherington (Vol. Ed.), *Handbook of child psychology: Vol. 4. Socialization, personality and social development* (4th ed., pp. 643–692). New York: Wiley.

Dweck, C., & Leggett, E. (1988). A social-cognitive approach to motivation and personality. *Psychological Review, 95*, 256–273.

Eccles, J., Midgley, C., & Adler, T. (1984). Grade-related changes in the school environment: Effects on achievement motivation. In J. Nicholls (Ed.), *Advances in motivation and achievement* (Vol. 3, pp. 283–331). New York: JAI.

Edmonds, R. (1979). Effective schools for the urban poor. *Educational Leadership, 37*, 15–23.

Escalante, J., & Dirmann, J. (1990). The Jaime Escalante math program. *Journal of Negro Education, 59*, 407–423.

Garmezy, N. (1983). Stressors in childhood. In N. Garmezy & M. Rutter (Eds.), *Stress, coping, and development in children* (pp. 43–84). New York: McGraw-Hill.

Goodenow, J. (1990). The socialization of cognition: What's involved? In J. Stigler, R. Schweder, & G. Herdt (Eds.), *Cultural psychology: Essays on comparative human development* (pp. 259–286). Chicago: University of Chicago Press.

Grusec, J., & Lytton, H. (1988). *Social development.* New York: Springer-Verlag.

Harrison, A., Wilson, M., Pine, C., Chan, S., & Buriel, R. (1990). Family ecologies and ethnic minority children. *Child Development, 61*, 347–362.

Hertz-Lazarowitz, R. (1992). Looking at six mirrors of the classroom. In R. Hertz-Lazarowitz & N. Miller (Eds.), *Interaction in cooperative groups: The theoretical anatomy of group learning* (pp. 71–101). New York: Cambridge University Press.

Holliday, B. (1985). Toward a model of teacher–child transactional processes affecting Black children's achievement. In M. Spencer, G. Brookins, & W. Allen (Eds.), *Beginnings: The social and affective development of Black children* (pp. 117–130). Hillsdale, NJ: Lawrence Erlbaum Associates.

Holloway, S. (1988). Concepts of ability and effort in Japan and the U.S. *Review of Educational Research, 58*, 327–345.

Jagacinski, C., & Nicholls, J. (1984). Conceptions of ability and related affects in task involvement and ego involvement. *Journal of Educational Psychology, 76*, 909–919.

Ladd, G., & Oden, S. (1979). The relationship between peer acceptance and children's ideas about helpfulness. *Child Development, 50*, 402–408.

Li, J. (1997). *The Chinese "Heart and Mind for Wanting to Learn" (Hao-Xue-Xin): A culturally based learning model.* Unpublished doctoral dissertation, Harvard University, Cambridge, MA.

Miller, A. (1986). Performance impairment after failure: Mechanism and sex differences. *Journal of Educational Psychology, 78*, 486–491.

Morgan, H. (1990). Assessment of students' behavioral interactions during on-task classroom activities. *Perceptual and Motor Skills, 70*, 563–569.

Nelson-Le Gall, S. (1981). Help-seeking: An understudied problem-solving skill in children. *Developmental Review, 1*, 224–246.

Nelson-Le Gall, S. (1992). Children's instrumental help-seeking: Its role in the social construction of knowledge. In R. Hertz-Lazarowitz & N. Miller (Eds.), *Interaction in cooperative groups: The theoretical anatomy of group learning* (pp. 49–68). New York: Cambridge University Press.

Nelson-Le Gall, S. (1993). Perceiving and displaying effort in achievement settings. In T. Tomlinson (Ed.), *Motivating students to learn: Overcoming barriers to high achievement* (pp. 225–244). Berkeley, CA: McCutchan Publishing.

Nelson-Le Gall, S., & Glor-Scheib, S. (1986). Academic help-seeking and peer relations in school. *Contemporary Educational Psychology, 11*, 187–193.

Nelson-Le Gall, S. & Jones, E. (1990). Cognitive-motivational influences on children's help-seeking. *Child Development, 61*, 581–589.

Nelson-Le Gall, S., & Jones, E. (1991). Classroom help-seeking behavior of African American children. *Education and Urban Society, 24*, 27–40.

Nelson-Le Gall, S., Kratzer, L., DeCooke, P., & Jones, E. (1990). Children's self-assessment of performance and task-related help seeking. *Journal of Experimental Child Psychology, 49*, 245–263.

Nelson-Le Gall, S., & Scott-Jones, D. (1985). Teachers' and young children's perceptions of appropriate work strategies. *Child Study Journal, 15*, 29–42.

Nicholls, J. (1979). Quality and equality in intellectual development: The role of motivation in education. *American Psychologist, 34*, 1071–1084.

Nicholls, J. (1984). Achievement motivation: Conceptions of ability, subjective experience, task choice, and performance. *Psychological Review, 91*, 328–346.

Ogbu, J. (1982). Socialization: A cultural ecological perspective. In K. Borman (Ed.), *The socialization of children in a changing society* (pp. 251–265). Hillsdale, NJ: Lawrence Erlbaum Associates.

Peak, L. (1986). Training learning skills and attitudes in Japanese early education settings. In E. Fowler (Ed.), *Early experience and the development of competence* (pp. 111–123). San Francisco: Jossey-Bass.

Peak, L. (1993). Academic effort in international perspective. In T. Tomlinson (Ed.), *Motivating students to learn: Overcoming barriers to high achievement* (pp. 41–59). Berkeley, CA: McCutchan Publishing.

Resnick, L. (1995). From aptitude to effort: A new foundation for our schools. *Daedalus, 124*, 55–62.

Resnick, L., & Nelson-Le Gall, S. (1997). Socializing intelligence. In L. Smith & P. Tomlinson (Eds.), *Piaget, Vygotsky and beyond* (pp. 145–158). London: Routledge.

Rosenholtz, S., & Simpson, C. (1984). Classroom organization and student stratification. *Elementary School Journal, 85,* 21–38.

Rotheram, M., & Phinney, J. (1987). Ethnic behavior patterns as an aspect of identity. In J. Phinney & M. Rotheram (Eds.), *Children's ethnic socialization* (pp. 201–218). Beverly Hills, CA: Sage.

Shade, B. (1978). Social psychological characteristics of achieving black children. *Negro Educational Review, 29,* 80–86.

Sivan, E. (1986). Motivation in social constructivist theory. *Educational Psychologist, 21,* 209–233.

Stevenson, H., & Lee, S. (1990). Contexts of achievement: A study of American, Chinese, and Japanese children. *Monographs of the Society for Research in Child Development, 55* (Whole No. 221).

Stevenson, H., & Stigler, J. (1992). *The learning gap: Why our schools are failing and what we can learn from Japanese and Chinese education.* New York: Summit Books.

Tharp, R. (1989). Psychocultural variables and constants: Effects on teaching and learning in schools. *American Psychologist, 44,* 349–359.

Tobin, J., Wu, D., & Davidson, D. (1989). *Preschool in three cultures: Japan, China, and the United States.* New Haven, CT: Yale University Press.

Tolson, T., & Wilson, M. (1990). The impact of two- and three-generational Black family structure on perceived family climate. *Child Development, 61,* 416–428.

Vygotsky, L. S. (1978). *Mind in society: The development of higher psychological processes* (M. Cole, V. John-Steiner, S. Scribner, & E. Souberman, Eds.). Cambridge, MA: Harvard University Press.

4

Relationship, Esteem, and Achievement Perspectives on Autonomous and Dependent Help Seeking

Arie Nadler
Tel Aviv University

Help-Seeking Dilemma: Definition and Present Focus

Although seeking other's help to overcome personal difficulties is likely to expedite effective coping, people are often reluctant to seek outside help. This has been demonstrated in educational (e.g., Karabenick & Knapp, 1988), organizational (e.g., Burke, Weir, & Duncan, 1976), and interpersonal contexts (e.g., Flett, Blankstein, Hicken, & Watson, 1995). Taking psychiatric symptomology as a case in point, studies estimate symptomology (mostly neurosis and personality disorders) to be about 21% in the general population (Neugebauer, Dohrenwend, & Dohrenwend, 1980). It is estimated that fully three-fourths of these individuals never sought help to cope with their difficulties (Link & Dohrenwend, 1980). Similarly, Garland and Zigler (1994) estimate that only 20% to 25% of children with psychiatric disorders receive the assistance of mental health services.

It seems, then, that many, if not all, problem situations involve a common dilemma as far as help seeking is concerned. On the one hand, from an instrumental perspective, the benefits associated with help seeking in terms of time, effort, and quality of coping would imply that individuals will readily seek available assistance whenever they encounter difficulties. On the other hand, oftentimes the seeking of others' help is associated with psychological costs. These costs are subtle and implicit. Seeking outside help often involves the open admission of inadequacy and, as such, may be threatening to self-esteem (e.g., Nadler, 1986), lead to feelings of embarrassment (e.g., Shapiro, 1983), or may be stigmatizing even, for the recipient of help (e.g., Blaine, Crocker, & Major, 1995). These psychological costs inhibit the seeking of help, to the detriment of the person who needs it. This tension between the instrumental benefits and psychological costs associated with help seeking was labeled the help seeking dilemma (Nadler, 1991). Much of the research on help seeking has been concerned with identifying the variables and processes that determine the resolution of this dilemma (DePaulo, Nadler, & Fisher, 1983; Nadler, 1991; Nadler, Fisher, & DePaulo, 1983; Wills, 1987; Wills & DePaulo, 1993).

This dilemma—between going alone and depending on others—involves an even more basic choice that people face throughout their lives. It reflects the unavoidable tension between the need to assert one's individuality and self-worth through independent action and the unavoidable necessity in social life of depending on more powerful and knowledgeable others. At the early stages of life, these powerful others are our parents; in later stages, they are our siblings, supervisors at work, and spouses; and in the last stages of our life, these may be our own children. Attesting to the great importance of this tension between individual and social action in coping, a number of personality theorists have viewed it as the crucible of personality development.

The present chapter suggests that the dilemma extends beyond seeking versus not seeking help. It is based on the premise that a richer and more parsimonious account of help seeking must distinguish between two distinct categories of help seeking: dependent and autonomous. Subsequent sections highlight the fact that, whereas some instances of help seeking imply dependence, others imply independence and autonomy. Although this dual meaning of help seeking was noted by a number of other authors (Asser, 1978; Nelson-Le Gall, 1985), it has not been systematically considered against the wealth of information available in the research. The present chapter provides such a systematic account. Before proposing a more systematic definition of these two categories of help seeking, I shall briefly review the relevant research traditions.

Help Seeking: Three Traditions of Research

Because of the relevance of the help seeking dilemma to a wide array of human social behavior, education researchers, experimental social psychologists, and researchers in the areas of health and coping have all been involved in studying the variables that affect people's willingness to seek help. Attesting to this diversity, the journals that published scientific research on help seeking in 1994 and 1995 include the Journal of

Personality and Social Psychology, Journal of Educational Psychology, American Journal of Orthopsychiatry, and Social Science and Medicine. I shall briefly outline three major research traditions that have focused on the help-seeking dilemma: social psychology, epidemiological research on help utilization, and research on support seeking as a coping response in times of stress.

Social psychologists have relied on experimental techniques to elucidate the variables that tip the scales of the help-seeking dilemma. For the most part, the dependent measure in these studies has been a behavioral index (e.g., amount of help sought or its latency) of the willingness to seek help to overcome an instrumental difficulty (e.g., completing an anagram test), and the theoretical account of the findings has been largely intrapsychological, either emotional or cognitive (e.g., threat to self-esteem, attributions of the need for help).

The epidemiological studies have relied mainly on archival indices of help seeking. A typical study in this tradition has focused on the seeking of medical or mental health help where the helper has been a professional (e.g., physician, psychologist) or an institutional helping service (e.g., Philips & Murrel, 1994). This research has emphasized the role of socio-cultural constructs (e.g., level of income, socioeconomic status, ethnic affiliation) and has couched the interpretation of its findings within sociological theories (Gourash, 1978; Greenley & Mechanic, 1976; Merton, Merton, & Barber, 1983).

The studies conducted by researchers interested in coping and social support have focused on individuals' willingness to use the support (i.e., emotional or instrumental) of close others (e.g., family or close friends) to cope with stressful life events. The indices of help seeking have been based on self-reports of the person's past behavior, and the explanatory concepts were borrowed from the research literature on stress and coping, (e.g., Aspinwall & Taylor, 1992; Lazarus & Folkman, 1984).

These different traditions of help-seeking research show considerable methodological and conceptual diversity. They have used different research methodologies, focused on different states of need, considered different types of helper, and employed different theoretical constructs to account for the empirical findings. Beyond this diversity, however, they all center on a similar question: What variables account for an individual's reported, or actual, decision or behavior to seek or not to seek help or support from others?

Autonomous and Dependent Help Seeking

Whereas help-seeking behavior is a unitary concept, the motives that drive it are different and contradictory. Autonomous help seeking occurs when individuals seek others' assistance to enable them to solve a problem on their own. Persons who seek autonomous help are motivated to retain their autonomy, and they use assistance to enable them to achieve on their own. Autonomous help seeking is predicated on the individual's motivation to solve the problem at hand, and the belief one is able to do so. Help seeking is a means to an end (i.e., solving the problem on one's own). Not seeking help in this case reflects the person's conviction that he or she does not need outside assistance to solve the problem.

Persons seeking dependent help do so out of passivity and lack of self-efficacy. They are motivated to terminate a painful situation, and they rely on others whom they believe can solve the problem for them. Being helped is an end in itself, and the failure to seek help reflects resignation to living with the problem. Persons who engage in dependent help seeking relinquish all their efforts to control their environment and put themselves in the hands of more powerful or knowledgeable others.

This distinction between dependent and autonomous help seeking suggests that if individuals seek help even though they can solve the problem on their own, they engage in dependent seeking and overutilize helping resources. If, however, they refrain from seeking help, even though their reluctance will slow or prevent the resolution of the problem, they underutilize helping resources. Finally, if individuals seek help when it can expedite and enable coping, but do not seek help when it will not expedite successful coping, they are autonomous help seekers and adequate utilizers of help.

Beyond enriching the simple dichotomy between seeking and not seeking help, this distinction between autonomous and dependent help seeking enables more direct examination of the links between help seeking and coping. Implied within this distinction is the idea that autonomous help seeking is associated with effective coping, but dependent help seeking, and the reluctance to seek help, which respectively reflect over and under utilization of help, would entail less effective coping.

RELATIONSHIPS, ESTEEM, AND ACHIEVEMENT
PERSPECTIVES ON DEPENDENT HELP SEEKING

A help-seeking context consists of an individual who needs assistance with a particular task, and seeks or does not seek it from a specific helper or helping agency. For the most part, reviews of help-seeking behavior employed this schematic representation and considered the effects of the characteristics of help seeker, the task with which help is needed, and the helper, on the willingness or reluctance to seek outside help (e.g., Nadler, 1991; Wills & DePaulo, 1993). The present focus goes beyond the question of whether help is sought to the psychological processes that underlie dependent versus autonomous help seeking. This review is thus structured around the psychological explanations that have been used in past research. It considers in turn *relationship-oriented* explanations, research on self-esteem processes, and explanations that emphasize cognitive processes in achievement settings as determinants of the willingness to seek help.

Relationship-Oriented Explanations

Two bodies of theory and research center on the quality of persons' social relationships as a central construct in the explanation of help seeking. The first has focused on impact of actual quality of the relationship between a person in need and the helper on help seeking. The second has examined how the help seeker's internal schema of interpersonal relations (e.g., that others are friendly and trustworthy or not) affects his or her willingness to seek help. Thus, for example, whereas a study within the first tradition would focus on differences between willingness to seek help from a stranger or a friend, a study in the second tradition might investigate how a general dispositional tendency to view others as friendly or not is related to help seeking. The first body of studies falls within the research on interpersonal behavior, the second within the boundaries of personality research.

Actual Relationships Between Helper and Help Seeker

Since seeking help is an interpersonal interaction, it is not surprising that much research has centered on the effects of the actual relationship between the helper and the help seeker on help seeking. Two lines of inquiry are relevant here: the social support literature that studied who people seek support from in times of need and the social psychological literature that examined willingness to seek help as affected by controlled variations of the helper's characteristics. The conclusions of these two lines of research are inconsistent. Whereas the social support research tells us that people prefer to seek help from socially close others (e.g., Corrigan, 1978; Cutrona, 1990), the social psychology research indicates that similarity or social proximity between helper and help seeker detracts from the willingness to seek help (Nadler & Fisher, 1986). I present some of these findings and show how the controversy can be resolved by applying the distinction between autonomous and dependent help seeking.

  Epidemiological studies on seeking psychological help (e.g., Fischer, Winer, & Abramowitz, 1983) and field studies on help seeking in academic contexts (e.g., Karabenick & Knapp, 1988) indicate that persons prefer seeking help from friends rather than strangers. In their introduction of the concept of "help-seeking pathways," Rogler and Cortes (1993) suggested that people in need first approach their spouse or close friend; only if this path proves unsatisfactory do they seek help from outside their close social circle. Summarizing this position, Rickwood and Braithwaite (1994) noted that one of the better predictors of support seeking during stress is the availability of close friends.

The experimental research in social psychology reaches the opposite conclusion. Here, a number of studies indicate that when encountering difficulties in completing an experimental task, individuals seek more help from a dissimilar than a similar other (i.e., Clark, Gotay, & Mills, 1974; Nadler, 1987) and feel more uneasy when receiving help from a similar other or friend than from a dissimilar other (Nadler, Fisher, & Streufert, 1976) or stranger (i.e., Nadler, Fisher, & Ben-Itzhak, 1983). The interpretation offered for these findings was that, in line with social comparison theory (Festinger, 1954) and other theoretical developments (Tesser, 1988), admitting inferiority by seeking help is more self-threatening when the helper is a meaningful other who serves for comparison purposes (i.e., a similar other or a friend). The fact that the inhibiting effects of social proximity on help seeking were evident only when the task was presented as relevant for self-evaluations (e.g., a test of creativity) was viewed as supporting this interpretation (e.g., Nadler & Fisher, 1986).

The distinction between autonomous and dependent help seeking offers a resolution to this empirical discrepancy. The research that showed a preference for seeking help from close others centered on long-term ongoing interactions between individuals. In such relationships, one is not faced with a dichotomous behavioral alternative between seeking or not seeking help. Rather, one can employ a variety of tactics to minimize the psychological costs of seeking help from another who serves as a source for meaningful comparison. One may mask the request of help by describing it as seeking assistance for someone else (Glidewell, Tucker, Todt, & Cox, 1983). One may ask for advice rather than help, thereby retaining a degree of independence. In short, the interpersonal context of an ongoing and long-term relationship makes autonomous help seeking a viable option. This is not the case in the experimental studies. There, the person was presented with a problem and confronted with a behavioral choice of seeking or not seeking help. In these studies, subjects could not negotiate the seeking of help. They did not have the freedom to seek assistance while maintaining their self-perceptions of independence, mastery, and control. The route of autonomous help seeking was blocked, and the only two alternatives were dependent help seeking versus no help seeking.

Taken together, this study suggests that when the person in need of help can employ autonomous help seeking, the helper's similarity or social proximity will increase the likelihood of help seeking. When, however, the path of autonomous help seeking is unavailable, and seeking help means dependent help seeking, social proximity will decrease the likelihood of help seeking. This proposition remains to be examined by research into the effects of the quality of the relationship between helper and help seeker on dependent and autonomous help seeking. Nevertheless, the previous argument demonstrates how the distinction between autonomous and dependent help seeking offers a parsimonious tool that clarifies the issue.

Inner Schemes: Gender, Dependent Personality, and Attachment Styles

The underlying assumption of the studies that have examined the help seeker's social orientation as a determinant of help seeking is that personality dispositions that are associated with greater openness to the social world and interconnectedness with others are positively related to a person's willingness to seek help. The personal orientations studied range from gender and gender-related characteristics (e.g., sex role orientation) through extroversion and attachment styles, to the dependent personality. The common element of these studies is that they all explain variations in the willingness to seek help as a function of a person's orientation toward social relationships. This research is more fully described elsewhere (Wills & DePaulo, 1993; Nadler, in press). The present chapter examines its conclusions in light of the distinction between autonomous and dependent help seeking.

Gender: Dependence or Effective Coping.

One of the most robust findings in the help-seeking literature is the greater willingness of females than males to seek help (Veroff, 1981; Nadler, 1991). The finding is commonly interpreted in terms of differences in the masculine and feminine gender-role orientation. It has been suggested that feminine gender-role orientation allows, and even encourages, dependency on others. Studies showing that femininity scores on scales measuring gender-role orientation (i.e., psychological gender) are also positively related to help seeking in both males and females support this interpretation (Nadler, Maler, & Friedman, 1984). In general, this gender difference has been taken as implying that compared to men, women overutilize help and engage in relatively more dependent help seeking. In fact, women have been said to seek help even if they could cope by themselves. The pejorative overtones of this view are captured in an observation by Greenglass (1993b). On the basis of her review of women's coping in the workplace she wrote that feminine social orientation has been traditionally "... delegated to the dependency field and thus has not been highly valued" (p. 156).

In terms of the present chapter, this view suggests that relative to men, women are dependent help seekers. Yet, examination of the links between help seeking by men and women, together with data on the differential effectiveness of their coping suggests otherwise. Greenglass (1993a) noted that, in addition to problem focus and emotion focus coping identified by Lazarus and Folkman (1984), one should consider a third strategy: social coping, of which help seeking is an integral part. Women employ this strategy more than men. Similarly, Hobfoll, Dunahoo, Ben-Porath, and Monnier (1994) suggested a dual axis model of coping: (a) passive versus active coping and (b) prosocial versus antisocial coping. Support seeking is viewed as being a prosocial/active mode of coping. More important, a number of studies have documented a positive link between social coping by means of seeking help from others and effective coping (Greenglass, 1993a; Hobfoll, et al., 1994; Long, 1988). This suggests that an active social orientation, of which femininity scores is one manifestation, is associated with autonomous rather than dependent help seeking.

This idea receives support from other bodies of theory and research. Studies of resilient children (Fisher, Kokes, Cole, Perkins, & Wynne, 1987; Garmezy, 1981; Milgram & Palti, 1993) render a similar conclusion. These are children who, despite deprivations in their formative years, cope well with environmental stressors in later life. They are characterized by a high level of sociability and empathy and exhibit high levels of both self-reliance and willingness to seek support. This dual emphasis on self-reliance and willingness to seek support from others accords well with the definition of autonomous help seeking. The fact that autonomous help seeking is related to high sociability supports the idea that it is a behavioral manifestation of an active social orientation.

This view of the long-term consequences of the decision not to seek help suggests that reliance on others may be either a primary or a secondary coping strategy. If primary, it is one employed close to the time when the difficulty is encountered. If secondary, the strategy is one employed after the use of a primary strategy that failed to solve the difficulty. This distinction implies that people who have an active social orientation seek help as a primary strategy, whereas those who are less socially oriented (e.g., shy individuals) seek help, if at all, only as a secondary strategy. In a similar vein, Butler (1993) suggested that an early request for help (i.e., help seeking as a primary coping response) is associated with an instrumental (rather than an ego-evaluative) perspective, which "... enhances help seeking by encouraging perceptions that this is adaptive strategy for mastery promotion" (p. 29). This line of thought implies that seeking help as a primary coping strategy is autonomous help seeking and that individuals with an active social orientation are more likely to seek autonomous help than individuals who are not so characterized. It suggests that whatever the specific manifestation (e.g., resilient children, gender), active social orientation results in better coping because it facilitates autonomous help seeking.

Further support for this conclusion is found in the work of Amirkhan, Risinger, and Swickert (1995), who viewed support help seeking as a form of active coping and described it in terms similar to the present conception of autonomous help seeking. Their findings indicate that extroverted individuals seek help more quickly than introverted ones. Employing the McRae and Costa (1986) distinction between neurotic coping and mature coping, they viewed support seeking as a form of mature coping. These findings agree well with our distinction between help seeking as a primary or secondary coping response. It suggests that individuals who are high on sociability (e.g., extroverts) would use autonomous help seeking as a primary coping strategy more than individuals low on sociability (e.g., introverts). Neither Amirkhan et al. (1995) nor other studies known to the author differentiate between autonomous and dependent help seeking or link them to the case of primary or secondary help seeking as a coping strategy. Yet, the logic of the present argument suggests that after time has elapsed and the difficulty persists, introverted individuals who had not sought help earlier might have to do so later. Because the problem is likely to be aggravated by the passage of time, their belated help seeking is likely to be dependent rather than autonomous. Somewhat paradoxically, the failure to seek help early (i.e., autonomous help seeking) may result in greater subsequent dependency (i.e., dependent help seeking).

Dependent Personality.   A socially oriented personality characteristic that is relevant to help seeking is the dependent personality. Employing Freud's thinking, researchers describe the dependent personality as one that is overly dependent on the support and assistance of others. Persons with dependent personalities are said to have high needs for support and nurturance by powerful and high-status others. Although there is no agreement over the exact mechanisms by which this personality disposition is acquired (cf. Bornstein, 1992 for a concise discussion of psychodynamic and social learning views), most descriptions of the dependent personality point to an individual who overutilizes help. Dependent individuals rely on others not only because of the value of assistance for better coping but also because of the desire to fulfill personal needs and secure nurturant relationships with powerful others. Fromm's (1947) description, cited by Bornstein (1992), of the dependent personality is especially poignant: " ... they are always in search of a magic helper. They show a particular kind of loyalty, at the bottom of which is the gratitude for the hand that feeds them and the fear of ever losing it" (pp. 62–63).

The various descriptions suggest that there should be a positive relationship between dependency scores and help seeking. Numerous studies have reported such a relationship in both laboratory (e.g., Shilkret & Masling, 1981) and field settings (e.g., Sroufe, Fox, & Pancake, 1983). The descriptions also suggest that highly dependent persons overutilize helping resources and their help seeking is dependent in nature. Yet, if the above argument that active social orientation promotes autonomous help seeking is correct, then it may be premature to equate dependent personality with dependent help seeking and overutilization of help. This link should be examined in light of data on the highly developed social skills of the dependent personality and more refined conceptions of the dependent personality.

Beyond the overall positive relationship of dependency with help seeking (e.g., Kagan & Mussen, 1956), findings show that individuals with high dependency are also interpersonally more sensitive than individuals low on dependency (Pincus & Gurtman, 1995) and are characterized by greater cooperativeness and willingness to help others (Bornstein, Krukonis, Manning, Mastrosimone & Rossner, 1993). If one bears in mind the previously described link between femininity scores and sociability, these findings are congruent with the fact that females score higher than males on the dependency scale (Birtchnell & Kennard, 1983).

Given their greater sociability, and our earlier claim that active social orientation is associated with autonomous help seeking as a primary coping strategy, it may be that the greater willingness of dependent individuals to seek help reflects autonomous help seeking and is associated with better coping. A similar argument has been made by Bornstein et al. (1993), who found a positive link between dependency scores and utilization of health services in a campus environment. Commenting on these findings, Bornstein et al. (1993) reminded us that the utilization of health services represents "... active rather than passive behavior on the part of the dependent person" (p. 274). Until we have data relating dependency scores to help seeking and coping effectiveness, we cannot ascertain whether the greater help seeking exhibited by dependent individuals represents dependent or autonomous help seeking.

One way of resolving this uncertainty is by examining the possible interaction between a person's dependency scores, the identity of the helper, and autonomous versus dependent help seeking. Both theoretical accounts and empirical findings (Bornstein, 1992) indicate that the dependent person's wish to be nurtured by and dependent on others is most aroused when the other is a high status person. This suggests that help seeking by individuals with high dependency would assume the characteristics of dependent help seeking when the helper is of high status. However, when the helper is either a peer or a relatively impersonal source of help (e.g., an institution), different dynamics may come into play. Then, the greater sociability of a person with high dependency may facilitate the utilization of external help as a primary coping strategy, thereby furthering autonomous help seeking and the more effective coping with which it is associated. The possible interaction between the helper's identity and the help seeker's dependency needs on help seeking behavior and coping remains to be examined.

A second way of clarifying the meaning of the links between dependency and help seeking is to consider a multifaceted rather than unitary approach to dependency. Such an approach was proposed by Pincus and Gurtman (1995) who empirically validated three distinct facets of interpersonal dependency: love dependency, which taps the dimension of high sociability, exploitable dependency, which taps increased evaluation apprehension, and submissive dependency which captures the dependent person's tendency to yield to high authority. Depending on what kind of dependency it is, high dependency may be linked to either autonomous or dependent help seeking. More specifically, whereas love dependency (i.e., the sociability component) should be associated with autonomous help seeking and better coping, submissive dependency should be associated with dependent help seeking, especially when the helper is of high status. Although this hypothesis awaits future research, it demonstrates the utility of considering theoretically and empirically the well established dependency-help seeking link in light of the distinction between autonomous and dependent help seeking.

Attachment Styles.   In the mid-1980s, Hazan and Shaver (1987) applied Bowlby's attachment theory to the study of interpersonal relationships. On the basis of Bowlby's theory (Bowlby, 1973) and related research (e.g., Ainsworth, Blehar, Waters, Waters, & Wall, 1978), they distinguished between three attachment styles that characterize adult interpersonal relations: the secure, the avoidant, and the anxious-ambivalent. These styles are said to reflect an individual's social orientation during times of stress. Secure individuals are said to view attachment figures (e.g., close friends, close family members) as being there for them when they need them. Insecure individuals have doubts about the availability of significant others during times of stress. Anxious-ambivalent persons adopt a watchful and guarded stance towards significant others, whereas avoidant individuals use denial and blocking of emotions as a way of coping with the insecurity about the availability of significant others. This tripartite distinction has stimulated much research designed to better understand the dynamics of interpersonal relations (e.g., Hazan & Shaver, 1987, 1990).

It is reasonable to believe that one's attachment style will affect one's readiness to seek help. A number of laboratory (Simpson, Rholes, & Nelligan, 1992) and field studies (e.g., Mikulnicer & Florian, 1995) support the hypothesis that as stress increases, securely attached individuals seek more help from significant others than persons with anxious or avoidant attachment styles. Simpson et al. (1992) found that avoidant individuals decreased their willingness to rely on significant others as stress increased. In terms of the present chapter, these individuals are consistent underutilizers of help. Findings on anxious-ambivalent persons are less consistent. Whereas one study found that individuals characterized as anxious-ambivalent showed a reluctance to seek help (Mikulnicer, Florian, & Weller, 1993), another study using a different situation found their help seeking to be relatively high (i.e., Mikulnicer & Florian, 1995). This variability suggests that the help seeking behavior of anxious-ambivalent individuals is affected to a greater degree than that of avoidant or secure individuals by situational variables that are unrelated to the degree of stress (e.g., whether other people share the stressful situation).

These help-seeking preferences can be subsumed under the distinction between autonomous versus dependent help seeking, and between the over-, under-, or adequate utilization of help. Secure individuals are adequate utilizers of help. Help seeking for them is a primary coping strategy, and when circumstances make other's assistance necessary (i.e., as stress increases), they seek help. They are autonomous help seekers. Avoidant individuals, on the other hand, are consistent underutilizers of help. For them, help seeking is neither a primary nor secondary coping strategy. Anxious-ambivalent individuals are more erratic in their behavior. Depending on factors such as the identity of helper, degree to which the stress is shared by others, and so forth, they can be overutilizers of help and engage in dependent help seeking, or they can exhibit a pattern of underutilization of assistance. In fact, the tripartite distinction between secure, avoidant, and anxious-ambivalent individuals seems to be a personality analog to adequate, under, and overutilization of help, respectively. Tzafrir, Nadler, and Friedland (1996) obtained experimental evidence supporting this idea.

Esteem-Oriented Explanations: Situational and Personality Moderators

Another major organizing construct in help seeking research has been the concept of threat to self-esteem. Much of the research on the social psychology of help seeking has been guided by the assumption that, in Western societies, which put a premium on self-reliance and independence, dependency on others may be a self-threatening experience. Relevant research has identified both situational and personality moderators of the threat to self-esteem associated with help seeking. It has indicated that, under certain conditions and for certain individuals, dependency is not self-threatening, whereas under other circumstances and for other persons, dependency poses a threat to self-esteem. It has been asserted that when dependency is self-threatening people will underutilize available help. We shall first review the research on situational and personality moderators of the self-threat in help seeking and then consider the findings in the light of the distinction between autonomous and dependent help seeking.

Situational Determinants of Self-Threat in Seeking Help

Normativeness. In one of the first experimental investigations of help-seeking behavior, Tessler and Schwartz (1972) studied the willingness to seek help on a novel task (i.e., detecting neuroticism from a taped conversation) from an impersonal source (i.e., guidelines placed conspicuously on the experimenter's desk). In their study, half the participants were told that seeking help is normative behavior, while the other half were told that help seeking is not normative behavior for the task (i.e., the first group were reminded that the number of participants who needed help in past administrations was very high; the second group, that it was very low). Arguing that the implications of low ability associated with help seeking are diluted by information that many others have also sought help, the authors hypothesized that people would seek more help when they know that many others need help under similar conditions (i.e., high normativeness). Their findings supported the hypothesis, as have studies by subsequent researchers (e.g. Broll, Gross, & Piliavin, 1974; Gross, Fisher, Nadler, Stiglitz, & Craig, 1979; Nadler & Porat, 1978).

On the other hand, Snyder and Ingram (1983) found that the effects of normativeness on help seeking depended on whether the person needing help was or was not symptomatic. For symptomatic individuals, afflicted by the symptoms for which help was needed, high normativeness facilitated help seeking. This pattern replicates the aforementioned effects of normativeness as facilitating help seeking. For nonsymptomatic individuals, however, low normativeness was associated with greater help seeking than when normativeness was said to be high. The interpretation for this unexpected finding was that a person who is unfamiliar with the problem (i.e., a nonsymptomatic individual) regards information that the problem is relatively rare (i.e., low normativeness) as implying that it is serious enough to merit seeking outside assistance in order to solve it. The contradictory findings on normativeness highlight the role of social comparison processes in help seeking. Information about other people's need for help colors the implications of dependency for one's self, thereby affecting help-seeking behavior. This is the main thrust of the next section.

Comparison Stress-Closeness That Threatens. The research on the effects of social proximity and similarity between helper and person in need on willingness to seek help has also focused on the role of social comparison processes. Because this research was reviewed earlier, I note here only what is relevant to the esteem-oriented explanations of help seeking. The research on the effects of donor–recipient similarity on help receiving and help seeking has consistently noted that social comparison processes may make dependency on a similar other a self-threatening experience. The findings show that, to maintain a positive self-esteem, individuals avoid this self-threatening dependency and show a relative reluctance to seek and accept help from a socially relevant other (Clark et al., 1974; Nadler, 1986, 1987). These effects were observed when social proximity was operationalized both by attitude similarity (e.g., Nadler, 1987) and by actual social closeness (i.e., friend vs. stranger; Nadler, Fisher and Ben-Itzhak, 1983). Nonetheless, social proximity is not the only factor that affects the self-threat inherent in help seeking.

Ego-Centrality. Some tasks are clearly relevant to most people's view of themselves (e.g., performance reflecting on IQ), whereas others are not (e.g., manual dexterity). Esteem-oriented explanations assert that help seeking that reflects dependency and inadequacy in ego-central psychological dimensions are potentially self-threatening. As self-threat is assumed to lead to reduced willingness to seek help, the general prediction has been that ego-centrality will inhibit help seeking. Research generally supports this prediction. In Tessler and

Schwartz's (1972) pioneering study, half the subjects were told that performance on the given task reflected ego-central qualities such as intelligence and mental hygiene, whereas the other half were told that success depended on chance factors' (i.e., ego-peripheral instructions). The results support the prediction that individuals are more reluctant to seek help on ego-central than on ego-peripheral tasks. A recurring helper similarity X ego-centrality interaction indicates that individuals seek less help from socially close others and respond more defensively to the receipt of such help only when the task on which it is needed is defined as ego-central (Nadler & Fisher, 1986).

The important role of ego-centrality in help seeking has also been observed in field settings. Nadler, Sheinberg, and Jaffe (1981) reported a positive link between acceptance of disability and willingness to seek help in a sample of males who are paraplegic. Acceptance of disability is conceptually similar to the concept of ego-centrality. It reflects the degree to which people who are parapalegic have shifted their ability to use their legs to the periphery of their self-concept and can say to themselves: "I am a worthwhile person, although I am disabled." Thus, high acceptance scores mean that their disabilities, which reflect their need for help, are ego-peripheral. A similar finding was reported by Nadler, Lewinstein, and Rahav (1991) who studied the willingness of parents of retarded children to seek outside help for their childrearing problems. Here, acceptance of retardation (e.g., an item reads "Although we have a retarded child, we are a normal and happy family") was positively associated with the willingness to seek outside help. If acceptance of disability is viewed as a dispositional analog to a noncentral task, these various findings also support the conclusion that ego-centrality inhibits help seeking and suggest that ego-peripherality should promote an instrumental rather than evaluative perspective and be associated with autonomous help seeking. The finding that parents who had high acceptance of retardation scores also exhibited a relatively high level of self-help efforts and help seeking supports this idea.

Self-Esteem as a Personality Moderator of Self-Threat in Help High or Low Self-Esteem.   Given the pivotal role of threat to self-esteem, individuals with high and low self-esteem should be differentially sensitive to the self-threat implications in help and exhibit different levels of help seeking. The direction of the difference may be predicted by either of two approaches (Nadler, 1986). A vulnerability approach suggests that because low self-esteem individuals possess relatively few positive self-cognitions, they will be more vulnerable to the self-threat in help than would be high self-esteem individuals and thus will be less willing to seek help. The consistency approach rests on the assumption that information about the self is threatening to the degree that it is inconsistent with existing self-knowledge. Because dependency is more inconsistent with the positive self-cognitions of the high self-esteem individual than with the self-cognitions of the low self-esteem person, high self-esteem individuals are likely to be more sensitive to the self-threat associated with interpersonal dependency and less likely to seek help.

Both the social psychological and the social support literatures provide empirical evidence on the effects of self-esteem on willingness to seek help. The social psychological studies provide fairly clear support to the consistency prediction. High self-esteem individuals were found to seek less help than low self-esteem individuals in studies using both paper and pencil and behavioral measures of help seeking (e.g., Nadler, Mayseless, Peri, & Tchemerinski, 1985). To be sure, the impact of self-esteem on help seeking was also modulated by self-threat. The lower help seeking exhibited by high self-esteem individuals was apparent only in ego-central tasks.

Overall, these findings imply that high self-esteem individuals underutilize available assistance, thereby resulting in poorer coping. Some support for this position is available in an experimental study by Weiss and Knight (1980). In that study, high and low self-esteem individuals worked on a task that required frequent mutual consultation. The high self-esteem individuals performed more poorly than their low self-esteem counterparts. The authors attributed the difference to the lower willingness of the high self-esteem individuals to seek help. They labeled this effect *the utility of humility*. In similar vein, Hobfoll and London (1986) discussed the costs of the reluctance of high self-esteem women to seek their family's support in times of stress (i.e., when their husbands were away on military duty in war time).

In terms of help seeking as a primary or secondary coping strategy, it may be suggested that in situations in which help seeking entails salient self-threat (e.g., ego-central help), individuals who are sensitive to this threat (e.g., high self-esteem) will use external assistance, if at all, as a secondary coping strategy. Their relatively rigid self-reliance results in the underutilization of available assistance and poorer coping. On the other hand, the humility that frees the individual of the need to appear independent to self and others may be instrumental and conducive to effective coping.

Reducing the Self-Threat in Help: Furthering Autonomous Help Seeking.   The logic behind the psychological dynamics described earlier is that, under certain circumstances, persons tend to view help seeking as abdicating control, and people who are sensitive to this threat will be particularly prone to viewing it this way. Under such conditions, these individuals will view help seeking as dependent help seeking and will choose not to seek help. This suggests that highlighting autonomous elements in the available assistance will encourage help seeking. There are several ways of doing so. Asser (1978) distinguished between didactic and negotiating styles of help seeking, and Nelson-Le Gall (1985), between executive and instrumental seeking. Negotiating and instrumental help seeking are partial requests for help, in which one seeks advice or assistance, but solves the problem on one's own. In didactic and executive help seeking, the person requests the full solution. Highlighting the instrumental or negotiating elements in the helping interaction will enable autonomous help seeking and encourage help seeking, especially by those who are sensitive to the implications of dependency.

Another strategy comes from research on help seeking and perceived opportunity to reciprocate. Help is more easily sought if the person in need expects to be able to reciprocate it (Hatfield & Sprecher, 1983). Phrased in the present terminology, seeking help that cannot be reciprocated is more likely to be perceived as dependent help seeking and is avoided, especially by high self-esteem individuals for whom such dependency is particularly self-threatening (Nadler et al., 1985). Making the opportunity to reciprocate in the future more concrete should color the help seeking as a more autonomous act. This will encourage help seeking and avert the dangers of underutilization of help. Expressing a similar idea, Harlow and Cantor (1995) called for the creation of psychological environments that promote a person's sense of mastery, thereby facilitating the seeking of needed assistance.

When the help is autonomous (i.e., instrumental elements are highlighted, the person perceives future reciprocity) and the person enjoys perceptions of efficacy and ability (i.e., high self esteem), seeking assistance is likely to be an *active, social* and *primary problem focused* coping strategy. Such seeking of assistance is likely to be pursued together with the investment in self-help effort which is active, individual and primary problem-focused coping strategy. Under such conditions, people are likely to alternate between investing effort themselves and autonomous help seeking. Research in the social support literature lends support to this contention. For example, Folkman and Lazarus (1985) reported a high positive correlation (r = .64) between problem-focused coping (i.e., exerting own efforts to solve the problem) and support seeking. Other studies have reported a positive relationship between optimism, perceptions of self-efficacy, and the effectiveness of coping with stress (e.g., Fleishman, 1984;

Taylor & Brown, 1988). Aspinwall and Taylor (1992) found that a primary mediator of the relationships between feeling good about oneself (i.e., high self-esteem, high self-efficacy, optimism) and effective coping is the active seeking of social support from one's network. Active seeking of social support is close in meaning to autonomous help seeking, as used here. As an example, an item on the scale used to measure active seeking of social support reads "I asked a relative or a friend I respect for advice" (Aspinwall & Taylor, 1992). This item emphasizes two elements that are associated with autonomous help seeking: Seeking advice from a friend or a family member. Advice implies partial-instrumental help, and friend or family members are helpers with whom one has long term relationships of which future reciprocity is an important characteristic (Clark & Mills, 1993a, 1993b).

Cognitive Processes Associated With Autonomous versus Dependent Help Seeking

The present section discusses the cognitive processes that are associated with help-seeking behavior in achievement contexts and considers their relationship to the seeking of autonomous or dependent help. Several theoretical conceptualizations deal with the cognitive processes in achievement contexts and provide some important insights. These conceptualizations are Dweck's theorizing on entity versus incremental personal theories in achievement contexts, Nicholls' differentiation between ego and task focus, and attributional analyses of achievement behavior (Weiner, 1979) and depression (Abramson, Seligman, & Teasdale, 1978).

The common element in these three, somewhat overlapping, approaches is their focus on the individual's subjective interpretation of outcomes in achievement contexts (e.g., success or failure), and their emphasis on the principle of active construal in social behavior (Ross & Nisbett, 1991). We begin by presenting the essentials of each of these approaches and then by considering their relevance to the issue of dependent versus autonomous help seeking.

Entity-Theorists Versus Incremental-Theorists: Dweck's Theory of Helpless- Versus Mastery-Oriented Children

Dweck (1991) distinguished between mastery-oriented and helpless-oriented patterns that characterize children in achievement contexts. Children in the helpless pattern view themselves as being constantly evaluated and tested, whereas children in the mastery pattern view performance as a stepping stone on the road toward further development and learning. Consequently, a child characterized by a helpless pattern sees failures as an indication of low ability, whereas the mastery-oriented child views it as a step on the ladder of new learning.

The two patterns can be situationally induced. For example, Elliott and Dweck (1988) induced the helpless- versus mastery-oriented patterns by emphasizing the evaluative versus value of learning perspective on the task. The patterns may also reflect dispositional tendencies. In subsequent research, Dweck and her colleagues distinguished between entity-theorists and incremental-theorists. *Entity theorists* are children who believe that intelligence is a fixed trait over which one has no control. They interpret good performance as an indication of high ability and poor performance as a sign of low intelligence and ability.

Incremental theorists are children who view intelligence as a malleable quality that can be developed by investing effort and learning. Whereas entity theorists consider outcomes in achievement settings as measures of their competence or intelligence, incremental theorists are more concerned with the process of learning. They feel capable and satisfied with themselves when they master something new, after having gone the full route of investing effort, falling, getting back on their feet, falling, and getting up again. They realize that effort and persistence are part of the process of mastering a new skill or acquiring new knowledge. Entity theorists, for whom the outcome is the measure of all things, therefore feel able and competent even if their success is on an easy task. Successful performance for them is an end; for incremental theorists, performance is a means toward gaining new skill or knowledge, which is their aim or end.

It may be suggested that performance perspective, whether induced situationally or manifested in a dispositional entity theory of achievement, which is associated with a strong evaluation apprehension, will render help seeking threatening. Individuals who are characterized by or induced to employ a performance perspective are likely to feel under evaluation and reluctant to demonstrate dependency for fear that it will reveal their inadequacies and will probably not adopt help seeking as a primary coping strategy. Incremental theorists, who do not feel that their intelligence is on the line, are less likely to fear dependency as evidence of some global personal inadequacy and are more likely to view it as an additional means of improving or developing their skills. Feeling that they are actively learning and thus in control of the situation, they are likely to view autonomous help seeking, combined with self-help coping efforts, as a primary coping strategy.

This dual emphasis on the motivation to better one's skills or knowledge and the belief that such skills are malleable and therefore controllable by the individual agrees with Nadler & Fisher's (1986) conceptualization of controllable self-threat in receiving help. This is defined as a situation in which the recipient of help views dependency as self-threatening and believes that one can solve the problem by exerting more efforts oneself. The self-threat is said to create a motivation to end one's dependency on others, and the perception that one can control the situation leads to increased self-help efforts. This is a motivational state not unlike that described by Dweck as characterizing incremental theorists. Although both Dweck (1991) and Nadler and Fisher (1986) highlighted the role of the individual's motivation for mastery and belief of control in achievement contexts, their predictions regarding help seeking were different. Dweck's theorizing would suggest that high motivation for mastery and the belief that one controls the situation would lead to greater willingness to seek help. In contrast, Nadler and Fisher suggested that the combination of self-perceptions of control and high motivation for mastery lead to increased self-help effort and low help seeking. Distinction between autonomous and dependent help seeking allows a resolution of this inconsistency. Help seeking in Nadler and Fisher's model was conceptualized as dependent help seeking, whereas the present application of Dweck's theorizing implies autonomous help seeking. Taken together, it may be suggested that controllable self-threat, or an incremental theory of achievement, would lead to a high degree of self-help efforts, autonomous help seeking, and low dependent help seeking.

Illustrating the importance of the entity versus incremental pattern for predicting performance in school settings, Henderson and Dweck (1991) investigated the grades of students after they had moved to junior high school. They found that children who were characterized as incrementalists tended to do as well or better in Grade 7 than in the Grade 6. Entity theorists, on the other hand, got worse grades in Grade 7 than in Grade 6. In describing these results, Dweck (1990) wrote:

> Overall, entity theorists who had been low achievers in the past remained so, and any of those who had been high achievers in the 6th grade were now among the lowest achievers. Prominent among the latter were many high confidence entity theorists. It may be that the challenge and confusion of transition are more threatening to those who believe that intelligence is fixed and have been accustomed to thinking of themselves as having it. (p. 211)

A possibility that is not considered by Dweck and her colleagues, but which is raised by the present discussion, is that this phenomenon may be, at least partly, explained by differential levels of help seeking. Children with high expectations of success, who are also more concerned about performance than learning goals (i.e., entity theorists), may be especially sensitive to the self-threat in asking for help. In the new environment of junior high school, these children, and especially those who have a positive self-image to protect (i.e., high achievers in Grade 6), may be particularly sensitive to others' evaluations of them and likely to view any help difficult task of adjusting to their new environment (i.e., junior high school) on their own, and, therefore, suffer decreased performance. These children may be characterized by the following pattern: (a) Initially, they invest only in self-help efforts; (b) if self-help efforts do not prove successful, they see their failure as indicative of overall inability to cope; and (c) this results in their subsequent dependent help-seeking. This possibility, that the decreased performance of high confidence-entity theorists is moderated by their relative reluctance to seek help, must be empirically validated.

Task Involvement versus Ego Involvement: Nicholls' Theory

Nicholls' (1984) differentiated and non-differentiated concepts of achievement are similar to Dweck's distinction between performance and mastery-oriented patterns. On a more general level, both theories differentiate between two basic psychological perspectives on task performance: evaluative and task perspectives. In the evaluative perspective, attention while performing the task is on the outcome and its consequences for one's feelings of self-worth. In the task perspective, attention is focused on the process of task completion, and one's concern is with the task rather than self-evaluation.

Nicholls' emphasis, however, is more interpersonal than Dweck's. Whereas Dweck discusses self-theories and conception of personal ability, Nicholls' pivotal distinction is between the judgment of one's ability in relation to one's perceived mastery (i.e., a less differentiated perception) and one's judgment relative to the ability of members of a normative reference group (i.e., a differentiated perception). The first orientation is termed task involvement because the concern is with improving mastery on a task rather than with how one performs compared to others. The second orientation emphasizes performance relative to others, and the person is concerned with whether he or she is better or worse than others. This orientation is termed the ego-involvement orientation.

It seems that in an ego-involvement conception of achievement, dependency on others for help could be inconsistent with the desire to gain their favorable evaluation. Ego-involved individuals are thus likely to avoid seeking help even when it is necessary to task completion. Findings that persons are more sensitive to unfavorable social comparisons (i.e., Nadler & Fisher, 1986; Tesser, 1988), and seek less help from a socially close other than a socially distant other (Nadler, 1987) in ego relevant tasks, are consistent with Nicholls' claim that ego-involvement is associated with self-judgments relative to others. They also suggest that the inhibitive effects of an ego-involved conception of achievement on help seeking are most likely to occur when the potential helper serves as a frame of reference for self-evaluation. Task-involved individuals, on the other hand, who are less concerned with others' evaluations and their relative standing, would probably be more likely to view others' assistance as an instrumental means toward gaining mastery and knowledge. They would probably engage in autonomous help seeking, seeking assistance when it is instrumental to task mastery, and avoiding it when it is not.

Nicholls noted that ego-involvement is enhanced by (a) presenting the task as test of a valued skill, (b) highlighting interpersonal competition, and (c) inducing self-awareness. This suggests that these conditions will be associated with the underutilization of help. The research showing that less help is sought when the task is ego-central (i. e., a test of valued skill) and there is a high level of donor-recipient similarity (which induces comparison stress related to interpersonal competition; Nadler, 1987) indicates that the same conditions that foster an ego-involved focus also contribute to the underutilization of help. Moreover, because self-awareness promotes increased self-evaluation, it should also be associated with lower willingness to seek help. This suggestion has received empirical support. Using scores on a self-consciousness scale (the personality analog of self-awareness), La Morto-Corse and Carver (1980) reported that individuals characterized as high in self-consciousness sought less help than those characterized as low. Thus, situations that induce ego-involved focus would also be linked to lower willingness to seek help. Butler and Neuman (1995) obtained direct support for the link between ego versus task involvement and help seeking. In their study, they experimentally manipulated ego versus task focus and found that children sought more help when task was involved than when ego was involved.

Extending his analysis, Nicholls (1984) suggested that the effects of task and ego involvement on achievement behavior depend on the person's perceived ability on the task in question and the certainty of these perceived abilities. This extension enables a further delineation of the variables associated with the under utilization or over utilization of help. According to Nicholls, under conditions that foster ego-involvement, persons who have low perceived ability but are uncertain of their self-perceptions might be expected to choose very difficult tasks. This is because they see a chance for success that will bring them praise if it materializes but will not bring blame if it does not. Applied to the present context, they are also likely to complete the task without any help. For, if they succeed without help, they are likely to be positively evaluated by themselves and others, and, if they fail, they can nonetheless congratulate themselves, and expect others to do the same for having put all they had into it.

Nicholls also suggested that ego-involved individuals who are certain of their low abilities are likely to choose a very easy task to assure their success. Applied to the present context, it may be suggested here that they are also likely to opt for the easiest route to problem solution: seeking dependent help. Persons who are convinced that they lack the ability to solve a problem on their own have only one way of overcoming the difficulties of the task: dependent help seeking (obtaining a complete solution to the problem).

Lastly, Nicholls suggested that under conditions that foster task-orientation, or when one enjoys perceptions of high ability, the individual is likely to choose moderately difficult tasks. This choice maximizes the chance of meaningful success (i.e., on a relatively challenging task), while minimizing the likelihood of failure (i.e., on an extremely difficult task). This instrumental perspective is likely to be associated with autonomous help seeking, which strikes a balance between avoiding the overutilization of help and unwarranted dependency of others, and shunning underutilization and ineffective reliance on self. Both choosing a task of moderate difficulty and seeking autonomous help epitomize the compromise between the opposite psychological dangers of failure or meaningless success on the one hand, and underutilization or overutilization of help on the other. Both these behavioral choices are more likely to occur when one is task-oriented and certain of one's high ability on the task.

The issues of ego versus task orientation and high versus low perceived ability are related to the findings reviewed previously in the esteem-oriented explanations to help seeking. I conclude this section with an exposition of the links. First, the seeking of help may or may not be related to one's self-evaluation. The esteem-related research tells us that help seeking has self-evaluative implications when the task on which help is needed is ego-central to the individual. Nicholls' theorizing similarly suggests that its implications are self-evaluative when the achievement situation is ego-relevant. In either case, the person is likely to underutilize external help and not employ help seeking as a primary coping response.

Second, by applying Nicholls' theorizing, I suggested that people who are certain of their low ability will exhibit dependent help seeking.

This suggestion is based on the assumption that low self-esteem scores represent a general and pervasive sense of inability, and the argument that persons who are certain of their low ability would choose easy tasks and seek complete solutions in achievement contexts. The proposed link is congruent with the findings that low self-esteem individuals consistently seek more external assistance than high self-esteem individuals and that the assistance they seek is of a dependent nature (i.e., complete solutions).

Attributional Analyses: Weiner and Ames

Attributional analysis of social behavior has been a major theoretical and empirical tool in social psychology since the 1970s. One of the most influential conceptualizations in this context is Weiner's attributional analysis of achievement situations, which has subsequently been applied to explain other psychological phenomena as well.

Wiener's pioneering contribution centered on the roles of external versus internal and stable versus unstable attributions in explaining outcomes in achievement contexts (Weiner et al., 1971). Subsequently, he refined and redefined this conceptualization by adding the dimensions of controllability and globality to those of locus (internal vs. external) and stability (stable vs. unstable; Wiener, 1979). Although a detailed exposition of these theoretical developments is beyond the scope of the present chapter, Weiner's research and thinking alerts us to the fact that the meaning of an outcome to the individual is determined by its subjective interpretation by the self and others rather than by its objective properties.

Extending Weiner's analysis to the domain of affective difficulties, Abramson et al. (1978) suggested an attributional model to account for the set of phenomena that is associated with helpless resignation to the problem versus the investment of effort to solve it. This theoretical extension is particularly relevant to our distinction between autonomous and dependent help seeking in that it centers on the cognitive processes that account for why some people initiate active efforts to solve their problems whereas others adopt a passive and helpless attitude.

The main concept that distinguishes Weiner's (1979) and Abramson et al.'s, (1978) analyses from earlier attributional accounts in achievement settings is the notion of the globality of attributions for failures or difficulties. Abramson et al. (1978) suggested that helplessness-like passivity is associated with the attribution of the problem to internal, stable and global causes. An example of this is blaming one's current emotional difficulties on an inadequate personality. Personality deficiency is (a) a global attribution that encompasses innumerable psychological dimensions, (b) refers to an internal locus, and (c) is stable over time in that one's overall personality is less changeable than a single personality feature. Global, internal, and stable explanations of a problem are associated with the conclusion that problems are beyond one's power to solve and the perception of noncontingency between one's actions and outcome, which precipitates the psychological helplessness described by Abramson et al. (1978). In contrast, the attribution of one's current difficulties to external, unstable, and specific causes is less likely to be associated with helplessness. For example, persons who attribute their emotional difficulties to a deficiency in assertiveness (i.e., an internal, stable, specific cause) could more easily envisage a specific and time-bound course of action to correct it (e.g., take a four week assertiveness training course). They are more likely to feel a motivation to control their situation by investing efforts and contingency between their actions and outcomes. Hence, they are more likely to put effort into solving the problem.

Ames and his colleagues applied these ideas to help seeking (Ames, 1983). Ames distinguished between help-relevant and help-irrelevant attributional patterns, the first leading to willingness to seek assistance to solve one's difficulties, the second resulting in reluctance to seek help. Help-relevant attributions include the beliefs that the difficulty or failure (a) does not reflect on one's global ability but is due rather to a lack of specific skill or information, or a lack of effort and (b) that external causes for the failure (e.g., bad luck) are irrelevant. The help-relevant attributions are epitomized in the following statement: "I am capable, but I did not try hard enough, and there are no external forces that would have inhibited me from doing better if I had put forth more effort" (Ames, 1983, p. 170). Ames suggests that both persons who hold help-relevant and those who hold help-irrelevant attributions may believe that they have low ability and that they differ in the degree to which they consider their low ability a global trait. Persons who make help-relevant attributions could explain their need by lack of effort or deficiency in a specific and malleable ability, rather than by a general and more or less permanent deficiency in an inherent personal quality.

To provide empirical support for their claims, Ames and Lau (1982) developed a questionnaire designed to tap help-relevant and help-irrelevant attributional patterns. The help relevant pattern included statements that tapped perceptions of adequate global ability, the attribution of the deficiency to low specific ability, viewed effort exertion as instrumental for success, and discounted external excuses as explanations for failure. Their study examined the links between the two attributional patterns and attendance at review sessions offered to students in an introductory psychology course. The data indicate that, of various students who performed poorly on a first test in the course, those who explained their performance by a help-relevant pattern were more likely to attend review sessions than those who had made help-irrelevant attributions.

The above attributional explanation of help seeking, however, is applicable only to the case of autonomous help seeking. Ames' conceptual definition of help seeking and Ames & Lau's (1982) operational definition of help seeking make this point clear. Commenting on Ames and Lau's (1982) data, Ames (1983) regarded help seeking as a specific case of achievement behavior: "The data from this study provide clear support for the relation of causal attributions to the achievement-related behavior of help seeking" (emphasis added; p. 174). Moreover, the help studied by Ames and Lau is autonomous. Students who attend a review session retain responsibility for and autonomy in their performance. They do not place themselves in the hands of a magic helper. The review session is an instrumental tool to further the chance of personal success and individual achievement. Finally, the help-relevant attributional pattern is no different from the attributional patterns that have been shown to be related to individual achievement behaviors, such as persistence and exertion of effort. Both the belief in the importance of effort and the belief that one's global self is adequate have been shown to predict exertion of effort on tasks in the face of difficulties.

In all, Ames' incisive attributional analysis seems to be related to only two of the three behavioral alternatives discussed in this chapter. It predicts autonomous help seeking (i.e., help-relevant attributions) and underutilization of help (i.e., help irrelevant attributions). The spirit of this model also suggests that low performers who did not seek help by attending review sessions had resigned themselves to a future low performance. In the language of Abramson et al., there was no contingency for them between effort and outcome.

CONCLUSIONS AND IMPLICATIONS

Research on help seeking has traditionally focused on the dichotomous alternatives of seeking help versus not seeking help. This chapter diverges from this traditional approach by proposing a tripartite distinction, identifying the processes and variables that result in (a) autonomous help seeking, (b) dependent help seeking, or (c) unwillingness to seek help. At the background of this approach was the emphasis on the links between seeking help and coping. Help seeking can be an ineffective coping strategy if it involves an overutilization or underutilization of the available helping resources (i.e., dependent help seeking and no help seeking, respectively), or it can be an effective coping strategy if it entails an adequate utilization of helping resources, as autonomous help seeking does. Similarly, any particular act of help seeking may have any of several very different and antagonistic motives. Its meaning derives from the specific personal and situational context in which it is undertaken.

Our review of the previous research centered on three broad and overlapping sets of explanations of help-seeking behavior: relationship explanations, self-esteem explanations, and cognitive explanations. The research on the impact of the quality of the actual relationship between helper and help seeker has yielded an inconsistent picture. Whereas the social support research has consistently found that persons are more willing to seek help from socially close others, the social psychological research has found just the opposite. The autonomous–dependent distinction was proposed as a resolution of this empirical conflict. Review of the literature suggests that help seeking is greater from socially close others when it is autonomous (e.g., partial requests, help that can be reciprocated) and allows the help seeker to retain his or her sense of control and perception of self-efficacy. When, however, the only route open for the person in need is to engage in dependent help seeking, the helper's social proximity engenders comparison stress that results in underutilization of help.

Various bodies of research on personality characteristics that reflect the quality of the person's relationship with the social world enable us to argue that feminine gender-role orientation, resilience, dependent personality, and secure attachment style all entail an active social orientation, and furthermore, that this orientation is associated with autonomous help seeking as a primary coping strategy that results in enhanced coping. The autonomous versus dependent distinction enabled me to make conceptual extensions of existing empirical findings. Thus, for example, in line with theorizing on the dependent personality, I argued that highly dependent individuals would engage in dependent help seeking when the helper is high status. Similarly, I suggested that secure, avoidant, and anxious-ambivalent attachment styles are the personality analog of adequate, underutilization, and overutilization patterns of help seeking, respectively.

Discussion of studies within the threat to self-esteem tradition was also enriched by the distinction between autonomous and dependent help seeking. Regarding situational determinants, it was noted that situational conditions, such as high normativeness of help seeking or the non-ego-centrality of the problem with which the help is needed, are likely to foster an instrumental perspective and encourage autonomous help seeking. Regarding the trait of self-esteem, the distinction between two types of help seeking was used to resolve the conflict between the recurring finding that, because high self-esteem individuals display a relatively rigid adherence to norms of self-reliance and independence, they underutilize assistance and other findings that show that high self-esteem is positively associated with seeking social support in time of need. I suggested that in the studies that found that high self-esteem individuals underutilize assistance, the help seeker would necessarily have been dependent and the need for help would threaten their self-perceptions as capable and self-reliant, whereas in studies that found the opposite, the seeking was autonomous.

The discussion of the cognitive processes in achievement contexts focused on three theoretical orientations: Dweck's theorizing on incremental versus entity theory of achievement, Nicholls' distinction between differentiated and undifferentiated conceptions of achievement, and Weiner's attributional analysis of achievement behavior. Notwithstanding their differences, these theories show a considerable degree of theoretical overlap in their implications for the help-seeking dilemma. An incremental theory of achievement, an undifferentiated conception of achievement, and help-seeking relevant attributions reflect an instrumental view of the need for help, whereas an entity theory of achievement, a differentiated conception of achievement, and help-irrelevant attributions reflect an ego-evaluative view of the need for help. If the goal of behavior is to outperform others, the person's global ability and sense of adequacy are on the line, and the task is viewed as a test of ego-relevant abilities. Under these conditions, individuals will probably refrain from seeking help and underutilize the available resources. If they do seek help, it will be as a secondary and delayed coping behavior and probably will be dependent help seeking, because their avoidance of assistance is likely to result in worsening the problem. If an instrumental perspective pervades and performance on the task is not viewed as an ultimate test of one's overall abilities, the help seeking is likely to be autonomous and undertaken in accord with objective need. It is likely to be pursued simultaneously with self-help efforts and be viewed as an additional instrumental means of gaining better knowledge and mastery. Phrased different: autonomous help seeking is an active, social, primary, and problem-focused coping strategy.

The various positions suggest that an important determinant of help seeking is the person's perceived control of the achievement context. An instrumental perspective is likely to be associated with greater feelings of personal control. This is true of incremental theorists who view skills as malleable, of the task focus of individuals who views their acts as means to self-development, and of persons who espouse help-seeking-relevant attributions and reject the notions of global inability or uncontrollable situational factors as explanations for their need for help. In fact, it seems that the perception of control in a given situation encourages an instrumental perspective and facilitates autonomous help seeking. In contrast, feeling helpless in the face of a problem is likely to result in underutilization of available assistance even at the cost of not being able to solve the problem or the cessation of trying and depending on others to solve the problem. In the first case, the effort to solve the problem on one's own, no matter what, may restore the person's sense of control and self-efficacy, but in a way that is detrimental to the self. The second reflects a helpless-like state where individuals have lost the perception that they can affect their outcomes. This analysis also highlights the role of two related concepts: motivation for self-development, rather than motivation to succeed on the task at hand; and the belief that one can control one's outcomes. Emphasis on a developmental rather than an outcome result and the belief in one's ability to control this process are likely to be associated with autonomous help seeking. Lacking perception of control and focusing on the outcome rather than the process of self-development are likely to be associated with either the underutilization of help or dependent help seeking.

REFERENCES

Abramson, L. Y., Seligman, M. E. P., & Teasdale, J. D. (1978). Learned helplessness in humans: Critique and reformulation. *Journal of Abnormal Psychology, 87*, 49–74.

Ainsworth, M., Blehar, M., Waters, E., Waters, E., & Wall, S. (1978). *Patterns of attachment*. Hillsdale, NJ: Lawrence Erlbaum Associates.

Ames, R., (1983). Help-seeking and achievement orientation: Perspectives from attribution theory. In B. M. DePaulo, A. Nadler, & J. D. Fisher, (Eds.), *New Directions in Helping: Help-seeking* Vol. 2. (pp. 165–186). New York: Academic Press.

Ames, R., & Lau S. (1982). An attributional analysis of help-seeking in academic settings. *Journal of Educational Psychology, 74*, 414–423.

Amirkhan, J. H., Risinger, R. T., & Swickert, R. J. (1995). Extroversion: A hidden personal factor in coping? *Journal of Personality, 63*, 189–212.

Aspinwall, L. G., & Taylor, S. E. (1992). Modeling cognitive adaptation: A longitudinal investigation of the impact of individual differences and coping on college adjustment and performance. *Journal of Personality and Social Psychology, 60*, 989–1003.

Asser, E. S. (1978). Social class and help-seeking behavior. *American Journal of Community Psychology, 6*, 465–474.

Birtchnell, J., & Kennard, J. (1983). What does the MMPI dependency really measure? *Journal of Clinical Psychology, 39*, 532–543.

Blaine, B., Crocker, J., & Major, B. (1995). The unintended negative consequences of sympathy for the stigmatized. *Journal of Applied Social Psychology, 25*, 889–905.

Bornstein, R. F. (1992). The dependent personality: Developmental, social and clinical perspectives. *Psychological Bulletin, 112*, 3–23.

Bornstein, R. F., Krukonis, A. B., Manning, K. A., Mastrosimone, C., & Rossner, S. (1993). Interpersonal dependency and health service utilization in college student sample. *Journal of Social and Clinical Psychology, 12*, 262–279.

Bowlby, J. (1973). *Attachment and loss: Separation, anxiety, and anger.* New York: Basic Books.

Broll, L., Gross, A. E., & Piliavin, I. (1974). Effects of offered and requested help on help seeking. *Journal of Applied Social Psychology, 4*, 244–258.

Burke, R. J., Weir, T., & Duncan, G. (1976). Informal helping relationships in work organizations. *Academy of Management Journal, 19*, 370–377.

Butler, R. (1993). Effects of task and ego achievement goals on information seeking during task engagement. *Journal of Personality and Social Psychology, 65*, 18–31.

Butler, R., & Neuman, O. (1995). Effects of task and ego achievement goals on help-seeking behaviors and attitudes. *Journal of Educational Psychology, 87*, 261–271.

Clark, M. S., Gotay, C. C., & Mills, J. (1974). Acceptance of help as a function of similarity of the potential helper and opportunity to repay. *Journal of Applied Social Psychology, 4*, 12–24.

Clark, M. S. & Mills, J. (1993a). Communal and exchange relations: What it is and is not. *Personality and Social Psychology Bulletin, 19*, 684–691.

Clark, M. S., & Mills, J. (1993b). Interpersonal attraction in exchange and communal relationships. *Journal of Personality and Social Psychology, 67*, 12–24.

Corrigan, J. D. (1978). Salient attributes of two types of helpers. *Journal of Counseling Psychology, 25*, 588–590.

Cutrona, C. E. (1990). Stress and social support: In search of optimal matching. *Journal of Social and Clinical Psychology, 9*, 3–14.

DePaulo, B. M., Nadler, A., & Fisher, J. D. (Eds.). (1983). *New directions in helping: Vol. 2. Help seeking.* New York: Academic Press.

Dweck, C. S. (1991). Self theories and goals: Their role in motivation, personality and development. In R. A. Dienstbier (Ed.): *Nebraska Symposium on Motivation,* (pp. 199–235). Lincoln, NE: Nebraska University Press.

Elliott, E. S., & Dweck, C. S. (1988). Goals: An approach to motivation and achievement. *Journal of Personality and Social Psychology, 54*, 5–12.

Festinger, L. (1954). A theory of social comparison processes. *Human Relations, 1*, 117–140.

Fischer, E. H., Winer, D., & Abramowitz, S. I. (1983). Seeking professional help for psychological problems. In A. Nadler, J. D. Fisher, & B. M. DePaulo (Eds.), *New directions in helping: Vol. 3. Applied perspectives on help seeking and receiving* (pp. 163–182). New York: Academic Press.

Fisher, L., Kokes, R. F., Cole, R. E., Perkins, P. M., & Wynne, L. C. (1987). Competent children at risk: A study of well functioning offspring of disturbed parents. In E. J. Anthony & B. J. Cohler (Eds.), *The invulnerable child* (pp. 211–228). New York: Guilford Press.

Fleishman, J. A. (1984). Personality characteristics and coping patterns. *Journal of Health and Social Behavior, 25*, 229–244.

Flett, G. L., Blankstein, K. R., Hicken, J. D., & Watson, M. S. (1995). Social support and help seeking in daily hassles versus major life events stress. *Journal of Applied Social Psychology, 25*, 49–58.

Folkman, S., & Lazarus, R. S. (1985). If it changes it must be a process: Study of emotion and coping during three stages of a college examination. *Journal of Personality and Social Psychology, 48*, 150–170.

Garland, A. F., & Zigler, E. F. (1994). Psychological correlates of help seeking attitudes among children and adolescents. *American Journal of Orthopsychiatry, 64*, 586–594.

Garmezy, N. (1981). Children under stress: Perspectives on antecedents and correlates of vulnerability and resistance to psychopathology. In A.I. Rabin, J. Aronoff, A. M. Barclay, & R. A. Zucker (Eds.), *Further explorations in personality* (pp. 196–269). New York: Wiley.

Glidewell, J. C., Tucker, S., Todt, M., & Cox, S. (1983). Professional support systems: The teaching profession. In A. Nadler, J. D. Fisher, & B. M. DePaulo (Eds.), *New directions in helping: Vol. 3. Applied perspectives on help seeking and receiving* (pp. 189–210). New York: Academic Press.

Gourash, N. (1978). Help seeking: A review of the literature. *American Journal of Community Psychology, 6,* 413–423.

Greenglass, E. R. (1993a). The contribution of social support to coping strategies. *Applied Psychology: An International Review, 42,* 323–340.

Greenglass, E. R. (1993b). Social support and coping of employed women. In B. C. Long & S. E. Kahn (Eds.), *Women, work, and coping* (pp. 154–169). Montreal, Canada: McGill-Queens.

Greenley, J. R., & Mechanic, D. (1976). Social selection in seeking help for psychological problems. *Journal of Health and Social Behavior, 17,* 249–262.

Gross, A. E., Fisher, J. D., Nadler, A., Stiglitz, E., & Craig, C. (1979). Correlates of help utilization at a women's counseling service. *Journal of Community Psychology, 7,* 42–49.

Harlow, R. E., & Cantor, N. (1995). To whom people turn when things go poorly? Task orientation and functional social contacts. *Journal of Personality and Social Psychology, 69,* 329–341.

Hatfield, E., & Sprecher, S. (1983). Equity theory and recipient reactions to aid. In J. D. Fisher, A. Nadler, & B. M. DePaulo (Eds.), *New directions in helping: Vol. 1. Recipient reactions to aid* (pp. 113–141). New York: Academic Press.

Hazan, C., & Shaver, P. (1987). Romantic love conceptualized as an attachment process. *Journal of Personality and Social Psychology, 52,* 511–524.

Hazan, C., & Shaver, P. (1990). Love at work: An attachment-theoretical perspective. *Journal of Personality and Social Psychology, 59,* 270–280.

Henderson, V., & Dweck, C. S. (1990). Adolescence and achievement. In S. Feldman & G. Elliot (Eds.), *At the threshold: Adolescent development.* Cambridge, MA: Harvard University Press.

Hobfoll, S. E., Dunahoo, C .L., Ben-Porath, Y., & Monnier, J. (1994). Gender and coping: The dual axis model of coping. *American Journal of Community Psychology, 22,* 49–82.

Hobfoll, S. E., & London, P. (1986). The relationship of self concept and social support to emotional distress among women during war. *Journal of Social and Clinical Psychology, 12,* 87–100.

Kagan, J., & Mussen, P. (1956). Dependency themes on the TAT and group conformity. *Journal of Consulting Psychology, 20,* 29–32.

Karabenick, S. A., & Knapp, J. R. (1988). Help-seeking and the need for academic assistance. *Journal of Educational Psychology, 80,* 406–408.

LaMorto-Corse, A. M., & Carver, C. S. (1980). Recipient reactions to aid: Effects of locus of initiation attributions and individual differences. *Bulletin of the Psychonomic Society, 16,* 265–268.

Lazarus, R. S., & Folkman, S. (1984). *Stress, appraisal, and coping.* New York: Springer.

Link, B., & Dohrenwend, B. P. (1980). Formulation of hypotheses about the ratio of untreated to treated cases in true prevalence studies of functional psychiatric disorders. In B. P. Dohrenwend, B. S. Dohrenwend, M. S Gould, B. Link, R. Neugebauer, & R. Wunsch-Hitzing (Eds.), *Mental illness in the United States: Epidemiological estimates.* New York: Praeger.

Long, B. C. (1988). Work-related stress and coping strategies of professional women. *Journal of Employment Counseling, 25,* 37–44.

McRae, R. R., & Costa, P. T., Jr. (1986). Personality, coping, and coping effectiveness in an adult sample. *Journal of Personality, 54,* 385–405.

Merton, V., Merton, R. K. & Barber, E. (1983). Client ambivalence in professional relationships: The problem of seeking help from strangers. In B. M. DePaulo, A. Nadler, & J. D. Fisher (Eds.), *New directions in helping: Vol. 2. Help seeking* (pp. 13–45). New York: Academic Press.

Mikulincer, M., & Florian, V. (1995). Appraisal and coping in a real life stressful situation: The contribution of attachment styles. *Personality and Social Psychology Bulletin, 21,* 406–414.

Mikulincer, M., Florian, V., & Weller, A. (1993). Attachment styles, coping strategies, and post-traumatic psychological distress: The impact of the Gulf War in Israel. *Journal* of Personality and Social Psychology, 64, 817–826.

Milgram, N. A., & Palti, G. (1993). Psychosocial characteristics of resilient children. *Journal of Research in Personality, 27,* 207–221.

Nadler, A. (1986). Self-esteem and the seeking and receiving of help: Theoretical and empirical perspectives. In B. Maher & W. Maher (Eds.), *Progress in experimental personality research* (Vol. 14, pp. 115–163). New York: Academic Press.

Nadler, A. (1987). Determinants of help-seeking behavior: The effects of helper's similarity, task centrality, and recipient's self-esteem. *European Journal of Social Psychology, 17,* 57–67.

Nadler, A. (1991). Help-seeking behavior: Psychological costs and instrumental benefits. In M. S. Clark (Ed.), *Review of personality and social psychology* (Vol. 12, pp. 290–312). New York: Sage.

Nadler, A. (in press). Personality and help seeking: Autonomous vs. dependent help seeking. In G. Pierce, B. Leakey, I. G. Sarason, & B. Sarason (Eds.), *Sourcebook of theory and research on social support and personality.* New York: Plenum.

Nadler, A., & Fisher, J. E., (1986). The role of threat to self-esteem and perceived control in recipient reactions to aid: Theory development and empirical validation. In L. Berkowitz (Ed.), *Advances in experimental social psychology,* (Vol. 19, pp. 81–123). New York: Academic Press.

Nadler, A., Fisher, J. D., & Ben-Itzhak, S. (1983). With a little help from my friend: Effects of single or multiple act aid as a function of donor and task characteristics. *Journal of Personality and Social Psychology, 44,* 310–321.

Nadler, A., Fisher, J. D., & DePaulo, B. M. (Eds.). (1983). *New directions in helping: Vol. 3. Applied perspectives on help seeking and receiving.* New York: Academic Press

Nadler, A., Fisher, J. D., & Streufert, S. (1976). When helping hurts: The effects of donor–recipient similarity and recipient self-esteem on reactions to aid. *Journal of Personality, 44,* 310–321.

Nadler, A., Lewinstein, E., & Rahav, G. (1991). Acceptance of retardation and help-seeking: Correlates of help-seeking preferences of mothers and fathers of retarded children. *Mental Retardation, 29,* 17–23.

Nadler, A., Maler, S., & Friedman, A. (1984). Effects of helper's sex, subject's sex, subject's androgyny, and self evaluation on males' and females' willingness to seek and receive help. *Sex Roles, 10,* 327–339.

Nadler, A., Mayseless, O., Peri, N., & Tchemerinski, A. (1985). Effects of self-esteem and ability to reciprocate on help-seeking behavior. *Journal of Personality, 53,* 23–36.

Nadler, A., & Porat, I. (1978). When names do not help: Effects of anonymity and locus of need attributions on help seeking behavior. *Personality and Social Psychology Bulletin, 4,* 624–628.

Nadler, A., Sheinberg, L., & Jaffe, Y. (1981). Coping with stress by help seeking: Help seeking and receiving behaviors in male paraplegics. In C. Spielberger, I. Sarason, & N. Milgram (Eds.), *Stress and anxiety* (Vol. 8, pp. 375–386). Washington, DC: Hemisphere.

Nelson-Le Gall, S. (1985). Help-seeking behavior in learning. In E. W. Gordon (Ed.), *Review of research in education,* (Vol. 12, pp. 55–90). Washington DC: American Educational Research Association.

Neugebauer, R., Dohrenwend, B. P., & Dohrenwend, B. S. (1980). Formulation of hypotheses about the true prevalence of functional psychiatric disorders among adults. In B. P. Dohrenwend, B. S. Dohrenwend, M. S. Gould, B. Link, R. Neugebauer, & R. Wunsch-Hitzing (Eds.), *Mental illness in the United States: Epidemiological estimates* (pp. 45–94). New York: Praeger.

Nicholls, J. G. (1984). Achievement motivation: Conceptions of ability, subjective experience, task choice, and performance. *Psychological Review, 91*, 328–346.

Philips, M. A., & Murrel, S. A. (1994). Impact of psychological and physical health, stressful events, and social support on subsequent mental health help seeking among older adults. *Journal of Consulting and Clinical Psychology, 62*, 270–275.

Pincus, A. L., & Gurtman, M. B. (1995). The three faces of interpersonal dependency: Structural analyses of self report dependency measures. *Journal of Personality and Social Psychology, 69*, 744–758.

Rickwood, D. J., & Braithwaite, V. A. (1994). Social psychological factors affecting help seeking for emotional problems. *Social Science and Medicine, 39*, 563–572.

Rogler, L. H., & Cortes, D. E. (1993). Help seeking pathways: A unifying concept in mental health care. *American Journal of Psychiatry, 150*, 554–562.

Ross, L., & Nisbett, R. E. (1991). *The person and the situation: Perspectives of social psychology.* Philadelphia, PA: Temple University Press.

Shapiro, G. E. (1983). Embarrassment and help seeking. In B. M. DePaulo, A. Nadler, & J. D. Fisher (Eds.), *New directions in helping: Vol. 2. Help seeking* (pp. 143–165). New York: Academic Press.

Shilkret, C. J., & Masling, J. M. (1981). Oral dependence and dependent behavior., *Journal of Personality Assessment, 45*, 125–129.

Simpson, J. A., Rholes, W. S., & Nelligan, J. S. (1992). Support seeking and support giving within couples in an anxiety provoking situation: The role of attachment styles. *Journal of Personality and Social Psychology, 62*, 434–446.

Snyder, C. R., & Ingram, R. E. (1983). "Company motivates the miserable": The impact of consensus information on help seeking for psychological problems. *Journal of Personality and Social Psychology, 45*, 1118–1126.

Sroufe, L. A., Fox, N. E., & Pancake, V. R. (1983). Attachment and dependency in developmental perspective. *Child Development, 54*, 1615–1627.

Taylor, S. E., & Brown, J. D. (1988). Illusion and well being: A social psychological perspective on mental health. *Psychological Bulletin, 103*, 193–210.

Tesser, A. (1988). Toward a self-evaluation maintenance model of social behavior. In L. Berkowitz (Ed.), *Advances in experimental social psychology* (Vol. 21, pp. 181–227). New York: Academic Press.

Tessler, R. C., & Schwartz, S. H. (1972). Help seeking, self esteem, and achievement motivation: An attributional analysis. *Journal of Personality and Social Psychology, 21*, 318–326.

Tzafrir, A., Nadler, A., & Friedland, N. (1996). *Attachment styles, self-esteem and help-seeking as a function of help's instrumentality.* Unpublished manuscript, Tel Aviv University.

Veroff, J. B. (1981). The dynamics of help-seeking in men and women. *Psychiatry, 44*, 189–200.

Weiner, B. (1979). A theory of achievement for some classroom experiences. *Journal of Educational Psychology, 71*, 3–25.

Weiner, B., Frieze, I., Kukla, A., Reed, L., Rest, S., & Rosenbaum, R. M. (1971). *Perceiving the causes of success and failure.* New York: General Learning Press.

Weiss, H. M., & Knight, P. A. (1980). The utility of humility: Self-esteem, information search, and problem-solving efficiency. *Organizational Behavior and Human Performance, 25*, 216–223.

Wills, T. A. (1987). Help seeking as a coping mechanism. In C. R. Snyder & C. Ford (Eds.), *Coping with negative life events: Clinical and social psychological perspectives* (pp. 19–50). New York: Plenum.

Wills, T. A., & DePaulo, B. M. (1993). Interpersonal analysis of the help-seeking process. In C. R. Snyder & D. R. Forsyth (Eds.), *Handbook of social and clinical psychology* (pp. 350–375). New York: Pergamon.

5

Student Goal Orientation and Help-Seeking Strategy Use

Amy Arbreton
Public/Private Ventures

Getting help from others is something that begins in early childhood and is expected as part of the learning process at that time. Parents provide guidance that enables their children to take on pieces of complex tasks while maintaining support from someone else. Parents differ in how sensitive they are to providing an appropriate level of intervention that is within their children's understanding but that is not overly directive. The supportive environment parents provide has been referred to as scaffolding (Wood, Bruner, & Ross, 1976). Although the complexity of parent help giving has been explored extensively, the variation in children's help seeking has been relatively neglected (Nelson-Le Gall, 1981). Similar to the variation that exists in parents' help giving, children's help-seeking behaviors can take many forms.

Studies of children's help-seeking strategies have drawn attention to variations in cognitive engagement that are related to the ways in which a student asks for help (Good, Slavings, Harel, & Emerson, 1987; Nelson-Le Gall & Glor-Scheib 1985; van der Meij, 1990). For example, some children may request hints, providing themselves the opportunity to continue their involvement in the problem-solving process even after they receive help. This type of engaged help seeking has been referred to as instrumental help seeking (Nelson-Le Gall, 1981; Nelson-Le Gall & Glor-Scheib, 1985; Nelson-Le Gall, Gumerman, & Scott-Jones, 1983) because when students ask for hints or clues, they are obtaining aid that will be instrumental in helping them to continue to solve the problem on their own. Asking for hints, examples, or first steps may be similar to strategies that have been referred to as deep level cognitive processing strategies (Nolen, 1988; Nolen & Haladyna, 1990). Students who utilize deep processing strategies try to figure out how problems fit with other relevant material (Nolen, 1988) and are actively engaged in the problem solving process (Meece, Blumenfeld, & Hoyle, 1988). On the other hand, some children may ask for help with the goal of getting the answer or finishing a task quickly. Asking for answers without first trying is a more cognitively passive approach to problem solving and could be considered parallel to measures of surface level cognitive processing strategies (Nolen & Haladyna, 1990) or superficial cognitive engagement strategies (Meece et al., 1988) because there is no transformation of the information for better understanding (Corno & Mandinach, 1983). This more passive means of seeking help has been referred to as executive help seeking, because the child seeks help with the intent of having someone else finish or do the problem for them (Nelson-Le Gall & Glor-Scheib, 1985).

Another inappropriate approach to problem solving is when children seek help prior to making any initial independent attempts at problem mastery (Nelson-Le Gall & Glor-Scheib, 1986) and is termed excessive help seeking. Children who do not try to work on tasks by themselves before they ask for help do not give themselves the opportunity to explore what type of help might lend sufficient scaffolding for their problem solving. It is these children who seek help, specifically before trying on their own, who are not showing independence in their work. Students who do not make independent attempts prior to asking for help are asking for help too soon and may be less likely to develop autonomous behaviors for solving subsequent (and more difficult) problems (Corno & Mandinach, 1983).

Instrumental, executive, and excessive help-seeking strategies represent different efforts by students to approach problems in the classroom by seeking others' advice and asking questions. In contrast, students may engage in strategies to avoid asking for help. Students may avoid asking for help because they are wary of potential threats or costs of seeking help, such as looking dumb (Karabenick & Knapp, 1991; Newman, 1990). They may also avoid asking for help because pursuing help may mean spending more time continuing to work on a challenging problem. By acting independently, some children may, in fact, get inadequate necessary help. These children may be striving for independence rather than striving for task mastery (Nelson-Le Gall, 1990).

Students' help seeking can thus be portrayed as a potentially motivated, proactive strategy, depending on the way in which the help is requested. In particular, students' instrumental, executive, and excessive use and avoidance of help seeking represent the diversity of help-seeking strategies students employ. Differentiating between help-seeking strategies this way provides a context for examining these achievement behaviors as stemming from distinct goal orientations (C. Ames, 1992; R. Ames, 1983; Maehr & Midgley, 1991).

In this chapter, a goal theory approach to understanding differences in help seeking is explored, with the notion that children can be responsible for enlisting an appropriate level of help from others to enable them to choose challenging tasks and to engage in active learning. Research based on a goal theory perspective is described in the first section. This discussion is followed by a presentation of empirical findings relating the personal and classroom goals students try to achieve to differences in the help-seeking strategies they utilize. Finally, issues for future research and implications for classroom practices are discussed.

GOAL THEORY

Goal theory emphasizes the different achievement goals students strive for and stresses how these salient goals or values influence other aspects of their classroom learning, such as the strategies they use for problem solving (C. Ames & Ames, 1984; Pintrich, 1989). Students who have learning-focused (Maehr & Midgley, 1991) or mastery (C. Ames & Archer, 1988) goals focus on accomplishment, task mastery, understanding the task, and self-improvement. For students who adopt a learning-focused goal orientation, learning is sought as an end in itself (Nicholls, Chung Cheung, Lauer, & Patashnick, 1989; Nicholls, 1992). In comparison, students who adopt a relative-ability focused goal concentrate on doing better than others (Nicholls, 1984). With this goal orientation, achieving is a way to show how smart or able one is, and a primary concern is demonstrating one's ability relative to others to prove this. Another goal students pursue in classrooms includes a concern with extrinsic aspects of achievement, such as caring a great deal about getting good grades or getting answers correct without regard to the process (C. Ames, 1990). Students with an extrinsic-focused goal are concerned about showing smartness and ability (similar to the relative-ability focused goal), but emphasize the importance of a completed task, regardless of how one achieves that solution.

In summary, the goals to which a person attends reflect different ways of thinking about achievement (C. Ames & Ames, 1984). In the first case, the student focus is on learning (and understanding)—referred to as a learning-focused goal orientation. In the second two cases, the focus of the student is on ability, either through the display of relative ability or by the attainment of extrinsic reinforcements, such as grades.

STRATEGY USE

The goals students adopt have been found to be related to their use of different learning strategies. Students who adopt learning-focused goals use more deep processing strategies for learning, such as monitoring comprehension, trying to relate new problems to old problems, and trying to solve problems in different ways (C. Ames & Archer, 1988; Maehr, 1984; Meece et al., 1988; Nolen, 1988). In contrast, students who hold extrinsic goals tend to use more surface processing strategies, such as guessing (Young, Arbreton, & Midgley, 1992), and fewer deep processing strategies (C. Ames & Archer, 1988). The relation of relative-ability goals to cognitive processing strategy use has been less clear. Nolen (1988) found no relation between a relative ability goal and either surface or deep processing strategy use for eighth-grade students on science tasks. Meece et al., however, found a positive relation between a construct combining relative-ability and social approval goals, and both active and superficial engagement in their study of fifth- and sixth-grade students in science classrooms. Superficial engagement was referred to as nonactive participation in problem solving, which they measured as "copying answers or asking for help."

In their study, Meece et al. (1988) did not differentiate different types of help that may have been related to more or less task engagement by students, calling asking for help nonactive. A similar framework to that of Meece et al. could be used, however, to examine the mediational role of students' personal goals on their strategy use, if different types of students' help seeking, those that may themselves be more or less superficial or active, were examined. Such a study would add to the existing literature on help seeking and motivational orientation by exploring the relation between children's goal orientation and the level of cognitive engagement of the help-seeking strategies children employ.

Very little research has examined the relation between personal goal orientation and children's help seeking. In one study, Newman (1991) found that at Grade 3, students' expressed likelihood of seeking help was negatively related to what Newman called learning goals (to learn and to become better) and was positively related to what he referred to as performance goals (to finish all problems and to get the work done on time). The relation for seventh graders was in the opposite direction. Further, there was no relation between students' goals and their general intentions to seek help for fifth-grade students. These findings provide a limited picture, however, because the study examined children's general intentions to seek help, rather than the particular kinds of help-seeking strategies children employed. In other words, it is not clear what type of help children at Grade 3, in contrast to children at Grade 7, might intend to request given different goal orientations.

In work with sixth- and seventh-grade students (Arbreton & Wood, 1992), children were asked about their use of help-seeking strategies and their learning preferences. Children's learning goals and their help seeking strategies were related, but the relation depended on the learning preference as well as on the strategy. There was a significant positive relation between a focus on learning new and challenging things and children's indications that they would seek help in the form of hints or clues rather than answers (i.e., instrumental help). Additionally, a positive relation was found between these sixth- and seventh-grade students' focus on demonstrating relative ability and their reports that the first thing they do when they cannot solve a problem is to ask for help (i.e., excessive help). Critical in that study was the finding that wanting hints was not related to ability-focus preferences and asking for help first was not related to learning-focus preferences. The picture that emerged showed that the significant relations between goals and help seeking depended on the type of help intended and were only evident when differences in strategy use were examined.

These findings support the need to look at the specific intentions inherent in different types of help seeking and not just children's general intentions to seek help. The relation between children's goal orientations and their intentions to seek help may be explained, in part, by children's help-seeking approaches that they themselves are more or less learning (i.e., hints) or performance (i.e. answers) oriented. Perhaps children of different ages express their likelihood of getting help based on what they mean by help at that age. Thus, the pattern of relations between learning goals and intentions may vary at different grade levels and may have been masked for the fifth-grade students in the Newman (1991) study with third-, fifth-, and seventh-grade students because the type of help intended was not specified. Studies that address goal orientation as well as the type of help students seek would add to our understanding of this developmental phenomenon.

CLASSROOM CONTEXT AND HELP SEEKING

In addition to the personal motivational goals students bring to the classroom that influence their achievement behaviors, achievement patterns are assumed to be further influenced by students' perceptions of different classroom goals stressed by their teachers (Dweck, 1992). For instance, a student may believe the teacher stresses learning and understanding, encourages participation of all students, and tries to relate materials that are introduced in terms of how they relate to the real world. In contrast, students may feel their teacher stresses comparisons among students, pays more attention to the smart children in the class, and thinks grades and right answers are more important than understanding. These descriptions relate to learning-focused and ability-focused classroom environments, respectively. C. Ames (1992) suggested that these classrooms represent "situation factors as well as instructional demands [that] can influence the salience of a particular goal and hence its adoption" (p. 330).

Newman and Schwager (1992) argued that both perceptions of the classroom and self-perceptions are critical to understanding whether students seek academic help. Both sets of perceptions are also likely to influence the different types of strategies they use. R. Ames (1983) provided a theoretical analysis proposing that classrooms in which there was a task or learning focus would lend themselves to more overall proactive help seeking; whereas in classrooms where competition and comparison were salient, students' help seeking would be more diversified.

In an experimental study, Butler and Neuman (1995) examined the extent to which learning- and ability-focused goal conditions affected children's choices to use instrumental or executive help to solve a puzzle task. Providing some support for R. Ames' analysis, Butler and Neuman (1995) found that children requested more hints (i.e., instrumental help) on the puzzle task when learning-focused goals were made salient than when ability-focused goals were introduced, but that requests for solutions (i.e., executive help) were not influenced by goal focus. No empirical work has been done in classroom settings, however, to examine the interrelations among classroom goal perceptions, personal goal perceptions, and students strategies for seeking help.

PERCEIVED TEACHER SUPPORT
FOR HELP SEEKING

Given that one large part of a learning-focused goal orientation very often includes an emphasis on independent task mastery (C. Ames & Archer, 1988; Boggiano & Barrett, 1991; Nolen & Haladyna, 1990), a classroom focus on learning and mastery may be necessary but not sufficient to promote children's use of help seeking as a means to persist at tasks. Nolen and Haladyna (1990), for example, measured students' perceptions of classroom learning goal orientation by combining items related to mastery, integration, and independent thinking. Their independent thinking construct included an item about the teacher wanting the students to solve problems on their own.

It is plausible that this item assesses students' perception of how the teacher evaluates achievement and whether they are led to believe achieving with the help of someone else is valued. Wentzel (1991) discussed the importance of the degree to which desired outcomes are valued within the classroom context. In order for children not to avoid asking for help when help is necessary, they may need to feel support from the teacher for asking for help as a potentially useful problem-solving strategy (Newman & Schwager, 1992), even in a classroom environment that otherwise is perceived to be focused on learning, understanding, and improvement.

Studies specifically examining the influence of teacher support for seeking help on intentions and likelihood of asking for help suggest that perceived support for seeking help is positively related to students' instrumental help seeking and negatively related to their avoiding asking for help. For example, Karabenick and Sharma (1994) found that for students in college classrooms, perceived teacher support for asking questions was related to students' increased likelihood of asking a question in class through its relation with students' being less inhibited about asking a question. Newman and Schwager (1995) also found a positive relation between perceived teacher support of help seeking and intentions to seek help for fifth- and seventh grade students, although the relation did not hold for third grade students.

It is not unlikely, however, that students' would interpret and act on teacher support for seeking help taking into account the other motivational and achievement goals the teacher stresses in the classroom. Help given by teachers provides salient information to students that they often use to interpret the ability level of the child who receives help (Graham and Barker, 1990; Weinstein, 1989). Further, in ability-focused classrooms, to the extent that the teachers compare students to one another and group them according to ability, ability levels are made more salient (C. Ames, 1987).

Therefore, in classrooms where students perceive an emphasis on comparative ability (a component of an ability-focused context), even if they also perceive support for seeking help, they may avoid asking for help to avoid giving a message to others that their receiving help indicates low ability. It is also conceivable that when students perceive the teacher as stressing getting tasks done, making no mistakes (another aspect of an ability-focused context), and seeking help, they may be more likely to seek executive help—to get answers. In contrast, in classrooms where students perceive the teacher's focus to be on learning, understanding and becoming interested in topics (aspects of a learning-focused classroom context), perceived support for seeking help should be associated with an increased likelihood that when students ask, they ask for instrumental help.

In summary, the influence of student's perceptions that their teacher supports seeking help on their help-seeking strategy use would be expected to be moderated by their perceptions of other classroom goals. Specifically, when students perceive support for seeking help within an ability-focused context, the likelihood of their seeking executive help or avoiding help should be greater. On the other hand, students who believe the teacher supports seeking help and also creates a learning-focused environment should have a greater tendency to seek instrumental help.

A STUDY OF GOAL ORIENTATION
AND STUDENTS' HELP-SEEKING STRATEGY USE

The study presented in this section was undertaken to explore more fully the relations between student goal orientation and help seeking, taking into account different types of help-seeking strategies—instrumental, executive, and avoidant—that students may employ. Specifically, students' personal goal orientation, perceived classroom goal orientation, and perceived support for seeking help from the teacher are examined in relation to students' help-seeking strategy use.

Students in Grade 5 were chosen as the subjects of the study for several reasons. First, in previous research in laboratory settings on help seeking, fifth-grade students, more than third-grade students, appeared to discriminate in terms of the type of help they preferred (direct or indirect) based on their particular need (Nelson-Le Gall, 1987; Nelson-Le Gall, DeCooke, & Jones, 1989; Nelson-Le Gall & Jones, 1990; Nelson-Le Gall, Kratzer, Jones, & DeCooke, 1990). Second, at Grade 5, but not at Grade 3, support for help seeking has been shown to influence children's intentions to seek help (Newman & Schwager, 1995). Finally, as referred to earlier, in the limited work that has been done on goals and help seeking, motivational goals and general intentions to seek help were found to be uncorrelated for fifth- grade students (Newman, 1991). However, the lack of correlation may have been due to the fact that children were asked about general intentions to seek help, rather than the specific type of help they intended to seek. If learning goals are positively related to instrumental help seeking and negatively related to executive help seeking, as proposed, then the effects of learning goals on intentions to seek help may have been masked for the fifth-grade students in the Newman (1991) study.

The study was conducted in math classrooms, in part because students tend to report difficulty and say that they need academic assistance in this domain (Newman & Goldin, 1990). Math is also a domain in which students believe that the mode of instruction is to be told how to do a problem (Stodolsky, 1985; Stodolsky, Salk, & Glaessner, 1991), and therefore students may have considered asking for help in math more than in other domains.

Research Subjects

Data for this study were collected as part of a larger study investigating the impact of the school environment on children's motivation (Midgley, 1990). Volunteer participants (172 girls and 212 boys) from 21 Grade 5 classrooms in six elementary schools from one district were administered questionnaire surveys in their classrooms in the spring of 1992. The students in this district were primarily from lower-class or working class families. Approximately 10% were African American, 89% White, and 1%, other racial and ethnic groups.

Research Procedure

Students were given a 40-minute survey in their classrooms. Two survey administrators were in each classroom, and all questions on the survey were read aloud. All questions were answered using a 5-point Likert-type scale. The scale anchors were 1 (*not at all true*) and 5 (*very true*). All questions referring to the classroom began with the statement, "In this class, our teacher...."

In order to control for the effect of subject area, questionnaire items asked students to focus on math class, math lessons, and their math teachers. Students were also told to think about times when they were doing a math lesson or working on a math problem in school, but not during a testing situation.

Measures

Help-Seeking Strategies. Fourteen items assessed students' help-seeking tendencies: executive help seeking (getting help to get the job done quickly or to have someone else do the problem for you); instrumental help seeking (getting help to continue the problem solving on one's own); and avoiding help seeking (skipping or avoiding tasks where help may be beneficial). It should be noted that, similar to Newman (1990), items were worded in the conditional sense (i.e., when I can't understand the math work) rather than as a general likelihood of occurrence in order to control for students' need for help.

TABLE 5.1

Sample Items, Constructs, and Cronbachs' Alpha Coefficients for Study Scales

Scale and Construct	Sample Item	No. Items	Cronbach's Alpha
Student Perceptions of Classroom Goal Orientation			
Ability focus	Our teacher makes it obvious which students are not doing well in math.	6	.71
Learning focus	Our teacher thinks mistakes are O.K. in math as long as we are learning.	6	.67
Teacher support for seeking help	Our teacher takes time to explain how to start a math problem if we ask for help.	5	.56
Personal Goal Orientation Measures			
Ability focus			
Extrinsic	I don't care whether I understand something or not in math, as long as I get the right answer.	3	.59
Relative-ability	I'd like to show my teacher that I'm smarter in math than the other kids in my class.	3	.65
Learning focus			
Learning goal	Understanding the work in math is more important to me than the grade I get.	4	.71
Help Seeking Measures			
Instrumental	If I need help in math, I ask my teacher to give me hints or clues rather than the answer.	5	.69
Avoidance	In math, if I need help to do a problem, I skip it.	6	.60
Executive	If I don't understand something in math, the first thing I do is ask the teacher to give me the answer.	3	.53

In addition, all the questions were framed with the teacher (rather than a classmate) as help giver. Sample items from this and subsequent scales are presented in Table 5.1.

Perceived Classroom Goal Orientation. Students rated their perceptions of the learning-focused or ability-focused goals they perceived their teacher to endorse. These constructs were measured using six items each that had been piloted in previous waves of the study. Items were adapted from other measures of classroom goals (C. Ames & Archer, 1988; Nolen & Haladyna, 1990).

Personal Goal Orientation. In contrast to classroom goal orientation, personal goal orientation items contained reference to I. Ten items were used to tap three types of personal motivational goals: learning-focused, relative-ability-focused, and extrinsic-focused. These items had been used in previous waves of the study and were adapted from other achievement goal measures (C. Ames & Archer, 1988; Meece et al., 1988; Nicholls, Cobb, Yackel, Wood & Wheatley, 1990; Nolen & Haladyna, 1990; Pintrich & DeGroot, 1990).

Support for Seeking Help From the Teacher. A five-item assessment of support from the teacher for asking for help was developed, drawing from the work of Newman and Schwager (1995) and Karabenick and Sharma (1994).

Standardized Achievement Scores. Data were collected from the students' record files, and the grade equivalent scores on the math section of the Comprehensive Test of Basic Skills (CTBS) were used in the analyses in order to control for the students' level of achievement. CTBS scores were chosen as a more objective measure of the student's ability level than the grade the teacher gave the student.

A series of regression analyses were conducted with each of the three help-seeking strategies as the dependent variables. The predictors were (1) Personal Goal Orientation (learning-focused, extrinsic-focused, and relative-ability-focused), (2) Perceived Classroom Goal Orientation (learning-focused and ability-focused), and (3) Perceived Support for Seeking Help. Gender and CTBS scores were also entered into the regression analyses. Results of the regression analyses are presented in Table 5.2.

Research Findings

Personal Goal Orientation and Help Seeking. Help-seeking patterns were related to personal goals. Instrumental help-seeking strategy use, for example, was endorsed more strongly by students who focused on learning and improvement, but was unrelated to other ability-focused personal goal orientations. This finding suggests that process type questioning (e.g., instrumental help seeking) is important to students who need help and are concerned with learning how to solve problems and with maintaining some independence even after they get help.

TABLE 5.2

Multiple Regression Analyses of Help-Seeking Strategy Use in Fifth Grade Math Classrooms

Predictor	Executive Help	Avoiding Help	Instrument Help
Personal Goal Orientation			
Relative-ability focused	.10*	.07	-.05
Extrinsic focused	.21***	.19***	-.03
Learning focused	-.14**	-.20***	.36***
Classroom context			
Ability focused	.19***	.25***	.16**
Learning focused	.02	-.01	.17**
Support for seeking help	.07	-.11*	.16**
Control Variables			
Math CTBS	-.15**	.02	-.12**
Female	-.08	.00	-.07
R-square	.23	.29	.30
$F(8,355)$	13.69***	18.43***	18.83***

*$p < .05$, **$p < .01$, ***$p < .001$.

On the other hand, the more that students focused on getting good grades and getting the work done quickly, the more likely they were to say they would ask for executive help—a strategy that results in answers being provided with little reflection on the process of understanding. A relative-ability goal was also positively related to intentions to seek executive help. Interestingly, students who were concerned with demonstrating their ability in comparison to others, did not appear to be concerned with how they would look if they sought help. These findings are consistent with correlational results of Meece et al. (1988) linking relative-ability/social goals to superficial engagement, which consisted of asking for help in general. However, they raise an interesting question: How can a focus on how you appear to others be accompanied by the use of an executive help-seeking strategy—a strategy that may be an indication to others that you do not know something?

One possible explanation of the relation between relative-ability goals and intentions to seek executive help would be that students concerned with demonstrating their ability focus on speed of completion as their means of success. In other words, they avoid putting in too much effort, or they want to reduce effort, so that their ability level will not be easily discernible (Covington, 1984; Nicholls, 1984; Nicholls et al., 1989). One way to avoid having others perceive your ability level would be to ask for help that will get the task done right away (e. g., executive help seeking) and also to ask for help before trying (e. g., excessive help seeking). By obtaining this information, the student could move on quickly to a different task and be more assured of doing the task in the right way, leaving less room for detection of ability. These results suggest that students seek out quick answers for two reasons related to a focus on ability: looking smart by getting the task done quickly and correctly and looking smart by avoiding showing inability relative to others. Students were more likely to say they would engage in strategies to avoid seeking help when they held extrinsic goals (i.e., focused on getting the answer right, regardless of understanding). These results appear counterintuitive, especially given that students with an extrinsic goal orientation are also more likely to endorse the use of executive help. One explanation for this finding might be that the students who are focused on grades and easy, effortless solutions avoid challenging tasks and avoid spending time on their work. As a result, they avoid situations where they might find it necessary to ask for help. Two items in particular reflect this effort avoiding strategy: "In math, if I need help to do a problem I skip it" and "I choose easy work in math so I will not have to ask for any help." It may be this aspect of avoiding help, which others have termed work avoidance strategies (Meece, 1991), to which these students are responding. Whether students with an extrinsic goal orientation avoid seeking help or seek executive help may depend on other beliefs such as the value they place on the task, or on the importance of the particular task to someone else, such as a teacher or a parent. Alternatively, whether students seek help when they have adopted an extrinsic goal may depend on the reward structure of the class. These relations deserve further exploration.

It is important to note that although neither an extrinsic-focused nor a relative ability-focused goal orientation was related to intentions of instrumental help seeking, a learning-focused goal orientation was significantly negatively related to ability-focused type help seeking. These results are important for classroom research because they suggest that it is the learning-focused goals that promote positive help-seeking strategy use and decrease use of shallow help-seeking strategies. These findings are consistent with other research on student goals. For example, C. Ames and Archer (1988) found that to the extent that students held a learning-focused goal, and regardless of whether or not they also held ability-focused goals, they were more likely to engage in deep level cognitive processing strategies.

Perceived Classroom Context Effects on Help Seeking.   T h e
perceived classroom environment variables were also significant predictors of students' help seeking. Students who felt that the teacher
focused on ability-type goals were more likely to indicate that they
would use all types of strategies for seeking help. In contrast, when
students felt the teacher stressed learning-type goals in the classroom,
they were more likely to report that they would seek instrumental help
only. These findings suggest that the way in which the teachers' goals
are interpreted by students influences help seeking above and beyond
the influence of their own personal motivational goals. This implies
that the way in which the student interprets what the teacher stresses
as important for success in the classroom provides an indication to
children of the appropriateness of asking for different types of help or
of avoiding asking for help.

An ability-focused classroom perception was a positive predictor of
both avoiding help seeking and seeking out executive help. Other
factors are important to explore in order to more fully understand this
complex relation. For example, the effects of lab manipulations set up
to represent an ability-focused context have been shown to influence
student responses and behaviors more negatively when students also
attribute their failure to lack of ability (Elliott & Dweck, 1988; Magnusson & Perry, 1992; Stipek & Kowalski, 1989). In perceived ability-
focused classrooms, where ability judgments are believed to be made
more salient by the teacher, children who attribute failure to help-relevant causes, such as effort (R. Ames, 1983), may seek executive help,
just to get the task completed. Other children who make help-irrelevant attributions, such as attributing failure to luck or lack of ability,
may avoid asking for help because they see no purpose to it. Ability-
focused beliefs may also interact with specific costs that children
perceive to be associated with seeking help, such as looking dumb and
getting the teacher annoyed (Newman, 1990), and with the level of
threat to self esteem that students perceive (Karabenick & Knapp,
1991). Future studies that include measures of students' attributions
and more fully explore students' perceived costs of seeking help would
add to our understanding of these relations between classroom perceptions and help seeking.

Teacher Support for Seeking Help.   The more students perceived support for seeking help, the more they indicated that they
would seek instrumental help, and the less they reported that they would
avoid help seeking, independent of the other perceptions they had of the
teacher's classroom goals. In other words, the effect of teacher support
for seeking help on students' help-seeking strategy use did not differ

according to their perceptions of the classroom as either ability-focused or learning-focused. These results suggest that when students perceive that their teachers support asking for help, then students are also more likely to indicate they would ask for learning-oriented help and less likely to avoid help seeking, which is consistent with Newman and Schwager (1992) and Karabenick and Sharma (1994). Of importance here, however, is that when students perceive that their teacher supports asking for help when necessary, they are not any more likely to indicate that they would seek executive help. Rather, students' indications that they would seek this kind of product-oriented help was found to be more a result of the individual student's perception of the teacher as having ability-focused classroom goals.

Gender and Student Help Seeking. It is interesting to note the relation found in this study between student gender and student help seeking. Mean level differences were found, with boys more than girls reporting that they would seek more executive help and avoid help. According to results of the regression analyses, however, once the difference between boys' and girls' personal motivational goals is held constant (with boys more likely than girls to have extrinsic goals), boys and girls did not differ in their reports of either of these help-seeking strategies.

Gender deserves attention with respect to this topic because the issues of independence, dependency, and learned helplessness are often expressed in terms of male and female behaviors or even characteristics of masculine versus feminine behavior (Gross & McMullen, 1983; Johnson, 1988; Mitchell, 1987). In general, the assumption is that males are more independent and females more dependent and therefore more likely to seek help. However, gender rarely appears as a significant predictor for student help seeking (Nelson-Le Gall & Glor-Scheib, 1986; Nelson-Le Gall & Jones, 1990; Newman, 1990; van der Meij, 1988, 1990) and may have more to do with differences in goal orientation between boys and girls than with who seeks more help. Additionally, differentiating types of help seeking means that whether one seeks more help than another is less critical than the strategy used for getting help.

SUMMARY AND CONCLUSIONS

Several conclusions can be drawn from these findings and the discussion presented in this chapter. First, children differentiate between seeking instrumental help, seeking executive help, and avoiding seeking help. This is a critical finding, as many studies have combined children's help-seeking strategies into one helpless (Boggiano & Barrett, 1991) or superficial engagement strategy (Meece et al., 1988) category. Just knowing children's general intent to seek help is less informative than understanding what type of help they specifically intend to seek. Of particular note, when fifth-grade students indicated strategies of seeking help that reflected different levels of cognitive engagement, a relation between fifth-grade students' achievement goals and help-seeking intentions became evident (Newman, 1991).

Further, the results of this study support a conceptualization of the different help-seeking strategies students intend to employ as linked to their own personal motivational goals as well as to the individual differences in their perceptions of the goals stressed in the classroom. Indeed, the type of strategies students report they would use when they ask for help was found to be related to their goals in a way that is similar to the relation found between achievement goals and students' deep-level and surface-level cognitive processing strategy use (Nolen & Haladyna, 1990) as well as to their use of strategies that display active and superficial engagement (Meece et al., 1988). This implies that students' help seeking may itself be conceptualized as focused more on the process (instrumental help seeking) or product (executive help seeking) of learning. Therefore, a conceptualization of help-seeking strategy use that moves beyond unidimensional categorization as a superficial engagement strategy or a learned helpless response to a situation is highly warranted. Additionally, the results of this study provide evidence that intentions to use different kinds of strategies are more revealing than general intentions to seek help when examining the relation between goals and help seeking (Newman, 1991).

ISSUES FOR THE FUTURE

The study reported here and previous work have focused on the potential for learning that occurs as long as children ask for necessary help and ask for certain types of indirect help that keep them engaged in the process of learning (Newman, 1991). Nevertheless, further research is needed to determine how much of an influence knowledge about, and engagement in, asking for help when necessary can have on an individual—either positively or negatively. It is not improbable, for instance, that effective help-seeking strategy use by children has potential to build their self-confidence by enabling them to complete more complex tasks than they would be able to without some guidance by others. Additionally, children who seek help in learning contexts may, in turn, feel more capable of pursuing other challenging tasks that might possibly necessitate some support from others. Therefore, a major area that needs to be addressed next concerns the link between help seeking behaviors and later achievement and to future success in school and in the workplace.

In one classroom study, Koehler (1990) found some provocative results related to children's help seeking and achievement. Koehler compared two classrooms of high ability students. In one classroom, girls were doing more poorly than in the other classroom. The biggest difference between the classrooms that Koehler observed was that in one classroom the teacher supported children's requests for help whereas in the other classroom the teacher discouraged children from asking for help. In the classroom where the teacher encouraged the students to seek help, girls, but not boys, were doing worse on high-level math problems. The question to consider is whether one can infer from this study that asking for help, even when it is necessary help, creates long-term deficits in achievement and learning. First, Koehler did not report either the kind of questions students asked or the kind of response to questions the teacher provided—critical information. Second, it is not clear that asking for help would have long-term negative consequences, even if there were short-term indicators that children who sought help did worse than other children. An alternate theory deserves further attention: The girls who were part of a supportive math environment may be more likely to go on in math than the girls from the classroom where help seeking was discouraged. In sum, it is critical to verify the long-term effects of asking for help, even when help is sought appropriately and instrumentally. Furthermore, although this discussion of Koehler's findings was pursued as one about gender difference, the argument can be generalized as well to the potential impact for other students on their willingness to engage in challenging tasks with knowledge of the support of others.

Future studies should consider the achievement, as well as the motivational consequences of the type of help children choose to use in different classrooms. Getting help by getting answers may be one way to achieve, and may work in one particular classroom context, but repetition of this strategy would likely prove difficult for future learning (Corno & Mandinach, 1983). In contrast, working out math problems by asking for hints, clues, and examples to continue to solve problems on one's own can be seen as an active and engaged strategy for continued future learning (Nelson-Le Gall, 1985) and deserves more attention by teachers and by researchers.

EDUCATIONAL IMPLICATIONS

The findings that students' help-seeking attempts reflect their own goals and their perceptions of their teachers' goals suggest several areas for intervention, especially for those students who actually need more help with their schoolwork. First, a learning-focused environment can help to promote adaptive, learning-oriented help-seeking strategy use by students and may be useful in curtailing children's use of more maladaptive help-seeking strategies, such as asking for answers or avoiding seeking help. On the other hand, when teachers emphasize comparative ability and product-oriented learning, students may be more likely to avoid asking for help that they might need to take on new tasks, or complete old ones. In an environment that stresses correct answers and no mistakes, students might also find it appropriate to approach the teacher for help with the explicit intent of eliciting the answer without concern for understanding. Thus, teachers are more likely to keep students cognitively engaged by de-emphasizing comparative ability and focusing more on understanding, collaboration, and participation.

Further, teachers should be aware that students are more inclined to ask for help when they believe their teacher values seeking help as an important part of the process of learning. Students are less likely to seek help to finish quickly or just to get the answer when teachers place an emphasis on seeking help to continue work on a problem or to approach a more challenging problem. In fact, students seem to be more likely to recognize that an alternative to giving up is available—seeking help in the form of hints or examples—so they remain involved in the task and move step-by-step toward accomplishing their goal. Teachers should consider spending a portion of each day encouraging questions, providing specific feedback, and modeling appropriate ways for their students to ask for hints rather than answers. Without these proactive steps, classrooms are less likely to foster full engagement in the learning process for children at all levels of skills and knowledge.

Teachers should recognize that the type of help a student seeks, more than the act of seeking help itself, is an important indicator of the student's involvement in the classroom lesson. Teachers may elicit instrumental help-seeking strategy use over executive help-seeking use by using teaching strategies that include problem solving with multiple steps rather than single answer, product-oriented questions. When students avoid certain learning opportunities because they wish to avoid seeking help, this should provide a message to teachers about their students and about the priorities that they may be implicitly or explicitly emphasizing in the classroom. One way that teachers might lessen a student's tendency to avoid seeking help would be to conduct lessons that specifically include a component that got students involved and working collaboratively and progressing step-by-step through a meaningful problem, while the teacher points out the progress that can be made with some guidance by others.

In addition to classroom practices that promote a learning-orientation and place a positive value on instrumental help seeking, other constructs that measure aspects of the classroom learning and instructional environment not assessed in the current study would further our understanding of (a) what teachers can do to decrease executive help seeking, (b) decrease student avoidance of seeking help, and (c) to increase instrumental help seeking when appropriate. Work by Meece (1991) delineates some areas to address. Meece observed several differences, for example, between classrooms in which the students' average learning-focused goals were high, medium, and low. Although much was the same across the classrooms in terms of the cognitive level of instruction, differences emerged in terms of the greater emphasis placed on the intrinsic value of the tasks and on the specific promotion of meaningful learning by the teachers whose students tended to be high on mastery-orientation. Teachers who had a higher classroom average of students' mastery-orientation were also more likely to adapt their instruction to the developmental levels and personal interests of the students and to establish learning structures that allowed for both student autonomy and work with peers.

Teachers should, therefore, strive to adapt instruction to the developmental levels and personal interests of their students. This may necessitate rethinking traditional methods of instruction that stress whole group lessons where all students progress at the same pace. In other words, the structure of the lesson may need to change to allow students access to some decisions about what is taught and when. Based on these results, it is also reasonable to suggest that students have more responsibility given to them in terms of checking their answers to problems or having hints available for those times when they are experiencing difficulty. Classroom measures that may be important to incorporate into future studies of classroom influences on students' help seeking include the amount of time available for approaching the teacher with questions, the structure of the classroom itself that may impede easy access to the teacher, as well as the type of tasks the students are given to complete in their math classrooms.

In conclusion, this chapter has presented an argument for the importance in future research of examining what type of help children pursue, rather than simply assessing whether they were seeking help. An understanding of help seeking from this perspective may be a critical link that will lead to educators' providing more healthy, supportive environments for all children to have a chance to learn and to complete challenging problems, with or without the help of others. This is not to say that children should not be autonomous learners in the classroom. However, it is not implausible that, given some guidelines and given a classroom environment that encourages children to focus on learning as well as on asking for needed help, that children in school could develop the ability in the academic domain to obtain help as necessary. Thus, children can become more autonomous, independent learners within the scaffolding their teacher and peers provide in the classroom.

REFERENCES

Ames, C. (1987). The enhancement of student motivation. In D. A. Kleiber & M. L. Maehr (Eds.), *Advances in motivation and achievement: Vol. 5. Enhancing motivation* (pp. 123–148). Greenwich, CT: JAI.

Ames, C. (1990, April). *Achievement goals and classroom structure: Developing a learning orientation.* Paper presented at the annual meeting of the American Educational Research Association, Boston, MA.

Ames, C. (1992). Achievement goals and the classroom motivational climate. In D. Schunk & J. Meece (Eds.), *Student perceptions in the classroom* (pp. 327–348). Hillsdale, NJ: Lawrence Erlbaum Associates.

Ames, C., & Ames, R. (1984). Systems of student and teacher motivation: Toward a qualitative definition. *Journal of Educational Psychology, 78*(4), 535–556.

Ames, C., & Archer, J. (1988). Achievement goals in the classroom: Students' learning strategies and motivation processes. *Journal of Educational Psychology, 80*(3), 260–267.

Ames, R. (1983). Help-seeking and achievement orientation: Perspectives from attribution theory. In B. M. DePaulo, A. Nadler, & J. D. Fisher (Eds.), *New directions in helping: Vol. 2. Help seeking* (pp. 165–186). New York: Academic Press.

Arbreton, A. J., & Wood, S. (1992, March). *Help-seeking behaviors and children's learning preferences in the middle school years.* Paper presented at the Biennial Meeting of the Society for Research on Adolescence, Washington, DC.

Boggiano, A. K., & Barrett, M. (1991). Strategies to motivate helpless and mastery-oriented children: The effect of gender-based expectancies. *Sex Roles, 25* (9/10), 487–510.

Butler, R., & Neuman, O. (1995). Effects of task and ego achievement goals on help-seeking behaviors and attitudes. *Journal of Educational Psychology, 87*(2), 261–271.

Corno, L., & Mandinach, E. B. (1983). The role of cognitive engagement in classroom learning and motivation. *Educational Psychologist, 13*(2), 88–103.

Covington, M. C. (1984). The motive for self worth. In R. Ames & C. Ames (Eds.), *Research on motivation in education: Student motivation* (pp. 77–113). New York: Academic Press.

Dweck, C. S. (1992). The study of goals in psychology. *Psychological Science, 3*(3), 165–167.

Elliott, E. S., & Dweck, C. S. (1988). Goals: An approach to motivation and achievement. *Journal of Personality and Social Psychology, 54*(1), 5–12.

Good, T. L., Slavings, R. L., Harel, K. H., & Emerson, H. (1987). Student passivity: A study of question asking in K–12 classrooms. *Sociology of Education, 60,* 181–199.

Graham, S., & Barker, G. P. (1990). The down side of help: An attributional-developmental analysis of helping behavior as a low-ability cue. *Journal of Educational Psychology, 82,* 7–14.

Gross, A. E., & McMullen, P. A. (1983). Models of the help-seeking process. In B. M. DePaulo, A. Nadler, & J. D. Fisher (Eds.), *New directions in helping: Vol. 2. Help seeking* (pp. 46–70). New York: Academic Press

Johnson, M. E. (1988). Influences of gender and sex role orientation on help-seeking attitudes. *Journal of Psychology, 122,* 237–241.

Karabenick, S. A., & Knapp, J. R. (1991). Relationship of academic help seeking to the use of learning strategies and other instrumental achievement behavior in college students. *Journal of Educational Psychology, 83*(2), 221–230.

Karabenick, S. A., & Sharma, R. (1994). Perceived teacher support of student questioning in the college classroom: Its relation to student characteristics and role in the classroom questioning process. *Journal of Educational Psychology, 86*(1), 90–103.

Koehler, M. S. (1990). Classrooms, teachers, and gender differences in mathematics. In E. Fennema & G. Leder (Eds.), *Mathematics and gender* (pp. 128–148). New York: Teachers College Press.

Maehr, M. L. (1984). Meaning and motivation: Toward a theory of personal investment. In R. Ames & C. Ames (Eds.), *Research on motivation in education: Vol. 1. Student motivation* (pp. 39–73). New York: Academic Press.

Maehr, M. L., & Midgley, C. (1991). Enhancing student motivation: A school-wide approach. *Educational Psychologist, 26*(3/4), 399–427.

Magnusson, J., & Perry, R. P. (1992). Academic help-seeking in the university setting: The effects of motivational set, attributional style, and help source characteristics. *Research in Higher Education, 33*(2), 227–245.

Meece, J. (1991). The classroom context and students' motivational goals. In M. L. Maehr & P. R. Pintrich (Eds.), *Advances in motivation and achievement: Vol. 7. Goals and self-regulatory processes* (pp. 261–286). Greenwich, CT: JAI.

Meece, J., Blumenfeld, P., & Hoyle, R., (1988). Students' goal orientation and cognitive engagement in classroom activities. *Journal of Educational Psychology, 80,* 514–523.

Midgley, C. (1990). Enhancing the motivation and learning of underachieving students: A school-wide approach (No. R215A00430, Innovation in Education Program), Washington, DC: U.S. Department of Education.

Mitchell, C. L. (1987). Relationship of femininity, masculinity, and gender to attribution of responsibility. *Sex Roles, 16,* 151–163.

Nelson-Le Gall, S. (1981). Help-seeking: An understudied problem-solving skill in children. *Developmental Review, 1,* 224–246.

Nelson-Le Gall, S.(1985). Help-seeking behavior in learning. In E. W. Gordon (Ed.), *Review of research in education* (Vol. 12, pp. 55–90).Washington, DC: American Educational Research Association.

Nelson-Le Gall, S. (1987). Necessary and unnecessary help-seeking in children. *Journal of Genetic Psychology, 148*(1), 53–62.

Nelson-Le Gall, S. (1990). Academic achievement orientation and help-seeking behavior in early adolescent girls. *Journal of Early Adolescence, 10*(2), 176–190.

Nelson-Le Gall, S., DeCooke, P., & Jones, E. (1989). Children's self-perceptions of competence and help seeking. *Journal of Genetic Psychology, 150*(4), 457–459.

Nelson-Le Gall, S., & Glor-Scheib, S. (1985). Help seeking in elementary classrooms: An observational study. *Contemporary Educational Psychology, 10,* 58–71.

Nelson-Le Gall, S., & Glor-Scheib, S. (1986). Academic help-seeking and peer relations in school. *Contemporary Educational Psychology, 11,* 187–193.

Nelson-Le Gall, S., Gumerman, R. A., & Scott-Jones, D. (1983). Instrumental help-seeking and everyday problem-solving: A developmental perspective. In B. M. DePaulo, A. Nadler, & J. D. Fisher (Eds.), *New directions in helping: Vol. 2. Help seeking,* (pp. 265–283). New York: Academic Press.

Nelson-Le Gall, S., & Jones, E. (1990). Cognitive-motivational influences on the task-related help-seeking behavior of Black children. *Child Development, 61,* 581–589.

Nelson-Le Gall, S., Kratzer, L., Jones, E., & DeCooke, P. (1990). Children's self-assessment of performance and task-related help seeking. *Journal of Experimental Child Psychology, 49,* 245–263.

Newman, R. S. (1990). Children's help-seeking in the classroom: The role of motivational factors and attitudes. *Journal of Educational Psychology, 82*(1), 71–80.

Newman, R. S. (1991). Goals and self-regulated learning: What motivates children to seek academic help? In M. L. Maehr & P. R. Pintrich (Eds.), *Advances in motivation and achievement: Vol. 7. Goals and self-regulatory processes* (pp.151–154). Greenwich, CT: JAI.

Newman, R. S., & Goldin, L. (1990). Children's reluctance to seek help with schoolwork. *Journal of Educational Psychology, 82*(1), 92–100.

Newman, R. S., & Schwager, M. T. (1992). Student perceptions and academic help-seeking. In D. H. Schunk & J. L. Meece (Eds.), *Students perceptions in the classroom: Causes and consequences* (pp. 123–146). Hillsdale, NJ: Lawrence Erlbaum Associates.

Newman, R. S., & Schwager, M. T. (1995). Students' perceptions of the teacher and classmates in relation to reported help seeking in math class. *Elementary School Journal, Vol. 94*(1), 3–17.

Nicholls, J. G. (1984). Achievement motivation: Conceptions of ability, subjective experience, task choice, and performance. *Psychological Review, 91*, 328–346.

Nicholls, J. G. (1992). Students as educational theorists. In D. H. Schunk & J. L. Meece (Eds.), *Students perceptions in the classroom: Causes and consequences* (pp. 267–286). Hillsdale, N J: Lawrence Erlbaum Associates.

Nicholls, J. G., Chung Cheung, P., Lauer, J., & Patashnick, M. (1989). Individual differences in academic motivation: Perceived ability, goals, beliefs, and values. *Learning and Individual Differences, 1*, 63–84.

Nicholls, J. G., Cobb, P., Yackel, E., Wood, T., & Wheately, G. (1990). Students' theories about mathematics and their mathematical knowledge: Multiple dimensions of assessment. In G. Kulm (Ed.), *Assessing higher order thinking in mathematics* (pp. 137–154). Washington, DC: American Association for the Advancement of Science.

Nolen, S. B. (1988). Reasons for studying: Motivational orientations and study strategies. *Cognition and Instruction, 5*(4), 269–287.

Nolen, S. B., & Haladyna, T. M. (1990). Personal and environmental influences on students' beliefs about effective study strategies. *Contemporary Educational Psychology, 15*, 116–130.

Pintrich, P. R. (1989). The dynamic interplay of student motivation and cognition in the college classroom. In C. Ames & M. Maehr (Eds.), *Advances in motivation and achievement: Vol. 6. Motivation enhancing environments* (pp. 117–160). Greenwich, CT: JAI.

Pintrich, P. R., & De Groot, E. V. (1990). Motivational and self-regulated learning components of classroom academic performance. *Journal of Educational Psychology, 82*(1), 33–40.

Stipek, D., & Kowalski, P. S. (1989). Learned helplessness in task-orienting versus performance-orienting testing conditions. *Journal of Educational Psychology, 81*(3), 384–391.

Stodolsky, S. S. (1985). Telling math: Origins of math aversion and anxiety. *Educational Psychologist, 93*(3), 409–428.

Stodolsky, S. S., Salk, S., & Glaessner, B. (1991). Student views about learning math and social studies. *American Educational Research Journal, 28*(1), 89–116.

van der Meij, H. (1988). Constraints on question asking in classrooms. *Journal of Educational Psychology, 80*(3), 401–405.

van der Meij, H. (1990). Question asking: To know that you do not know is not enough. *Journal of Educational Psychology, 82*(3), 505–512.

Weinstein, R. S. (1989). Perceptions of classroom processes and student motivation: Children's views of self-fulfilling prophecies. In C. Ames & R. Ames (Eds.), *Research on motivation in education. Vol. 3. Goals and cognition* (pp.187–221). New York: Academic Press.

Wentzel, K. (1991). Social and academic goals at school: motivation and achievement in context. In M. L. Maehr & P.R. Pintrich (Eds.), *Advances in motivation and achievement: Goals and self-regulatory processes* Vol. 7. (pp. 185–212). Greenwich, CT: JAI.

Wood, D., Bruner, J. S., & Ross, G. (1976). The role of tutoring in problem solving. *Journal of Child Psychology and Psychiatry, 17*, 89–100.

Young, A., Arbreton, A., & Midgley, C. (1992, April). *All content areas are not created equal.* Paper presented at the annual meeting of the American Educational Association, San Francisco.

6
Achievement and Social Motivational Influences on Help Seeking in the Classroom

Allison M. Ryan
University of Michigan

Paul R. Pintrich
University of Michigan

There is a growing viewpoint among educators and researchers that asking for help when one truly needs it is an adaptive strategy for learning, not a reflection of student dependency (Arbreton, 1993; Karabenick & Knapp, 1991; McCaslin & Good, 1996; Nelson-Le Gall, 1981, 1985; Newman, 1991, 1994). The ability to utilize others as a resource to cope with ambiguity and difficulty in the learning process can be an important self-regulatory strategy in the classroom. When students encounter difficulty and ask for help that is limited to the amount and type necessary to allow them to solve the problem independently (e.g., asking for hints or clarification rather than the solution), help seeking fosters learning and understanding (Arbreton, 1993; Karabenick & Knapp, 1991; Nelson-Le Gall, 1981, 1985; Newman, 1991, 1994).

Students' achievement motivation has been shown to be important to understanding their help-seeking behavior in the classroom (Arbreton, 1993; Karabenick & Knapp, 1991; Nelson-Le Gall, 1985; Nelson-Le Gall & Jones, 1990; Newman, 1990, 1991, 1994). Students' achievement goals and perceptions of cognitive competence are critical determinants of their attitudes toward help seeking and their help-seeking behavior (Arbreton, 1993; Butler & Neuman, 1995; Newman, 1990, 1991, 1994; Ryan, Hicks, & Midgley, 1997; Ryan & Pintrich,

1997). However, help seeking is different from some other self-regulatory strategies in that it often involves other people and it is both a learning strategy and a social interaction (Nelson-Le Gall, 1981, 1985; Newman, 1991, 1994). Thus, it is likely that social, as well as achievement, motives will influence help seeking. The purpose of this chapter is to further explore the relations between motivation and help-seeking by examining social motivation as well as achievement motivation influences on help-seeking. In addition, we are interested in help seeking as it occurs in an inherently social setting: the classroom. A second aim of this chapter is to describe how various dimensions of the classroom context influence students' achievement and social motivation, and, in turn, their help-seeking attitudes and behavior.

This chapter is organized in three sections. Figure 6.1 displays the overall model that guides our discussion. First, we discuss the help-seeking process for students in the classroom, paying particular attention to how achievement and social motivational characteristics

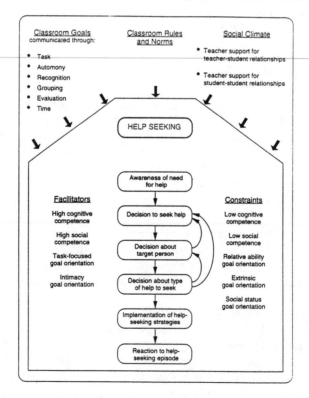

FIG. 6.1. Model of contextual influences on student motivation and help seeking in the classroom.

of students may facilitate or constrain help-seeking behavior. The inner box in Fig. 6.1 depicts the influence of students' personal motivational characteristics on help seeking. In the next section, we explore how various dimensions of the classroom might influence students' personal achievement and social motivation, as well as help-seeking attitudes and behaviors. The outer box in Figure 6.1 depicts the influence of classroom contextual features on students' personal motivational characteristics and their help-seeking. Finally, we discuss directions for future research and implications for educational practice.

STUDENT MOTIVATION
AND THE HELP-SEEKING PROCESS

The help-seeking process begins with an individual's awareness of their need for help. van der Meij (1994) and Dillon (1988, 1990) have described this stage as perplexity. Perplexity refers to a state of puzzlement or uncertainty that arises when there is a discrepancy between personal knowledge and new information or expectations. For example, a student may solve a math problem only to find that the solution in the back of the book is different. Or, a student may think of an example that contradicts a statement that the teacher presents in class. These two examples highlight that awareness of the need for help may be externally or internally generated. External cues are abundant in the classroom. For example, verbal responses by the teacher and graded assignments are external indications to students of how well they understand a given concept. The availability of such external cues may vary greatly between classes, and there is evidence to suggest that this type of information may change as students move through grades in school (Eccles et al., 1993). For example, at the middle or junior high school level, there is an increased emphasis on grades and social comparison (Eccles et al., 1993; Feldlaufer, Midgley, & Eccles, 1988).

At the same time, students' ability to internally monitor their comprehension increases as they age (Wigfield, Eccles, & Pintrich, 1996; Myers & Paris, 1978). Nelson-Le Gall (1981, 1985) and Newman (1991, 1994) have reviewed how children's cognitive development influences their ability to determine their need for help. In this chapter, we focus on adolescent help seeking. By adolescence, students have improved metacognitive and self-regulatory strategies and are better able to monitor and reflect on their performance (Keating, 1990; Myers & Paris, 1978; Paris & Newman, 1993; Wigfield et al., 1996). Thus, most adolescents have available the metacognitive and self-regulatory strategies to determine their need for help in academic situations. A key issue is how different motivational beliefs may facilitate or constrain the use of these strategies in the help-seeking process.

Nelson-Le Gall (1981, 1985) and Newman (1991, 1994) outlined a general model that describes the decisions and actions that make up the help-seeking process following an individual's awareness of their need for help. This model identifies the cognitive and behavioral aspects of help seeking prior to, during, and after seeking help and is displayed in Fig. 6.1. A brief summary of the model is

- The individual decides to seek help from another person.
- The individual decides on a target person from whom to seek the help.
- The individual decides what type of help to seek (e.g., formulation of a particular type of question).
- The individual implements strategies for engaging another person's help (e.g., expression of the question at a particular time with a particular tone).
- The individual reacts to the help-seeking episode (e.g., evaluates the success or failure of the help-seeking attempt, including the helpfulness or nonhelpfulness of the helper and the adequacy or inadequacy of the help obtained).

Motivational characteristics of students are likely to facilitate or constrain all stages of the help-seeking process. However, in this chapter we focus our discussion on how students' achievement and social motivation influences the first two steps in the process, the decision to seek help, and the decision regarding whom to ask for help.

Decision to Seek Help

When students become aware that they need help, they must decide whether to actually seek help. Considerable research has identified this stage as a critical juncture in the overall help-seeking process. Dillon (1988) wrote "95 per cent of the questions that we have in mind to ask we never go on to utter ... we may think the better of it and follow one of the numerous other paths available. These include keeping quiet and giving off that we know and understand" (p. 20). In the classroom, many students do not seek help with their academic work when needed (Good, Slavings, Harel, & Emerson, 1987; Newman, 1990; Newman & Goldin, 1990; Ryan, Hicks, & Midgley, 1997; Ryan & Pintrich, 1997).

Why do many students decide not to seek help when they know they need it? Personal characteristics of students such as self-esteem, perceptions of competence, and performance level have been linked with the decision to seek help. These are displayed as facilitators or constraints on the decision to seek help in Fig. 6.1. In academic settings, research has shown that the need for help is most threatening when students have low levels of self-esteem, perceptions of cognitive competence, and poor performance (Karabenick & Knapp, 1991; Newman, 1990; Newman & Goldin, 1990; Ryan, Hicks, & Midgley, 1997; Ryan & Pintrich, 1997). Students who are low achievers or who have perceptions of their competence as low are concerned that others will think that their need for help indicates that they are unable and, therefore, they are less likely to seek help. In contrast, when students who are high achievers or have perceptions of high cognitive competence encounter failure or difficulty, they do not worry that others will attribute it to their lack of ability and are more likely to secure the necessary help (Butler & Neuman, 1995; Karabenick & Knapp, 1991; Newman, 1990; Newman & Goldin, 1990; Ryan, Hicks, & Midgley, 1997; Ryan & Pintrich, 1997).

A similar relation exists between perceptions of social competence and help seeking (Ryan & Pintrich, 1997). Feeling comfortable and skillful in relating to others lessens the perception that there will be negative fallout (e.g., negative reaction or judgment from the helper) from help seeking. Ryan and Pintrich (1997) found that adolescents who perceived themselves as socially competent were less likely to feel threatened by help seeking and were more likely to ask for help. This relation was independent of the relation between cognitive competence and help seeking, suggesting an independent role of perceptions of social competence. It appears that if individuals feel comfortable and skillful in relating to others socially, then they feel more confident in their ability to ask for help without incurring a negative reaction from the helper. Accordingly, it is not just perceptions of cognitive competence that can influence the help-seeking process, but also perceptions of social competence. This pattern of results highlights the importance of considering help seeking, not just as an academic self-regulatory strategy, but also as a social interaction with others and of recognizing that social motivational constructs such as perceptions of social competence can play a role in the dynamics of help seeking.

Besides perceptions of competence, students' achievement goals are also related to the decision to seek help. Achievement goals concern the purpose and meaning that an individual ascribes to achievement behavior (see Ames, 1992 for a review). Three achievement goals have been examined in relation to help-seeking: task-focused goals, extrinsic goals, and relative ability goals.[1] Task-focused

---

[1]Task-focused and relative ability goals have been referred to elsewhere as mastery and performance goals (Ames, 1992), task and ego goals (Nolen, 1988) and learning and performance goals (Dweck, 1986).

goals refer to the desire to gain understanding, insight or skill; learning is valued as an end in itself. Extrinsic goals refer to the desire to engage in learning tasks to garner consequences external to the task itself (e.g., receiving rewards or avoiding punishment). Finally, relative ability goals refer to the desire to demonstrate high ability or gain favorable judgments of one's abilities in relation to others. These three achievement goals represent disparate reasons for involvement and different conceptions of success regarding academic tasks and have been linked to different help-seeking beliefs and behaviors.

Task-focused goals concern a desire for mastery and a belief that effort leads to mastery and, as such, are negatively related to perceived threat regarding help seeking and avoidance of help seeking when needed (Butler & Neuman, 1995; Newman, 1991, 1994; Ryan, Hicks, & Midgley, 1997; Ryan & Pintrich, 1997). In contrast, when students pursue relative ability or extrinsic goals, learning is viewed as a means to an end. A sense of accomplishment is derived from outperforming others, avoiding negative ability judgments, or receiving external rewards, regardless of the learning involved. Students with such goals are concerned about how others will evaluate them because external evaluation will determine how they compare to others or if they receive rewards. Such concerns are positively related to perceived threat associated with help seeking and reported avoidance of help seeking (Butler & Neuman, 1995; Newman, 1991, 1994; Ryan et al., 1997; Ryan & Pintrich, 1997).

In addition to academic goals, students pursue social goals in the classroom (Hicks 1996, 1997, Urdan & Maehr, 1995; Wentzel, 1989). Social goals concern the purpose and meaning that students ascribe to their social behavior in the classroom. Drawing on a large body of literature that demonstrates that young adolescents value both the opinions and companionship of their peers (e.g., Berndt, 1982; Brown, 1990; Hartup, 1989; Parker & Asher, 1987), Hicks postulated two social goals: social intimacy goals and social status goals (1996, 1997). These two goals concern two types of alliances adolescents have with their peers. Intimacy goals concern the desire to form and maintain positive peer relationships. Such goals include students' desire for both general acceptance and for closer and more inter-personal friendship. In contrast, social status goals concern the desire for social visibility and prestige within the larger peer group. Social status goals are related to the emergence of an elite social crowd in early adolescence, typically labeled popular, that various researchers have documented (e.g., Brown, Mory, & Kinney, 1994; Coleman, 1961; Eder, 1985; Kinney, 1993). Group membership, in these terms, does not necessarily equate with students' friendship selections or with their actual interaction patterns, but is related more to an individual's reputation within the larger peer group

(Brown & Lohr, 1987; Eder, 1985).

Social status and intimacy goals also have been related to the decision to seek help. Status goals are similar to relative ability goals in that both concern maintaining a certain image; relative ability goals concern a student's image of academic ability whereas status goals concern a student's social image or reputation. In both cases, there is a heightened awareness of the self relative to others and a potential need to protect self-worth. Because help seeking is a public behavior that has the potential to garner attention and evaluation from one's peers, students who hold status goals perceive help seeking as threatening to their self-worth and are more likely to avoid seeking help when they need it (Ryan, Hicks, & Midgley, 1997). In contrast, students' intimacy goals represent their desire to interact with and form relationships with peers. Seeking help within the classroom provides an opportunity for legitimate peer interaction, and the goal to form and maintain positive peer relationships is negatively related to avoidance of help seeking (Ryan, Hicks, & Midgley, 1997). These findings parallel the findings for social competence and reinforce the proposition that social motivational constructs are linked to help seeking and that help seeking needs to be considered both a self-regulatory strategy as well as a social interaction.

The discussion to this point has focused on main effects of perceptions of competence and goals, but research suggests that it is important to consider both students' perceptions of competence and their goals when investigating help-seeking attitudes and behaviors in the classroom. Ryan and Pintrich (1997) found significant interactions between extrinsic goals and perceptions of cognitive competence in predicting threat from help seeking for middle-school children. The pursuit of extrinsic goals exacerbated the vulnerability of students with low perceptions of their own cognitive competence. That is, as adolescents' perceptions of cognitive competence decreased, the endorsement of extrinsic goals was associated with higher levels of perceived threat from both peers and teachers regarding help seeking. Thus, students who did their math work to stay out of trouble or to receive rewards but believed they were not competent at math were particularly vulnerable to worries and concerns about others' reactions if they asked for help.

In another study, Ryan, Hicks, and Midgley (1997) found that the relation between adolescents' relative ability goals and their help-seeking behavior depended on their actual level of achievement. As grade point average decreased, the endorsement of relative ability goals was related to higher levels of perceived threat associated with help seeking and avoidance of help seeking. Thus, when students adopt a goal to outperform others but receive information that they are not achieving that goal, they are particularly vulnerable to negative perceptions about help seeking and more likely to avoid it. These findings are in line with the results of an experimental study by Butler and Neuman (1995), which found a similar interaction between initial competence at solving puzzles and relative ability goals. These findings are troubling but provide some insight as to which students in the classroom do not seek help when they need it. First, lower achieving students feel more threatened and report more avoidance of help seeking when needed than do higher achieving students. Furthermore, when students who are lower achievers endorse relative ability goals, the discrepancies become even greater. The very children who need help the most, seek it the least and pursuit of relative ability goals exacerbates this situation.

The finding that actual academic achievement moderates the impact of relative ability goals on help-seeking attitudes and behaviors suggests that a student's social situation might moderate the impact of social status goals on help-seeking variables. The desire to be popular might impact help-seeking attitudes and behavior differently depending on whether a student actually is liked and respected by their peers. An interesting question for future research is whether adolescents' sociometric status would moderate the impact of social status goals on help-seeking threat and behavior.

Much of our discussion of how students' motivation influences their decision to seek help has focused on student perceptions of threat associated with help seeking. However, students also perceive benefits to help seeking (Newman, 1990; Ryan & Pintrich, 1997). Students recognize that help-seeking can be a useful strategy that promotes learning. Newman (1991, 1994) suggested that the decision to seek help involves weighing the costs and benefits of that strategy in a given situation. Ryan and Pintrich (1997) found that students who endorsed task-focused goals were more likely to perceive benefits of help seeking and less likely to avoid help seeking when they needed it. Interestingly, when controlling for achievement goals, perceptions of cognitive and social competence were unrelated to students' perceptions of benefits associated with help seeking.

Decision Regarding a Target Person

Once a student has become aware of the need for help and has made the decision to seek help, a helper must be chosen. Several studies have used open-ended interviews to investigate children's preferences and rationale concerning choice of helpers (Barnett, Darcie, Holland, & Kobasigawa, 1982; Nelson-Le Gall & Gumerman, 1984; van der Meij, 1988; Wintre, Hicks, McVey, & Fox, 1988). Results suggest that choosing a helper is a complex decision that involves the consideration of many factors. Taken together, the results suggest that the following questions are common concerns that influence the choice of a helper:

- Is this person competent? Do they understand the problem at hand?
- Can this person instruct or communicate with me in a way that will help me understand?
- Is it appropriate to ask this person for help?
- Is this person willing to help me?
- What will this person think of me if I ask him or her for help?

If students want assistance in the classroom, their choice is most often between the teacher and their classmates. How do the concerns identified above influence students' choice of a helper in the classroom? Newman and his colleagues (Newman & Goldin, 1990; Newman & Schwager, 1993) have found that generally students believe that help from the teacher is more likely to foster learning than help from peers, suggesting that students view the teacher as more competent and better able to instruct. However, students do view peers as a potentially fruitful source of help and for pragmatic reasons it is likely that students often turn to their peers (Knapp & Karabenick, 1988). Indeed, this was the case in an observational study conducted by Nelson-Le Gall and Glor-Scheib (1985) that found that 83% of student bids for help were directed toward peers compared to 17% directed toward the teacher. This suggests that the decision often made by students is which peer to ask for help.

Regarding appropriateness and willingness of potential helpers, students are likely to consider the relationship they have with the helper. Familiarity, positive relations, and role duty (i.e., friends help each other, the teacher's job is to help) are factors that increase a student's belief that it is appropriate and the person will help them (Nelson-Le Gall & Gumerman, 1984; Newman & Schwager, 1993; Wintre et al., 1988). Finally, students consider the reaction of the helper before they ask a person for help. As discussed earlier, many students' self-worth is threatened by asking for help, in that they think others will think their need for help indicates they are dumb. However, students feelings of threat from the teacher are distinct from their feelings of threat from their peers. Ryan and Pintrich (1997) asked adolescents analogous questions about threat from teachers and peers (i.e., "I think the teacher will think I am dumb if I ask for help with my math work"; "I think other students will think I am dumb if I ask for help with my math work"). Although highly correlated, factor analysis provided evidence that threat from teachers and threat from peers were distinct constructs. This seems logical in that students' relationships with peers and teachers are qualitatively different. The content and power dynamics that characterize social interactions among peers is different from social interactions between students and teachers (Hartup, 1989). Concerns about the reactions and judgments of one's peers regarding help seeking are different from concerns about reactions and judgments from one's teacher regarding help seeking. Thus, the nature of the threat from teachers and peers is different and is likely to impact who a student approaches for help.

Additionally, the motivational influences on threat from peers and teachers seems to be different. Ryan and Pintrich (1997) found that, although relative ability goals heightened both of the negative attitudes of threat from peers and threat from teachers, task-focused goals were a negative influence on threat from teachers only. In contrast, perceived social competence was a negative influence on threat from peers only. Students focused on learning and mastery do not believe that asking for help will result in the teacher thinking negatively of them. The linkage between threat from peers and perceptions of social competence suggests that when students feel confident of their ability to relate to others, they worry less that their bid for help will incur negative evaluations from their peers. Interestingly, the negative attitude of threat from teachers is related to an academic motivational belief, task-focused goals, whereas threat from peers is related to a social motivational belief, perceptions of social competence.

Students' social status goals also may influence who they ask for help. Status goals refer to the desire to attain a position of visibility and social prestige among one's peers. Students who endorse status goals are selective about with whom they socialize, and may not want to associate with someone whom the popular crowd finds unacceptable (Hicks, 1997). Status goals might limit a student's choice for acceptable helpers in the classroom. A student may not want to interact with a student they find uncool and this reluctance may consequently interfere with selection of the best helper for fostering learning. The most competent helper may not be the most popular student in the classroom. Additionally, depending on what behaviors are associated with popularity, status goals may impact whether a student asks the teacher for help. For example, asking a teacher for help may be perceived as being overly concerned about academics or, more colloquially, as nerdy. However, there is a need for classroom research on how status goals may undermine a student's decision of whom to ask for help.

Students' intimacy goals may also influence whom they ask for help. Intimacy goals represent the desire to interact with and form relationships with peers (Hicks, 1997). In addition to yielding information, a successful help-seeking interaction garners support and responsiveness from a person. Support and responsiveness are important aspects of adolescent relationships and may influence the choice of a helper. When considering whom to approach, students' desires for relationships may have an impact. As already noted, familiarity, positive relations, and friendship influence whether a student views a person as appropriate and willing to help. Thus, choice of a helper may reflect a desire to continue a relationship with a peer. If a positive relation is already established, it is likely that the helper will be willing and react kindly to requests for help. However, students may also use help-seeking interactions to initiate relationships with peers. Help seeking provides the opportunity for a social interaction and also provides a chance for another peer to show investment in the relationship. A student may ask for help in the hopes of starting a friendship with the help exchange. Thus, students who pursue intimacy goals may view asking a peer for help as a means to achieve this social goal, not just the academic goal of being able to do their school work. However, as with status goals, there is still a need for empirical research to investigate the role of intimacy goals regarding whom students ask for help in the classroom.

CLASSROOM CONTEXT, STUDENT MOTIVATION, AND HELP-SEEKING

Taken together, research and theory suggest that both students' goals and their perceptions of competence can influence the help-seeking process. Moreover, it is not just achievement goals and achievement competence perceptions that are important. Students' social goals and social competence perceptions are relevant as well. Thus, both students academic and social characteristics need to be considered in models of help seeking. However, it is also important to consider how the classroom context may influence help seeking (Nelson-Le Gall, 1985; Newman, 1991, 1994). Teachers may set up environments that vary greatly in regards to fostering or discouraging students' help seeking. We discuss three dimensions of classrooms that are likely to affect student help-seeking: (1) classroom rules and norms, (2) classroom goals, and (3) the social/interpersonal climate of the classroom.

Classroom Rules and Norms

The rules and norms teachers establish in the classroom are likely to influence the opportunity structure for student help seeking. For example, Karabenick and Sharma (1994) found that college students' perceptions of the amount of support the instructor provided in the class were linked to students asking of questions, even when controlling for the students' level of confusion. In their model, teacher support included providing opportunities for question asking, specific instructions to the students on how to ask questions and reward–punishment contingencies (aspects of rules), as well as teachers' informational or procedural responses to questions, emotional responses to questions, and the value placed on questions by the teachers (aspects of norms).

In interviews we conducted with seventh and eighth grade students, they often referred to such rules and norms when asked about help seeking in the classroom (Ryan, 1996). For example, students told us "Like if the teacher is giving a lecture she doesn't want you to raise your hand and start talking"; "Usually there is a time [for questions] when, after she gives instructions"; and "Most of the time at the end of class if you really don't understand something you can go up and ask the teacher." Such procedures may or may not be explicitly stated but students' perceptions of such rules and norms are likely to influence the timing and manner in which help is sought, as Karabenick and Sharma (1994) showed for the college classroom.

In addition to rules and norms specific to help seeking, rules and norms for completing tasks, participating in class, and interacting with students are also likely to impact help seeking (Karabenick & Sharma, 1994; McCaslin & Good, 1996). A student might be aware that they need help but the rules and norms of the environment will be an important determinant in how the student reacts to this awareness. For example, some teachers allow students to talk to others during seat work in order to receive help. In such a classroom, help seeking should be facilitated. In other classrooms, talking to other students during seat work may be prohibited by the classroom rules because it is construed as cheating or not doing your own work and should constrain help-seeking behavior. Thus, the model of help seeking presented earlier in this chapter must be considered in the context of such rules and norms. Classroom rules and norms interact with students' personal motivational characteristics to influence help seeking. Rules and norms are likely to reflect two dimensions of the classroom: achievement goals and the social/interpersonal climate.

Achievement Goals Emphasized in the Classroom

In a previous section of this chapter we discussed how students' personal achievement goals influence their help seeking. Given that students' personal goals are so intimately related to their help seeking, it is important to examine the antecedents of students' personal goals. Research on student goals has shown that, although students exhibit individual differences in the goals they pursue, the classroom context exerts a powerful influence in shaping goals (Ames, 1992; Ames &

Archer, 1988; Anderman & Maehr, 1994; Maehr & Midgley, 1996; Meece, Blumenfeld, & Hoyle, 1988). When a teacher emphasizes mastery and self-improvement, students are more likely to adopt task-focused goals. In comparison, an emphasis on performance relative to others and competition in a classroom will increase the probability of students adopting relative ability goals. Additionally, teachers that emphasize the importance of doing work for grades and rewards are more likely to have students who endorse extrinsic goals. Epstein (1988), Ames (1992), and Anderman and Maehr (1994) identified six dimensions of the learning environment that impact student motivation and engagement: task, authority, recognition, grouping, evaluation, and time. We use this framework to explore how various instructional practices create an environment that is task-focused and thus fosters adaptive help-seeking attitudes and behaviors or an environment that is relative ability or extrinsic focused and thus hinders adaptive help-seeking attitudes and behaviors.

Tasks. The manner in which teachers structure tasks and learning activities can have important influences on students' goals and help seeking. First, an appropriate level of challenge and instructional support fosters task-focused goals and perceptions of cognitive competence (Ames, 1992; Brophy, 1983; McCaslin & Good, 1996; Meece, 1991; Pintrich & Schunk, 1996). If a task is too easy, students will be bored. On the other hand, if a task is too hard, students will feel overwhelmed and anxious. When task difficulty is optimal, students will feel challenged but also perceive that with effort they can master the task. Instructional support such as presenting tasks in terms of specific and short-term goals can enhance students' beliefs that they can master challenging tasks (Schunk, 1984). Additionally, such instructional support is likely to aid students' monitoring of their progress in their work and their awareness of their need for help. The appropriate level of challenge is likely to vary greatly between students in a particular class. Tasks that involve variety and diversity in the process and product have increased probability to be appropriate for more students. Also, tasks that involve variety and diversity decrease opportunities for social comparison among students (Marshall & Weinstein, 1984). By decreasing social comparison such tasks should decrease threat to self-worth associated with help seeking and, therefore, increase the likelihood students will secure help when they need it.

Authority. This dimension, as defined by Ames (1992), refers to the degree to which teachers involve students in the decision-making process in the classroom. Giving students some choice and control over their work is likely to encourage them to take an active role in their mastery of the material. Thus, when students encounter difficulty they are more likely to be responsible for identifying the problem and securing the necessary help to continue the learning process.

Grouping. Grouping refers to tasks and learning activities that take place in small groups within a classroom. The design, purpose, and extent of grouping in a classroom has been shown to influence student motivation and cognitive engagement (Johnson & Johnson, 1985; McCaslin & Good, 1996; Slavin, 1983; Webb & Palincsar, 1996). Grouping may occur in classrooms for dramatically different reasons. Teachers may use ability groups, which usually involves the teacher instructing small groups of students with homogeneous ability levels, followed by individual seat work (similar to traditional reading groups; Good, Grouws, Mason, Slavings, & Cramer, 1990). Such grouping practices draw attention to the relative ability of students, which would increase threat associated with help seeking for many students. Another potential drawback is that students are likely to have less opportunity to ask the teacher questions because the teacher is occupied making multiple presentations to many groups.

Alternatively, teachers may use small groups for students to collaborate on tasks and activities. When groups are structured cooperatively, in that students' goals and rewards are interdependent with their group members, responsibility for learning is shared among members. Such situations reduce students' concerns and anxiety about failure and evaluation (Davidson & Kroll, 1991) and increase interest, expectations for success, and persistence (Johnson & Johnson, 1985). Thus, with the right conditions, cooperative learning groups can foster task-focused goals. Cooperative learning groups have also been found to foster help seeking (Davidson & Kroll, 1991; Nelson-Le Gall & Glor-Scheib, 1985; Webb, 1982). In comparison to whole class instruction or individual seat work, cooperative learning groups make it easier for students to ask for help. When designed and implemented properly, students are supposed to interact and help one another. Thus, students are exposed to the benefits of help seeking. Slavin (1983) emphasized the importance of incorporating individual accountability within cooperative groups to ensure that all members be involved in the learning process. This should further encourage students to secure help if they need it.

Evaluation/Recognition. The standards, criteria, and methods that a teacher uses to recognize and evaluate students in the classroom has implications for the goals students adopt as well as their help-seeking beliefs and behaviors. The extent to which teachers engage in social comparison among the students, such as displaying public charts of student papers and scores and announcing the highest and lowest marks, draws attention to the relative performance of students and is likely to foster relative ability goals. When such information is made public, students are much more conscious of how able they appear to others and more likely to be concerned about how to maintain an image of high ability in the class. Students who are concerned with maintaining such an image of ability are likely to feel more threatened about the need for help.

Time. The use of time in a classroom has implications for students' goals and help seeking. A rigid time schedule is likely to work against students' mastery of and intrinsic interest in a task. For example, if students have 15 minutes to finish an assignment, they are likely to be conscious of completing their work in the allotted time rather than being thoughtful and creative with their work. Additionally, students may work at different paces and a rigid time schedule may leave some students bored and other students frustrated that they are not able to finish. If students are under a rigid time schedule, they may not take the time to ask for adaptive help. If they do ask for help, they may be more interested in just getting the answer rather than asking for hints, examples, or clues.

Social/Interpersonal Climate of the Classroom

Help seeking combines aspects of social and cognitive engagement, in that it is both a learning strategy and a social interaction with others (Nelson-Le Gall, 1981, 1985). Previously, we discussed how various social constructs, such as social competence and social goals, are related to student help seeking in the classroom. Familiarity as well as positive relations increase the likelihood that a student will ask another person for help (Nelson-Le Gall & Gumerman, 1984; Newman & Schwager, 1993; Wintre et al., 1988). Additionally, when students perceive themselves as comfortable and skillful in relating to others, they are more likely to seek help (Ryan & Pintrich, 1997). Finally, students who are concerned with forming and maintaining close friendships are more likely to seek help, whereas students who are concerned with their social image or status among their peers are less likely to ask for help (Ryan, Hicks, & Midgley, 1997).

Given the social nature of help seeking, it is likely that the social climate of the classroom influences students' help-seeking behavior. One dimension of the social climate that has received attention is teacher social support. Teacher support has been defined slightly differently by different researchers, but generally involves characteristics such as caring, friendliness, understanding, dedication, and dependability. Thus, teacher social support concerns the extent to which teachers value and establish personal relationships with students. Teacher support has been linked to student achievement motivation in the classroom. When students perceive their teacher as supportive, they report higher levels of interest and enjoyment (Feldlaufer et al., 1988; Fraser & Fisher, 1982; Goodenow, 1993; Midgley, Feldlaufer, & Eccles, 1989; Skinner & Belmont, 1993; Tricket & Moos, 1974) as well as expectancies for success in the classroom (Goodenow, 1993).

In addition to teachers' valuing and establishing teacher–student relationships, another dimension of the social climate of the classroom is the extent to which teachers value and encourage student–student relationships in the classroom. The way teachers structure tasks and procedures in the classroom provides different opportunities for students to interact with each other. Additionally, teachers may vary in the values that they communicate to students about relationships with peers. An observational study of classroom interactions between students and between the teacher and students provides support for this point (Anderson, Stevens, Prawat, & Nickerson, 1988). Whereas some classrooms were characterized by positive and comfortable relationships and frequent prosocial and cooperative interactions, some classrooms had an unpleasant affective tone and frequent negative interactions such as bickering, criticism, and insults. Interestingly, a positive social climate was highly correlated to student independence and initiative regarding classroom tasks and procedures (e.g., lining up, turning in assignments, and checking work). This suggests that this dimension of the social climate is intricately related to student motivation in the classroom.

It is likely that the social climate influences students' perceptions of their social competence as well as the social goals they endorse. In a classroom characterized as caring, supportive, and friendly, students are likely to feel more comfortable and skillful in relating to others. It may also be that when a teacher works to establish personal relationships with students they in turn will value relationships. If a teacher emphasizes the importance of getting along and respecting ones' classmates, then students may be more interested in establishing positive student relationships in the classroom.

Directly, and indirectly through achievement and social motivation, the social climate of a classroom is likely to influence student help seeking. Classrooms characterized as caring, supportive, and friendly are likely to make students feel more comfortable interacting with the teacher and other students as well as desiring and forming personal relationships with the teacher and peers. Increased perceptions of social competence, intimacy goals, positive relations, and familiarity have all been positively linked to help seeking (Nelson-Le Gall & Gumerman, 1984; Newman & Schwager, 1993; Ryan et al., 1997; Ryan & Pintrich, 1997; Wintre et al., 1988). It may be that in an environment in which students feel that others know and relate to them beyond their academic abilities, they feel less threatened that asking for help will incur negative judgments. This view is supported by the findings of two studies. Newman and Schwager (1993) found that student ratings of how much they liked their teacher and how much their teacher liked them were related to students' intentions to seek help when they needed it. In addition, Karabenick and Sharma (1994) found that teacher support of question asking, in terms of conveying positive emotions towards the students, resulted in more question asking by students.

However, more research is needed to fully understand how the social climate of a classroom influences help seeking. Additionally, it has been suggested that although negative emotional classroom climates are related to lower achievement, neutral emotional climates are just as supportive of achievement as warm emotional climates (Brophy & Good, 1986). Thus, the critical level of social climate variables may be important to consider. Further research in this area could add to our understanding about how teachers create a social climate that facilitates students help seeking.

DIRECTIONS FOR FUTURE RESEARCH AND IMPLICATIONS FOR CLASSROOMS

In this chapter, we have discussed how individual as well as classroom characteristics may influence student help seeking. Incorporating individual as well as contextual factors into a view of student help seeking is consistent with previous research on help seeking (e.g., Arbreton, 1993; Karabenick, 1994; Karabenick & Sharma, 1994; Nelson-Le Gall, 1985; Nelson-Le Gall & Glor-Scheib, 1985; Newman, 1991, 1994; Newman & Schwager, 1993). In our discussion of student help seeking, we integrated findings from research on achievement motivation and help seeking and also proposed that social motivational constructs are important for a full understanding of help seeking in the classroom. Initial investigations of social motivational constructs in models of help seeking have provided partial support for our viewpoint (Ryan, Hicks, & Midgley, 1997; Ryan & Pintrich, 1997). However, additional research is needed to fully understand the relation between social motivation and student help seeking.

We focused on how students' social motivation may influence the first two stages of the help-seeking process (as outlined by Nelson-Le Gall 1981, 1985 and Newman 1991, 1994, and summarized in the beginning of this chapter). Namely, we discussed students' decisions regarding whether to seek help when they need it, and regarding whom to seek help from. Whereas there is initial evidence that student perceptions of social competence and social goals are related to the overall decision to seek help (Ryan, Hicks, & Midgley, 1997; Ryan & Pintrich, 1997), no studies have examined how students' social motivation is related to their decision regarding whom to ask for help. Further, although not discussed in this chapter, students' social motivation is likely to be important in all stages in the help-seeking process. Previous work has distinguished between requests for help that foster independence (termed adaptive or instrumental help seeking) and requests that foster dependence (termed maladaptive or executive help seeking; Nelson-Le Gall 1981, 1985; Newman, 1994; Ryan & Pintrich, 1997). An important direction for future work is to examine how social motivational constructs influence the type of help that is sought. Additionally, the actual implementation of strategies to engage another person's help (e.g., expression of a question at a particular time and with a particular tone) and the evaluation of the success or failure of the help-seeking exchange have social aspects to them and are likely influenced by students' social motivation. Attention to these issues could increase our understanding of the relation between students' social motivation and help seeking.

There is also a need for more research on how the various contextual factors displayed in Fig. 6.1 can facilitate or constrain help seeking. In our model, these contextual factors may have a direct effect on the help-seeking process through the creation of a general climate and structure that makes it easier or harder for students to engage in the various phases of the help-seeking process. At the same time, as we have suggested in this chapter, there may be indirect effects of the contextual factors on help seeking as the various contextual factors influence the achievement and social motivation constructs such as goals and competency beliefs, which, in turn, have a direct influence on the help-seeking process. There has been very little research that has examined the full range of contextual and personal factors, and there is a clear need for this type of research in order to tease out the direct and indirect effects of context on help seeking. Investigating classroom contextual effects on student help seeking involves the exploration of hierarchical relationships (i.e., relationships between classroom-level variables and student-level variables). Recent developments in hierarchical linear models (HLM) now provide appropriate tools for modeling within- and between- classroom effects (Bryk & Raudenbush, 1992).

HLM allows simultaneous examination of contextual and individual influences on help seeking and thus could clarify multilevel influences. Such methodology could increase current understanding of student help seeking in the classroom.

An understanding of contextual influences on help seeking is especially important if we want to make suggestions to teachers regarding how to facilitate student motivation and help seeking. Findings regarding how students' individual characteristics relate to their help seeking can provide useful information for teachers about student help-seeking behavior. However, it is a challenging task to attend to each students' individual needs. Suggestions about instructional practices that will have a positive influence on all students' motivation and help seeking may be more pragmatic for practitioners (although still challenging to implement, see Maehr & Midgley, 1996). Maehr and Midgley (1996) and Anderman and Maehr (1994) have discussed how various dimensions of the classroom context—task, authority, grouping, evaluation/recognition, and time (TARGET)—can be structured to foster positive motivational beliefs. We have added the social dimension. We conclude our chapter by briefly summarizing how instructional practices are likely to influence student motivation and help seeking.

1. *Tasks*—Tasks with an appropriate level of challenge and instructional support fosters task-focused goals and perceptions of cognitive competence. Presenting tasks in terms of specific and short-term goals can enhance students' beliefs that they can master challenging tasks and aid in students' monitoring of their progress in their work and their awareness of their need for help.

2. *Authority*—Giving students some choice and control over their work is likely to encourage them to take an active role in their mastery of the material. Thus, when students encounter difficulty, they are more likely to be responsible for identifying the problem and securing the necessary help to continue the learning process.

3. *Grouping*—Ability groups that highlight ability differences are likely to foster relative ability goals in students and increase threat associated with help seeking for many students. Alternatively, groups that are structured for students to collaborate on tasks have potential to foster task-focused goals and also make it easier for students to seek help when they need it.

4. *Evaluation/Recognition*—The extent to which teachers engage in social comparison among students draws attention to the relative performance of students and is likely to foster relative ability goals. Students who are concerned with maintaining such an image of ability are likely to feel more threatened about the need for help.

5. *Time*—An overly rigid time schedule is likely to work against students' mastery of and intrinsic interest in a task. With rigid time constraints, students may not take the time to ask for help. If they do ask for help,

they may be more interested in just getting the answer than asking for the type of help that will foster true understanding.

6. *Social*—Classrooms characterized as caring and supportive are likely to make students feel more comfortable interacting with the teacher and other students. Thus, instructional practices that allow the formation of positive relationships and that legitimize mutual help and task-related interactions among peers should support students' efforts to seek help when it is needed. In contrast, instructional practices that make help seeking especially public or unusual are likely to threaten students' social competence and social status in the classroom and inhibit students from securing the help they need.

These suggestions are not always easy to implement, given the nature of schools and classrooms (see Maehr & Midgley, 1996). However, such changes should increase the probability that students will seek help when they need it. Facilitating and encouraging students to ask for help when they need it in the classroom should promote learning and performance.

REFERENCES

Ames, C. (1992). Classrooms: Goals, structures, and student motivation. *Journal of Educational Psychology, 84*, 261–271.

Ames, C., & Archer, J. (1988). Achievement goals in the classroom, students' learning strategies, and motivation processes. *Journal of Educational Psychology, 80*, 260–267.

Anderman, E., & Maehr, M. L. (1994). Motivation and schooling in the middle grades. *Review of Educational Research, 64*, 287–309.

Anderson, L. M., Stevens, D. D., Prawat, R. S., & Nickerson, J. (1988). Classroom task environments and students' task-related beliefs. *Elementary School Journal, 88*, 281–295.

Arbreton, A. (1993). *When getting help is helpful: Developmental, cognitive, and motivational influences on students' academic help-seeking.* Unpublished doctoral dissertation, University of Michigan.

Barnett, K., Darcie, G., Holland, C. J., & Kobasigawa, A. (1982). Children's cognitions about effective helping. *Developmental Psychology, 18*, 267–277.

Berndt, T. J. (1982). The features and effects of friendship in early adolescence. *Child Development, 53*, 147–1460.

Brophy, J. (1983). Conceptualizing student motivation. *Educational Psychologist, 18*, 200–215.

Brophy, J., & Good, T. L. (1986). Teacher behavior and student achievement. In M. C. Wittrock (Ed.), *Handbook of research on teaching* (3rd ed., pp. 328–375). New York: Macmillan.

Brown, B. B. (1990). Peer groups and peer culture. In S. S. Feldman & G. R. Elliott (Eds.), *At the threshold: The developing adolescent* (pp. 171–196). Cambridge, MA: Harvard University Press.

Brown, B. B., & Lohr, M. (1987). Peer group affiliation and adolescent self-esteem: An integration of ego-identity and symbolic interaction theories. *Journal of Personality and Social Psychology, 52*, 47–55.

Brown, B. B., Mory, M. S., & Kinney, D. (1994). Casting adolescent crowds in an relational perspective: Caricature, channel, and context. In R. Montemayor, G. R. Adams, & T. P. Gullotta (Eds.), *Personal relationships during adolescence: Vol. 6. Advances in adolescent development* (pp. 123–167). Thousand Oaks, CA: Sage.

Bryk, A. S., & Raudenbush, S. W. (1992). *Hierarchical linear models: Applications and data-analysis methods.* Beverly Hills, CA: Sage.

Butler, R., & Neuman, O. (1995). Effects of task and ego achievement goals on help-seeking behaviors and attitudes. *Journal of Educational Psychology, 87,* 261–271.

Coleman, J. S. (1961). *The adolescent society.* New York: Free Press.

Davidson, N., & Kroll, D. L. (1991). An overview of research on cooperative learning related to mathematics. *Journal for Research in Mathematics Education, 22,* 362–365.

Dillon, J. T. (1988). *Questioning and teaching: A manual of practice.* New York: Teachers College.

Dillon, J. T. (1990). *The practice of questioning.* New York: Routledge.

Dweck, C. S. (1986). Motivational processes affecting learning. *American Psychologist, 41,* 1040–1048.

Eccles, J., Midgley, C., Wigfield, A., Buchanan, C. M., Reuman, D., Flanagan, C., & MacIver, D. (1993). Development during adolescence: The impact of stage-environment fit on young adolescents' experience in schools and families. *American Psychologist, 48,* 90–101.

Eder, D. (1985). The cycle of popularity: Interpersonal relations among female adolescents. *Sociology of Education, 58,* 154–165.

Epstein, J. L. (1988). Effective schools of effective students: Dealing with diversity. In R. Haskins & D. MacRae (Eds.), *Policies for America's public schools: Teacher equity indicators* (pp. 89–126). Norwood, NJ: Ablex.

Feldlaufer, H., Midgley, C., & Eccles, J. (1988). Student, teacher, and observer perceptions of classroom environment before and after the transition to junior high school. *Journal of Early Adolescence, 8,* 133–156.

Fraser, B. J., & Fisher, D. L. (1982). Predicting student outcomes from their perceptions of classroom psychosocial environment. *American Educational Research Journal, 19,* 498–518.

Good, T. L., Grouws, D. A., Mason, D. A., Slavings, R. L., & Cramer, K. (1990). An observational study of small-group mathematics instruction in elementary school. *American Educational Research Journal, 25,* 755–782.

Good, T. L., Slavings, R. L., Harel, K. H., & Emerson, H. (1987). Student passivity: A study of question-asking in K–12 classrooms. *Sociology of Education, 60,* 181–199.

Goodenow, C. (1993). Classroom belonging among early adolescent students: Relationships to motivation and achievement. *Journal of Early Adolescence, 13,* 21–43.

Hartup, W. W. (1989). Social relationships and their developmental significance. *American Psychologist, 44,* 120–126.

Hicks, L. (1996). *Social goals in early adolescence: Development, gender, and schooling as contexts.* Unpublished doctoral dissertation, University of Michigan.

Hicks, L. (1997). Academic motivation and peer relationships–how do they mix in an adolescent's world? *Middle School Journal, 28,* 18—22.

Johnson, D., & Johnson, R. (1985). Motivational processes in cooperative, competitive, and individualistic learning situations. In C. Ames & R. Ames (Eds.), *Research on motivation in education* (Vol. 2, pp. 249–286). New York: Academic Press.

Karabenick, S. A. (1994). Relation of perceived teacher support of student questioning to students' beliefs about teacher attributions for questioning and perceived classroom learning environment. *Learning and Individual Differences, 6,* 187–204.

Karabenick, S. A., & Knapp, J. R. (1991). Relationship of academic help-seeking to the use of learning strategies and other achievement behavior in college students. *Journal of Educational Psychology, 83,* 221–230.

Karabenick, S. A., & Sharma, R. (1994). Seeking academic assistance as a strategic learning resource. In P. R. Pintrich, D. R. Brown, & C. E. Weinstein (Eds.), *Student motivation, cognition, and learning: Essays in honor of Wilbert J. McKeachie* (pp. 189–211). Hillsdale, NJ: Lawrence Erlbaum Associates.

Keating, D. P. (1990). Adolescent thinking. In S. S. Feldman & G. R. Elliot (Eds.), *At the threshold: The developing adolescent* (pp. 54–89). Cambridge, MA: Harvard University Press.

Kinney, D. A. (1993). From "nerds" to "normals": Adolescent identity recovery within a changing social system. *Sociology of Education, 66,* 21–40.

Knapp, J. R., & Karabenick, S. A. (1988). Incidence of formal and informal help-seeking in higher education. *Journal of College Student Development, 29,* 223–227.

Maehr, M. L., & Midgley, C. (1996). *Transforming school culture.* Boulder, CO: Westview Press.

Marshall, H., & Weinstein, R .S. (1984). Classroom factors affecting students' self-evaluations: An interactional model. *Review of Educational Research, 54,* 301–325.

McCaslin, M., & Good, T. L. (1996). The informal curriculum. In D. Berliner and R. Calfee (Eds.), *Handbook of educational psychology* (pp. 622–670). New York: Macmillan.

Meece, J. L. (1991). The classroom context and students' motivational goals. In M. L. Maehr & P.R. Pintrich (Eds.), *Advances in motivation and achievement: Vol. 7. Goals and self-regulatory processes (pp. 261—286).* Greenwich, CT: JAI .

Meece, J. L., Blumenfeld, P. C., & Hoyle, R. H. (1988). Students' goals and cognitive engagement in classroom activities. *Journal of Educational Psychology, 80,* 514–523.

Midgley, C., Feldlaufer, H., & Eccles, J. S. (1989). Student/teacher relations and attitudes toward mathematics before and after the transition to junior high school. *Child Development, 60,* 981–992.

Myers, M., & Paris, S. G. (1978). Children's metacognitive knowledge about reading. *Journal of Educational Psychology, 70,* 680–690.

Nelson-Le Gall, S. (1981). Help-seeking: An understudied problem solving skill in children. *Developmental Review, 1,* 224–246.

Nelson-Le Gall, S. (1985). Help-seeking behavior in learning. In E. W. Gordon (Ed.), *Review of research in education* (Vol. 12, pp. 55–90). Washington, DC: American Educational Research Association.

Nelson-Le Gall, S., & Glor-Scheib, S. (1985). Academic help-seeking and peer relations in school. *Contemporary Educational Psychology, 11,* 187–193.

Nelson-Le Gall, S., & Gumerman, R. A. (1984). Children's perceptions of helpers and helper motivation. *Journal of Applied Developmental Psychology, 5,* 1–12.

Nelson-Le Gall, S., & Jones, E. (1990). Cognitive-motivational influences on the task-related help-seeking behavior of Black children. *Child Development, 61,* 581–589.

Newman, R. S. (1990). Children's help-seeking in the classroom: The role of motivational factors and attitudes. *Journal of Educational Psychology, 82,* 71–80.

Newman, R. S. (1991). Goals and self-regulated learning: What motivates children to seek academic help? In M. L. Maehr & P. R. Pintrich (Eds.), *Advances in motivation and achievement: Vol. 7. Goals and self-regulatory processes (pp. 151–183).* Greenwich, CT: JAI.

Newman, R. S. (1994). Adaptive help-seeking: A strategy of self-regulated learning. In D. Schunk and B. Zimmerman (Eds.), *Self-Regulation of learning and performance: issues and educational applications* (pp. 283–301). Hillsdale, NJ: Lawrence Erlbaum Associates.

Newman, R. S., & Goldin, L. (1990). Children's reluctance to seek help with schoolwork. *Journal of Educational Psychology, 82,* 92–100.

Newman, R. S., & Schwager, M. T. (1993). Student perceptions of the teacher and classmates in relation to reported help-seeking in math class. *Elementary School Journal, 94,* 3–17.

Nolen, S. B. (1988). Reasons for studying: Motivational orientations and study strategies. *Cognition and Instruction, 5,* 269–287.

Paris, S. G., & Newman, R. S. (1990). Developmental aspects of self-regulated learning. *Educational Psychologist, 25,* 87–102.

Parker, J. G., & Asher, S. R. (1987). Peer relations and later personal adjustment: Are low-accepted children at risk? *Psychological Bulletin, 102,* 357–389.

Pintrich, P. R., & Schunk, D. H. (1996). *Motivation in education: Theory, research, and applications.* Englewood Cliffs, NJ: Merrill Prentice-Hall.

Ryan, A. M. (1996). [Interviews with adolescent students]. Unpublished data.

Ryan, A. M., Hicks, L., & Midgley, C. (1997). Social goals, academic goals, and avoiding seeking help in the classroom. *Journal of Early Adolescence, 17*, 152–171.

Ryan, A. M., & Pintrich, P. R. (1997). Should I ask for help?: The role of motivation and attitudes in adolescents' help seeking in math class. *Journal of Educational Psychology, 89*, 329–341.

Schunk, D. H. (1984). Sequential attributional feedback and children's achievement behaviors. *Journal of Educational Psychology, 76*, 1159–1169.

Skinner, E. A., & Belmont, M. J. (1993). Motivation in the classroom: Reciprocal effects of teacher behavior and student engagement across the school year. *Journal of Educational Psychology, 85*, 571–581.

Slavin, R. (1983). *Cooperative learning*. New York: Longman.

Trickett, E., & Moos, R. H. (1974). Personal correlates of contrasting environments: Student satisfaction in high school classrooms. *American Journal of Community Psychology, 2*, 1–12.

Urdan, T. C., & Maehr, M. L. (1995). Beyond a two goal theory of motivation and achievement: A case for social goals. *Review of Educational Research, 65*, 213–243.

van der Meij, H. (1988). Constraints on question-asking in classrooms. *Journal of Educational Psychology, 80*, 401–405.

van der Meij, H. (1994). Student questioning: A componential analysis. *Learning and Individual Differences, 6*, 137–161.

Webb, N. L. (1982). Student interaction and learning in small groups. *Review of Educational Research, 52*, 421–455.

Webb, N. L., & Palincsar, A. (1996). Group processes in the classroom. In D. Berliner & R. Calfee (Eds.), *Handbook of educational psychology* (pp. 841–873). New York: Macmillan.

Wentzel, K. R. (1989). Adolescent classroom goals, standards for performance, and academic achievement: An interactionist perspective. *Journal of Educational Psychology, 81*, 131–142.

Wigfield, A., Eccles, J. S., & Pintrich, P. R. (1996). Development between the ages of 11 and 25. In D. Berliner & R. Calfee (Eds.), *Handbook of educational psychology* (pp. 148–185). New York: Macmillan.

Wintre, M. G., Hicks, R., McVey, G., & Fox, J. (1988). Age and sex differences in choice of consultant for various types of problems. *Child Development, 59*, 1046–1055.

Help Seeking in the Japanese College Classroom: Cultural, Developmental, and Social-Psychological Influences

David W. Shwalb
University of Utah

Seisoh Sukemune
Mukogawa Women's University

Cross-cultural is a buzzword among social scientists, but too few in the field of psychology study or understand cultural influences. In fact, psychology is perhaps the most culture-bound of the sciences (Azuma, 1996; D. Shwalb & B. Shwalb, 1996), having developed in the traditions and values of Europe and the United States. It is the intersection of cultures that we can best appreciate the limitations of psychology as a universal science. Some psychologists sometimes see a value in non-Western research that broadens the data base or tests the universality of theories, but even this view assumes that ideas from outside the United States and Europe are mere supplements to psychological knowledge. After reading this chapter, we encourage you to reread the other chapters and to question the cultural assumptions held by each contributor. To ignore the fact that culture influences help-seeking behavior and education with regard to every chapter in this volume is to ignore a crucial causal variable.

BACKGROUND

Since the 1970s, Japanese education has been a frequent target of comparison in discussions of cultural influences on learning (D. Shwalb & B. Shwalb, 1996). The Japanese educational system, at least at the primary and secondary levels, is recognized as highly effective and efficient in international comparisons of academic achievement. U.S. scholars have shown that one can learn from the educational successes of Japanese and other Asian societies and have conducted excellent empirical research on Japanese schooling (e.g., Stevenson & Stigler, 1992). Japan is an ideal place for Westerners to study cultural influences on education because (a) Japanese education seems to work well, (b) some Japanese values and traditions differ from those in the West, and (c) there are excellent Japanese research collaborators available in the fields of educational and developmental psychology (Nakazawa & Shwalb, 1997).

Unfortunately, there are also at least three weaknesses in cross-cultural research on Japanese education. First is the neglect of college-age populations, as both Japanese and Westerners researchers have assumed that there is little of value to be studied about Japanese university education. This negative image was fostered by Michio Nagai's (1971) critique of Japanese higher education, aptly entitled Higher Education in Japan: Its Take-Off and Crash. Scholars in other fields (sociology, history of education, etc.) have written about college-age populations, but U.S. educational and developmental psychologists stop short at the college gateway when studying Japanese education and human development. This is generally the case among Japanese psychologists as well.

A second weakness is the tendency to focus on either positive or negative outcomes of Japanese education. Too much value judgment is involved, perhaps to emphasize implications for educators who want to emulate the Japanese. The third weakness is the preoccupation of Western educational scholars with academic achievement. When we ask Japanese parents what concerns them most about their children's schooling, they typically discuss issues of personality and socialization, such as bullying, peer relations, loss of free time, loss of individuality, and forfeiture of parental control over children's priorities. U.S. funding agencies are duly concerned with questions such as why Japanese students outachieve U.S. children academically, but the Japanese public is relatively more concerned with young people's social and identity development.

We mention these three limitations because they help us understand why the research literature on help-seeking behavior in Japanese college classrooms is so sparse. There has been almost no objective research on classroom communication in higher education. In addition, colleges are frequently criticized for the low quality of teaching, and research on teaching and faculty development is a new subject area. And although Japanese educators are preoccupied with outcomes such as the numbers of graduates who gain employment at prestigious companies, they pay only lip service to the importance of personal development among Japanese college students. Thus, our topic is seldom written about in Japan.

OVERVIEW: QUESTIONS TO BE ADDRESSED

Japanese Cultural Values and Norms

We can identify several patterns of Japanese normative behavior that relate to the topic of help seeking. Several questions arise in this discussion: What cultural values and norms encourage help-seeking and helping behavior? What values and norms discourage these behaviors? What socialization goals and values are fostered in college life?

Pre-College Socialization

As developmental psychologists, we are interested in the developmental origins of adult behavior. We summarize current knowledge on how help seeking and helping behavior are learned in Japan between early childhood and early adulthood. The following questions are addressed: What experiences at home and at school foster help seeking and helping behavior? How does socialization for cooperativeness relate to help seeking and helping? Are there school-level differences in pupils' experiences, relevant to help seeking and helping? Is there continuity or discontinuity in socialization for help seeking and helping between secondary and post-secondary education?

Personal and Situational Influences

Thirdly, we consider how help seeking and helping depend, in Japan, on the individual or on situational factors. The first two sets of questions lead to generalizations about Japanese values and experiences, whereas this third section shows the limitations of the generalities. When are Japanese college students more or less likely to help or seek help? Which individuals are more or less likely to help or seek help? Are these personal or situational variables in any way unique to Japanese students?

Implications

In the final section, we discuss the implications of this chapter. What are the implications for Japanese higher education and society? What are the implications for educators outside of Japan? Is the information provided here of limited relevance outside of Japan? What are the general implications for future research on help-seeking and helping behavior?

JAPANESE CULTURAL VALUES AND NORMS

The following is an assessment of the cultural values that are empha-sized by the Japanese educational system. What is the most impressive to us is the continuity of the goals across school levels. For instance, socialization in preschool is preparation for primary school, but the values that are emphasized in early childhood education are empha-sized consistently throughout childhood, adolescence, and adulthood.

Dependency

In the prospectus written for this volume, Karabenick wrote that "seeking help ... *despite its reliance on others* [italics added] can provide the foundation for autonomous achievement." This phrasing reflects the Western assumption that reliance on others is not as desirable as autonomous achievement (Ames, 1983; Nelson-Le Gall, 1985). As discussed over the past generation by Doi (1973, 1996), dependency *(amae)* is a universal human behavior that is especially valued in Japan. In Japanese schools, dependent behavior is not only permitted, but it is actually a desirable aspect of teacher–pupil rela-tionships because it is natural for learners to depend on their teachers (Azuma, 1996). In Japan, from preschool, where teachers are mater-nal figures (Peak, 1992), through college, where students sleep in class and beg for extra help before examinations, it is normal for learners to rely on their instructors.

Independence

One insightful school teacher told us, "I enjoy teaching third and fourth graders best, because that is their last chance to be individuals ... . From 5th grade parents pressure them to fit into the entrance exami-nation mold and they do nothing but study, but in middle elementary school children can still be themselves" (Y. Tsukamoto, personal communication, March 22, 1996). Children may lose their individu-ality, yet schools advocate individualism as a matter of public policy at every level of education. Even though every child is forced to study the same curriculum to pass the same entrance examinations, all educational institutions state that their goals include individuality (*kohsei*) and autonomy (*jisshusei*). Parents can easily see through this lip service paid to autonomy and complain at Parent Teacher Associa-tion (PTA) meetings that studying alone makes a child feel isolated rather than unique. Particularly from Grade 8, emphasis on small group learning gives way to individual competition (Sugie, 1995).

Empathy

Japanese people are encouraged from early childhood to show empathy (*kyokan*) and sympathy (*omoiyari*) toward others. Azuma (1996) illustrated this in his United States/Japan comparative study of childrearing, observing that Japanese mothers focused their preschool children on the effects of their behavior on others. At preschool, children also learn to empathize with their classmates and teachers (Lewis, 1995). An elementary school teacher informed of us of an incident that demonstrated socialization for empathy (K. Harada, personal communication, January 20, 1996). Five 4th-grade girls were involved in a series of intense disputes, leading up to a punching match in the girl's room. The teacher, rather than contacting their parents or punishing anyone, spent two hours diagraming the girls' different versions of the story on the blackboard in front of the entire class, and the entire class analyzed and role-played the communication problems. The five girls had to write reflection essays (hansei-bun) focusing on their adversaries' points of view.

Diligence

In attribution studies, Japanese children tend to emphasize effort and put relatively less emphasis on innate ability (Holloway, 1988). From a very early age, they are encouraged to always give their maximum effort (*gambaru*). For instance at the beginning of the annual Sports Day meet, an event held at every school, a student representative pledges everyone's effort (*doryoku*), and at the closing ceremony, the principal or other authority praises everyone's collective effort rather than focusing on the winners. In the classroom, teachers need to spend very little time disciplining or controlling children's behavior (Hamilton, Blumenfeld, & Miura, 1990), and most students work diligently whenever that is the desire of the teacher.

Group Achievement

Asked at a 1995 lecture by a Japanese student why the United States is "a more developed and superior" society compared with Japan (the student cited overwhelming numbers of U.S. Nobel Prize winners), psychological anthropologist Tom Weisner remarked that "Japanese are by no means inferior. It is just that many of their greatest achievements are accomplished as groups. Japanese excel internationally when they set collective goals." As a member of a family, a preschool or elementary school homeroom class, a secondary school club, or a college seminar class, Japanese participants have a strong sense of belongingness (Lebra, 1976). Groups nonetheless differ in degree of coherence—a college seminar class may be the main source of a student's identity and friendships for three years, whereas a lecture class may provide no sense of group awareness.

Cooperativeness and Competitiveness

Children are socialized to have a cooperative spirit (kyodoshin), which may involve conformity (kyochosei, e.g., a cooperative child listens quietly), or work toward group goals (kyoryokusei). On the other hand, aggressiveness (kogekisei) is explicitly discouraged, and although competition (kyososhin) is encouraged by many teachers from elementary school and on, it is not an official goal of schooling. Every student knows that beginning in elementary school entrance examinations are competitive, and, at college, students know that competition for jobs after graduation is severe. As a result socialization is for both cooperation and competition (D. Shwalb, B. Shwalb, & Nakazawa, 1995).

Role Perfection

At school, work, and everywhere, Japanese people are told to perform their roles to perfection (DeVos, 1973). The role of pupil/student is serious and is the central activity of life from preschool through graduate school. At college, however, students take on a greater diversity of other roles, so their commitment of time and energy is more diffused than in primary and secondary school. Teaching duties may also be less central in the work of professors than for primary and secondary school teachers, and for many university professors the role of researcher is more important to their identities than that of teacher. Nevertheless, all instructors and students know well that the sensei is the superior and the student is the inferior in a vertical relationship.

Values Stressed in College Education

The goals of college education in Japan depend on the institution and the individual student. Undergraduate colleges usually claim to value both the academic and personal development of the individual. One common image of Japanese college students is that, because they struggled throughout secondary school for admission to college, they tend to relax and study as little as possible in college. This is true of some students, although there are wide variations in the study habits of individual students (Sakamoto, 1985). Yet, the college's prestige level sets the range of employment possibilities after graduation (few students transfer between colleges). Credits and a diploma are the primary goals for many students, rather than learning. Only 15% of Japanese college students go on to graduate studies, so the undergraduate degree is, for most, the terminal degree. Therefore, while universities officially stress the development of the individual personality, we believe that, in reality, colleges mainly cultivate the kind of individual who can serve a company. In sum, the goals of college education are graduation, a job, and a business-like team attitude.

PRE-COLLEGE SOCIALIZATION
OF HELP SEEKING AND HELPING

All of the cultural values and norms mentioned thus far are related to help seeking, question asking, and helping behavior. The following section concerns pupils' experiences in helping and help seeking before they reach college. These activities are likely to influence the thinking and behavior of college students.

Cooperativeness and Helping

Help seeking and help giving are two sides of the same coin, and as is shown next, help-giving behavior is an important aspect of cooperativeness. As noted earlier, cooperativeness is a highly valued trait for all age groups. From an information acquisition standpoint, we expect to see help seeking at school in group study, asking questions of peers or teachers, and so forth. From a social standpoint, helping is also common, for instance, when pupils assist peers or teachers. To illuminate the precise contents of cooperation and helping behavior in Japanese schools, B. Shwalb and D. Shwalb (1985) documented the changing nature of prosocial behavior across school levels in a national survey of teachers. A sample of 55 teachers generated 453 free responses, and from these, a 30-item cooperative behavior scale was developed. An independent sample of 575 teachers then ranked the top ten of these items in terms of best representing a cooperative pupil. Their responses were factor analyzed and produced eight cooperation dimensions. Data based on these indexes were compared between three school levels (elementary, middle, and high school). The items are listed in Table 7.1 for each dimension along with school level comparisons.

The dimensions of cooperativeness were as follows:

1. Harmony (nakayoshi—harmonious peer relationships).
2. Friendship (yujin kankei—friendly or helpful contacts with peers).
3. Clubs or teams (kurabu katsudo ya taiku—participation in sports/team activities).
4. Small group involvement (han katsudo—participation in committees or group projects).
5. Diligence (sunao/kinben—obedience and seriousness).

TABLE 7.1
Cooperation in Japanese Primary and Secondary Schools: School-Level Comparisons

Factor (Composite) + Items	Total	Elem.	J.H.S.	H.S.	F	p
Harmony	11.0 (1)	8.9 (1)	12.7 (2)	11.9 (1)	19.24	<.001
Gets along well with any partner	11.9	9.6	13.5	13.0		
Friendly and harmonious with peers	10.1	8.3	11.9	10.7		
Friendliness	12.2 (2)	11.3 (2)	12.9 (3)	12.5 (3)	4.05	<.05
Contacts friends about school matters	15.2	16.7	14.3	14.3		
Friendly and harmonious with peers	10.1	8.3	11.9	10.7		
Plays with friends in free school time	11.1	9.2	12.5	12.0		
Helps out sick or injured friend	12.1	11.0	12.7	12.9		
Clubs & Teams	13.1(3)	15.4 (4)	11.6 (1)	12.0 (2)	28.40	<.001
Active in clubs	13.3	15.8	11.1	12.3		
Participates in gym/athletic meets	13.0	15.1	12.0	11.6		
Group Involvement	15.1 (4)	15.2 (3)	14.6 (4)	15.3 (5)	1.64	NS
Join group rather than do own thing	12.0	12.0	11.8	12.2		
Follows group though disagrees	12.6	13.9	10.8	12.4		
Does group experiments and projects	17.3	16.8	17.6	17.5		
Active in class/school government	16.1	17.9	14.8	15.1		
Gives constructive discuss. opinions	16.0	16.4	15.0	16.3		
Does group projects to completion	14.6	13.7	14.8	15.3		
Active in cleaning & committee work	14.2	13.2	13.9	15.2		

					F	p
Helps others after own work is done	18.2	17.6	18.4	18.5		
Diligence	16.2 (5)	16.2 (6)	16.2 (6)	16.3 (6)	0.12	NS
Studies hard	18.4	18.3	19.1	18.2		
Doesn't make trouble for friends	15.5	15.5	14.9	16.0		
Obeys school rules & behaves soberly	14.7	17.8	18.3	18.4		
Peer Communication	16.6 (6)	19.6 (8)	16.3 (5)	14.1 (4)	80.17	<.001
Discusses classes or future with peers	16.9	19.9	16.3	14.4		
Counsels emotionally troubled peer	16.4	19.2	16.3	13.8		
Peer's Work	17.0 (7)	15.9 (5)	17.1 (7)	17.9 (8)	12.62	<.001
Warns others who stray from group task	15.5	15.6	17.8	19.1		
Helps out peer weak in studies	16.4	16.1	16.5	16.6		
Helping	18.1 (8)	18.0 (7)	18.7 (8)	7.7 (7)	6.73	<.05
Keeps the school and classroom clean	17.4	18.0	18.4	16.4		
Does volunteer activities	18.3	19.2	18.6	17.3		
Helps the teacher with his/her work	18.3	17.2	19.4	18.5		
Helps out younger pupils	18.1	17.8	18.3	18.4		

Note. Teachers ($N = 575$) ranked 30 items 1 through 10 for representativeness of a cooperative pupil. Unranked items were scored as 20. Relative rankings of each composite are given in parentheses for each school level. All ANOVA *dfs* = 2,573. From "The Development of Cooperation and Competition in Japanese Schools: Two National Surveys," by B. J. Shwalb and D. W. Shwalb, 1995, *Evaluation in Education, 9,* pp. 285–299. Copyright © 1985 by Pergamon Press. Adapted with permission.

Personal helping (tasukeau—counseling or helping with non-academic matters).

7. Helping with studies (oshieau—assisting peers with academics).
8. Other Helping (tetsudai—assisting the teacher, younger students, etc).

Most of these eight involved helping behavior.

School level comparisons of the Table 7.1 composites indicated four trends. First, harmony and friendship were ranked highest for elementary school children in importance. This reflects the strong value placed on positive classmate relations in childhood (Lewis, 1995). Helping with studies was also of significantly greater importance at the primary school level. There is evidence that small group learning declines in importance in secondary school as study becomes more individualized and isolated (Sugie, 1995). Second, clubs and teams, and personal helping, were more important in secondary school. As adolescents become more introspective and concerned with intimate relations or the future, these two aspects of helping grow in importance. Club membership becomes mandatory in middle school, requiring students to remain at school until early evening and to attend six days a week (Fukuzawa, 1994). Third, teachers ranked small group involvement, diligence, and other helping as of equal importance across school levels. Fourth, harmony, friendship, and clubs and teams were ranked the highest of all items. The latter two findings reflect a degree of continuity in the socialization of prosocial behavior. As this study showed, pupils are systematically given experiences that stress the importance of helping others throughout their years of schooling. The school level differences also showed that the nature and contents of cooperation and of helping behavior can be changed depending on the overall goals of schooling. Thus, while the effects of these activities might carry over to college life, if the goals and atmosphere of college classrooms differ significantly from those in primary and secondary schools, helping and help-seeking behavior could also change after high school.

Study Skills

Another line of research has focused on information-acquisition behavior concerning study skills, that is, learning strategies. Sakamoto (1985) conducted a national survey of study skills among elementary, middle, and high school pupils ($N = 2967$), to see how strategies change over the years of schooling. Pupils rated how often they used each of 30 skills (selected by factor analysis from a pool of 520 skill items), and Sakamoto analyzed the factor structure of study skills for each level of schooling. His data indicated that, in elementary school, there are three types of study skills: cognitive (e.g., when I read, I think about the main idea), human contact (e.g., I study with friends), and searching (e.g., I use a dictionary to study). For the middle school data, factor analysis replicated the cognitive and human contact factors, but replaced searching skills with those of visual cueing (e.g., when I read, I mark or underline the important points). High school student data revealed the same cognitive and visual cueing factors, but human contact skills were replaced by voicing skills (e.g., I memorize by saying things aloud). These findings show how classroom behavior changes across school levels, from social learning (I study with friends) toward memorization of complex material (I memorize …). It was apparent from the school-level comparisons that information acquisition gradually becomes an isolated activity. In elementary school, pupils study together and help one another. But, as described by Rohlen (1983) and others, high school students help themselves first.

These findings confirm our informal observation that, in Japanese classrooms, questioning behavior disappears in secondary school. Peer interaction and learning through social activities are encouraged through elementary school, but, even at this level, teachers strongly control the classroom dynamics. For instance, on one classroom observation day (*jugyo sankanbi*), we witnessed a Grade four teacher who told the class when, to whom, and about what children should ask their questions. Children asked each other many questions at the appointed time, but there were no other questions during the remainder of the class. In secondary school, there is some use of group inquiry, but both students and teachers come increasingly under the control of the difficult curriculum, which leaves very little class time for give-and-take or question and answer.

In addition, from upper elementary school, more children attend private after school review classes at *juku*. Pupils often have a close relationship with the juku teacher, who answers individuals' questions as children restudy their school materials in preparation for entrance examinations (S. Sugie, personal communication, July 3, 1995). Although there is very little objective research data on *juku* education (Harnisch, 1993), the implication of our informal observations is that help-seeking behavior may be forced out of schools and into the *juku*.

RESEARCH ON JAPANESE COLLEGE STUDENTS AND TEACHERS

As described earlier, Japanese cultural values emphasize cooperative behavior, dependency, and empathy. Unfortunately, little is known about the socialization of these values in higher education (McVeigh, 1997). Only since 1993 did the Japanese Ministry of Education mandate research on undergraduate teaching and research. This bureauc-

TABLE 7.2

Reasons College Students Ask Questions in Class: Teacher Versus Student Responses

	Rating					Means		
Reason	5	4	3	2	1	Teacher	Student	X^2
Cannot understand the lecture	50 (83)	22 (14)	25 (00)	03 (03)	00 (00)	4.19 <	4.78	34.97
To validate whether their ideas are correct	19 (42)	34 (42)	31 (08)	6 (08)	09 (00)	3.47 <	4.17	32.36
The teacher elicits questions	28 (17)	19 (25)	28 (33)	03 (19)	05 (06)	3.25 =	3.28	
To improve their grades	13 (08)	28 (27)	28 (30)	16 (24)	16 (11)	3.06 =	3.19	
To make the class more interesting for all	06 (03)	03 (14)	16 (42)	31 (28)	44 (14)	1.97 <	2.64	35.45
To please the teacher	00 (00)	03 (03)	22 (34)	28 (37)	47 (26)	1.81 =	2.14	9.86
To get the attention of classmates	00 (00)	00 (03)	19 (03)	13 (43)	69 (51)	1.75	1.57	31.74
For no reason whatsoever	00 (03)	03 (03)	25 (11)	03 (13)	69 (70)	1.63 =	1.52	14.02
To gain recognition from classmates	00 (00)	00 (03)	16 (03)	25 (43)	59 (51)	1.56 =	1.78	15.56

Note. Data are percentages of responses (teacher, $n = 34$; student, $n = 38$). Five-point rating scale: 5, (A major reason); 1 (Not at all a reason). Modal responses are italicized; student percentages are given in parentheses. From "Are There Any Questions?—A Japan/USA Survey on the Psychology of Classroom Communication," by D. Shwalb, 1995, *Cross-Culture: The Bulletin of Koryo Women's College, 13*, pp. 43–57. Copyright © 1995, Koryo Women's College. Adapted with permission.

racy dictates many of the educational priorities of every school and college in Japan. Because the size of the Japanese college age population is now declining sharply and many private colleges and junior colleges are projected to close during the next generation. As a result, colleges want to improve the quality of undergraduate teaching in order to attract students. Research on college teaching in Japan should appear in the next decade, but, currently, data on classroom processes including help-seeking and question-asking behavior are lacking.

Study Skills

Sakamoto, Matsuda, and Muta (1985) replicated the study skill survey in an international comparison of college students in nine countries (N = 3075). They reported that students used passive study skills (e.g., "I take notes while listening in class") more often than active study skills (e.g., "I use charts and tables when preparing for class"), in all nine countries, including the United States. Their Japanese student subsample (n = 961) reported having the lowest cognitive study skills of any national subsample. For example, Japanese students reported that they seldom focused on the main point or emphasized their own ideas, when they were reading, listening, or problem solving. In both of Sakamoto's surveys, help-seeking behavior and question asking were included on the questionnaire (e.g., "If I don't understand my teacher, I ask him questions"), but they did not emerge in analyses as part of any important study skill factor. In fact, question asking was correlated with low study motivation among Japanese pupils. Sakamoto (personal communication, May 13, 1996) speculates that "Japanese students are very timid and passive learners. Therefore, they may think that asking questions is not so important." In our own observations, when most college teachers ask, Are there any questions? this expression is merely a transitional phrase signifying progression to the next part of the lecture. They do not really expect any questions and may not even consider question asking to be important.

Question Asking by College Students

D. Shwalb (1995) conducted a pilot study that was concerned with question-asking in the classroom, using 34 college teachers and 38 female undergraduates in Aichi Prefecture. Comparisons between reasons for questioning and non-questioning behavior given by these two subsamples are presented in Tables 7. 2 and 7.3. Participants rated each on a 5-point scale: 5, (a major reason) and 1, (not at all a reason). Teachers' and students' reasons for asking questions (Table 7.2) were similar. For instance, "cannot understand the lecture" and

TABLE 7.3

Why College Students Do Not Ask Questions: Teacher Versus Student Responses

Reason	Rating					Means		X^2
	5	4	3	2	1	Teacher	Student	
Students lack confidence	41 (30)	26 (32)	15 (35)	06 (00)	09 (03)	3.88	3.86	20.17
Students are shy	42(57)	21(30)	12(11)	12(03)	12(00)	3.70	4.38	21.30
It is difficult to speak out in front of everybody	34 (56)	29 (36)	12 (06)	09 (03)	16 (00)	3.58 <	4.44	27.13
Students do not want to make mistakes	30 (29)	24 (51)	24 (20)	12 (00)	12 (00)	3.48 <	4.09	34.10
There are too many students in the class	27 (17)	27 (31)	24 (28)	06 (22)	15 (03)	3.45	3.36	20.00
Students lack interest in the class contents	24 (11)	29 (28)	26 (36)	06 (19)	15 (06)	3.41	3.19	17.08
Course materials are difficult	13 (11)	25 (36)	34 (36)	12 (14)	15 (03)	3.06	3.39	8.74
Course materials are not well suited for questioning	13 (30)	25 (46)	21 (19)	16 (03)	25 (03)	2.88 <	3.97	39.21
Not asking questions is a Japanese cultural trait	18 (05)	26 (14)	15 (27)	09 (27)	32 (27)	2.88	2.88	23.80
Students learn in high school not to ask questions	18 (03)	18 (05)	15 (14)	15 (19)	34 (59)	2.73 >	1.73	25.28
Students are afraid of teachers	09 (00)	03 (14)	22 (43)	31 (26)	34 (17)	2.22	2.54	29.01
Teachers are poor at taking questions	06 (00)	12 (08)	21 (31)	21 (39)	41 (22)	2.21	2.20	19.85

There is a big status difference between students and teachers	06 (00)	06 (05)	34 (31)	16 (42)	38 (22)	1.97	2.19	22.16
Questions are seen as a waste of time	06 (00)	09 (03)	15 (00)	14 (42)	55 (56)	1.97 >	1.39	38.01
Teachers do not like questions	03 (00)	06 (05)	09 (05)	18 (53)	64 (37)	1.67	1.79	28.70
Course materials are too easy	00 (14)	00 (19)	12 (42)	27 (19)	59 (06)	1.53 <	3.17	94.26

Note. Data are percentages of responses (teacher $n = 34$; student $n = 38$). Five-point rating scale: 5, (A major reason); 1, (Not at all a reason). Modal responses are italicized; student percentages are given in parentheses. From "Are There Any Questions?—A Japan/USA Survey on the Psychology of Classroom Communication," by D. Shwalb, 1995, Cross-Culture: The Bulletin of Koryo Women's College, 13, pp. 43–57. Copyright © 1995, Koryo Women's College. Adapted with permission.

"to validate whether their ideas are correct" were the most common reasons in both subsamples, followed in order of frequency by "the teacher elicits questions" and "to improve their grades." Three of these four reasons are goal-oriented or related to information seeking. "To make the class more interesting for all" was rated as significantly more important by students than by teachers and is an example of how students and teachers perceive questioning differently. It is clear from Table 7.2 that the social function of questioning ("to please the teacher," "to get the attention of classmates," etc.) is of secondary importance compared with the information seeking function. Some of the questionnaire items relate to social functions (improving one's grades, gaining attention or recognition, etc.) that might appear socially undesirable to students, but there was no reason for professors to misrepresent their thinking about such items.

Apparently, the main function of question asking is information acquisition rather than to facilitate communicative abilities or other social functions. Students and teachers tend to see communication as one-way *(ippoteki)*, with teachers the dispensers and students the recipients of knowledge, particularly in lecture classes. These classes seldom include methods such as discussion or teacher–student dialogue.

There were more complex results on the reasons for lack of questions in the classroom. Table 7.3 reveals both similarities and differences between students' and professors' responses. The first four items were rated in the same order of importance by both teachers and students, focusing on students' concerns about speaking out (confidence, shyness, fear of mistakes). Both subsamples downplayed items that assigned responsibility for lack of questioning to the teachers (e.g., "teachers do not like questions," "teachers are poor at taking questions," etc.). Faculty members and undergraduate students also reported that class size is an important variable and were evenly divided on the issue of whether non questioning is a Japanese cultural trait. One notable difference between instructor and student responses was that students thought significantly more than did teachers that course materials influenced questioning behavior ("course materials are too easy," "course materials are not well suited for questioning"). Finally, more teachers than students thought that students "learn in high school not to ask questions," and that "questions are seen as a waste of time."

According to these data, both students and professors attached primary responsibility for lack of questions to the students rather than to the teacher. They attributed students' silence first to shyness, embarrassment, and cultural norms favoring politeness and quietness, reinforcing silence on the part of students. The lack of responsibility assigned to teachers may reflect a tendency of students to be self-critical. In addition, teachers are often openly critical of their students for not asking questions. The positive ratings of course materials by students might have been an indirect expression of blame on their teachers (students are highly critical of many instructors in private) because the instructor is responsible for course materials. Other differences between the reasoning of students and professors suggest the need for greater empathy on the part of teachers, and faculty in-service training about the student point of view. We talked informally with many of the students and professors who took part in this survey, and none could recall a single instance in which a Japanese professor blamed him or herself publicly for communication problems with students.

To better understand the thinking and behavior of teachers, additional questionnaire items focused on the professor's own experiences as students. Only half of the faculty members reported working as teaching assistants (TA) when they were in graduate school. The former TAs generally were the younger faculty members in the sample, but their work as TAs consisted almost entirely of grading papers and other clerical functions. As one (H. Nagayama, personal communication, February 5, 1994) remarked, "A TA in Japan is unfortunately a 'teacher's assistant' and not a 'teaching assistant'." Few professors in our sample reported experiences in classroom teaching, leading discussions, or in Q & A before they became faculty members.

When asked about their own school days, specifically, whether they asked their teachers questions when they were students, approximately half of the professors said that they "often asked questions" of their teachers between high school and graduate school. However, fewer than one third recalled that they often asked questions outside of class during high school, and only one in five recalled asking questions during class time as undergraduates. This suggests two settings in which help seeking may be least welcomed. It is not surprising that questions are not elicited during college classes—college teachers were apparently taught when they were undergraduates not to ask questions. But why not outside of class in high school? An anecdote may help clarify this finding. While observing high school classes in Tokyo, the senior author had the following whispered conversation with one bright student during a complex physics lecture:

Author: What is he [the teacher] talking about?

Student: I have no idea.

Author: Do your friends understand him?

TABLE 7.4
Reasons Students Do Not Ask Questions: Students' Free Responses

Reason	Frequency	Percent
I want to ask questions but am shy or embarrassed	871	67.1
I just don't have much interest in asking questions	462	35.6
I want to ask questions but due to the timing etc. I miss the chance to ask	266	20.5
I can't fully understand the contents of the class	246	19.0
I want to ask questions but the teacher discourages me from doing so	244	18.8
I don't have the custom or habit of asking questions	170	13.1
It is easier to ask questions of my friends	158	12.7
I would rather ask questions individually later	148	11.4
It is bothersome to ask	134	10.3
I don't know what to ask	117	9.0
I don't know how to ask questions	84	6.5
I lack the courage to ask questions	73	5.6
I'd rather solve the problem myself than ask for help	53	4.1
If I asked questions people would think I was stupid	33	2.5
I don't need to ask because I already understand the class contents	33	2.5
I don't ask because nobody else asks questions	31	2.4
I don't ask because there are too many students in the class	11	0.8
I have so many questions I cannot focus on one to ask	6	0.5

Note. N = 1298 undergraduate and junior college students. From "Hattatsu to Kyoiku. Honyo no Daigakusei no Mushitsumon Kodo ni Kansuru Shinfigakuteki Kenyu" (Dai-ipo) [A Study of Why Japanese College Students Do Not Ask Questions in the Classroom (Part 1)], by S. Sukemune, 1995, Research Reports, No. 13, Mukogawa Women's University, Institute for Education, Nishinomiya City, Hyogo, Japan, pp. 1–46. Copyright © 1995 by Mukogawa Women's University. Adapted with permission.

Student: Maybe one out of ten understand any of it.

Author: Why don't you say something, or ask him to slow down?

Student: My friends and I will put our notes together later and figure it out. Or we can ask our *juku* teacher.

Teachers may not need to answer or discourage questions because high school students have alternative sources for answers. A junior college student once told us, "We were very, very close personally with our homeroom teacher and cried for two hours together in the classroom on graduation day .... At college the professors are 'doctors' and we don't see them so often. So we keep a certain distance." Although the homeroom teacher in secondary school is very close to the pupils, other academic teachers are specialized professionals who do not need to know students as individuals.

Most college teachers in our sample rated themselves as fairly good at eliciting questions (mean = 3.41 on a scale from 1, very skilled to 5, very poor). They also reported that they seldom had the problem of facing too many questions (mean = 2.18 on a scale from 1, big problem to 5, no problem). Finally, a majority of teachers claimed that they often asked questions of their students (mean = 3.53 on a scale from 1, often question to 5, never question). Although these three self-evaluations are favorable, we cannot be certain of whether they reflect actual positive teacher–student communication. Teachers may consider themselves relatively good at responding to questions because students rate them favorably on course rating forms. However, we would prefer to see objective data on the effectiveness of teacher's skills in eliciting and responding to questions. Further, although many teachers say that they often ask their students questions, teachers may be asking questions out of frustration at the lack of questions from students.

Students' Reasons for Nonquestioning

Sukemune (1995) collected open-ended responses from a sample of 1,298 undergraduate students in the Kobe/Osaka region (see Table 7.4). He elicited reasons students do not ask questions in the classroom. Confirming the findings of D. Shwalb (1995), shyness/embarrassment was by far most frequently cited. But the second ("I just don't have much interest") and third ("I want to ask questions, but due to timing I miss my chance") most common reasons were not options on the Shwalb (1995) questionnaire. Lack of interest and inability to time one's question are two reasons for nonquestioning to students, but these variables are affected by the nature of the class (e.g., whether the class is required or an elective) and the instructor's (most often lecture style) classroom techniques. The fifth most common reason ("I want to ask questions, but the teacher discourages me … ") was not rated as an important factor in Shwalb (1995). Overall, Sukemune's findings supplement those of D. Shwalb (1995) and suggest additional student-centered reasons for the lack of questions. This partially confirms the image of some Japanese students as unmotivated or disinterested in learning. It may also reflect the inability of teachers to lecture in a manner that allows for effective questioning. For instance, some teachers wait at every class meeting until the final 3 minutes of a 90 minute lecture to solicit questions.

Foreigners' Views of the Japanese College Classroom

Non-Japanese students and faculty who have studied or taught in Japan offer a cross-cultural perspective on help-seeking behavior. Because such individuals were originally educated in their native cultures, they provide an outsider's view of Japanese classroom processes. When cultures and educational systems clash, we can clearly identify cultural influences on questioning behavior. Sukemune (1995) collected free response opinions about why Japanese college students do or do not ask questions in the classroom. The following opinions are excerpted from that report:

> In Brazil education is not as high-quality as it is in Japan, but our students are allowed to give their opinions and bring something new and personal to the debate during classes. Since I came to Japan I haven't been asked for my opinions about things. All that's expected of me is rote learning. I must admit that in the beginning I was really irritated about this system, but I also must concede that in the end I learned much more than I expected. (Brazilian undergraduate, p. 31)

Comment: This suggests that students' ideas, opinions and questions are not welcomed. It also occurred to this student that, while memorization is the key to information acquisition in Japanese colleges, the strategy is effective for its purposes.

> In Australia, we don't have an atmosphere in class that the professor has all the knowledge. But in Japan, the *sensei* has absolute knowledge, and few students have the courage to contradict him. (Australian undergraduate, p. 31)

> Students in Japan respect the *sensei*. And part of what respect means here is to never oppose what the sensei is saying. (Indonesian undergraduate, p. 32)

Comment: It appears from these two examples that communication is one way, but this example also indicates that students may be afraid to express disagreement or disrespect toward a professor. Asking a question draws attention and time away from the sensei , which could be thought of as impolite or confrontational.

Because there is so much competition, Japanese students must be scared to ask a question. (Morrocan undergraduate, p. 32)

Comment: If there is a competitive atmosphere in the classroom, it discourages questioning. Competition for grades is seen in that the percentages of students who fail some classes are high in Japanese universities (often over 50%). In addition, many students (often over 20%) must attend an extra year to graduate, which fosters competition and discourages helping.

Many Japanese students in middle school only study exactly what is in the textbook, to prepare for entrance examinations. In high school most students cannot concentrate during classes, as they think about sleep, fooling around or studying outside class. Because of these experiences, they have little or no spirit of inquiry by the time they get to college. (Australian undergraduate #2, p. 32)

Comment: A veteran university colleague (personal communication, T. Uemura, April 2, 1993) once told us a similar thing: that the three things students did during most lectures were "sleep, talk with friends, and take notes." Very rarely is credit toward one's grade given for classroom participation, so students are not rewarded for speaking out in class. Students work for grades and credits and have little appreciation for the intrinsic value of communication (Nakano, 1994).

In Japanese there is a saying, "The nail that sticks out gets hammered in." This means that it is wrong to do better or worse than others. ... People are brought up to believe that the best person is the average person, and that to stand out in public is an annoyance to others. ... So students learn not to ask questions unless they know the other person very well. (Korean undergraduate, p. 33)

Comment: This saying is used to illustrate the power of conformity in Japan. It is a social norm not to ask questions or seek help from the teacher, and so even bright and inquisitive students feel little dissonance when they are silent. As is discussed in the next section, help giving or help seeking is more likely to occur with someone the student knows very well than with the professor.

... the typical Japanese pattern of being quiet and reserved may not reflect enduring personality traits so much as it reflects those students' conception of the proper role of being a student in a classroom. ... Japanese students show less consistency in behavioral patterns than American students. Most Japanese are quiet and reserved in class, but show wider variation in personality styles in more relaxed informal settings, for example with friends ... (U.S. visiting professor of psychology, p. 38)

Comment: This comment relates question asking to situational factors. As did the preceding comment by the Korean student, it implies that the primary reason that Japanese students give for non questioning ("I'm shy") may only be true in public settings and in communication with people of higher status.

> During lectures, I believe students have a lot of questions in the back of their minds. They cannot however directly ask their questions to the professor because of the time constraint resulting from verbatim lecturing which takes place during class. Students' questions may therefore remain in their minds because of the difficulty of finding the appropriate time.... I believe that Japanese college students will be able to ask many questions if the style of class presentation provides them a chance to do so. This is so because most Japanese students are typically inquisitive when they have the chance to inquire.... (Philippine visiting professor of education, p. 35)

Comment: This comment is related to the finding by Sukemune (1995) that students do not ask questions because they cannot time their questions skillfully. It also contradicts the view that students are disinterested and have no questions. Rather, students ask questions when the classroom atmosphere and communication norms support help seeking.

PERSONAL AND SITUATIONAL INFLUENCES

As shown by the previous comments by the Philippine and U.S. educators, helping and help-seeking behavior are influenced by both individual differences and situational variations. The following section summarizes the research on such influences in Japan. Social-psychological influences might be more modifiable compared with more deep-seated cultural values.

Degree of Shyness

Inagaki, Ohshima-Takane, and Hatano (1978) studied individual differences in the question-asking behavior of college students. They found that students assessed on personality measures to be shy were less likely to seek help or information from others. So, although not all Japanese students conform to the stereotype of shyness, those who are shy ask fewer questions. Shy (hazukashii) is a very common descriptor of Japanese people of all ages, beginning when little children are cautious toward strangers. It is also interesting to note that the Japanese term hazukashii means both shy and embarrassed. So this expression refers to inner anxieties and other-directed shame. Another difference between Japanese and Western shyness concepts is that, in Japanese people, shyness is not considered a character flaw or weakness. Indeed, it is socially desirable (Mutoh, Kubo, & Ohshima, 1980). Females' self-assertion is considered to be selfish and un-feminine and for males the silent type (mono wo iwanai) is a positive image. Thus, in Japan, shyness may be more desirable than help seeking.

Ability Level and Difficulty

Miyake and Norman (1979) found an interaction between student ability level and difficulty of course materials, in an experimental study about question-asking behavior. They observed that high-ability college students in Tokyo asked more questions when they perceived the study materials as difficult. By contrast, lower ability students tended to ask more questions when they thought the materials were easy. Question asking may depend not only on the contents of course materials but also on the individual student's perception of the materials.

Class Size

Teachers in the survey by D. Shwalb (1995) reported that questions from students were most frequent (mean = 3.00 on a 5-point scale between 1, never and 5, very often) after small classes, slightly more than during small classes (mean = 2.82) or after a large lecture (mean = 2.81), but were quite rarely expected during a large class (mean = 1.87, 81% as hardly ever or never). This revealed the clear distinction between questioning during a small and large class, and during vs. after class. Some students attributed this distinction to the increase in self-consciousness in a larger and less intimate group; others explained it as diffusion of responsibility so that nobody in a large class felt individually obligated to help the teacher by asking a question.

Degree of Closeness to Recipient of Help

Ibusuki and Naito (1991), in another experiment, related Tokyo college students' moral judgments and prosocial (i.e., helping) behavior to the relationship between the giver and recipient of help. Specifically, they found that female students' thinking about prosocial behavior was influenced more by situational and relational factors than by universal principles of helping or giving. Among women more than men, help giving and help seeking were correlated with the degree of closeness in the relationship. This gender by relationship interaction was precisely the same finding that appeared in Asakawa and Shwalb's (1985) study of empathy in fourth- and seventh-grade students, where females empathized more with friends than with strangers. Helping and help seeking thus depend on whether one is familiar with the other person.

A 5-Factor Model of Help Seeking

Muto, Kubo, and Ohshima (1980) surveyed 227 Tokyo college students, and their multiple regression analysis of numerous personality, attitudinal and other measures revealed five mechanisms that predicted self-reports of help seeking and question asking in learning situations. The first predictor was affirmation of the information acquisition value of questions. When this function was operative, students asked questions to deepen their understanding or make discussions more lively. In such a case, questioning has intrinsic worth for learning. The second predictor was the individual's personality, mainly shyness, and, to a lesser degree, one's competitiveness or perfectionist tendency. The third mechanism was the questioner's relationship to the other individual. On the positive side, questioning was seen as a way to make a favorable impression or give personal feedback to the teacher, whereas on the negative side, some would not ask questions because they were afraid of disturbing or harming others. The fourth predictor concerned relations with classmates as a group, as the student who asks a question was either being sensitive in not upsetting the flow of the class by interrupting the teacher, or wanted to gain recognition from peers. Finally, the discrepancy between one's personal norms favoring questioning and general social norms predicted questioning behavior. Muto, Kubo, and Ohshima (1980) concluded that the mentality by which the Japanese people strictly avoid disturbing or confronting others is a major obstacle that stifles help-seeking behavior. Muto (1994) also observed that Japanese pupils and college students are not trained at school in metacognitive skills that foster a spirit of inquiry.

PERSONAL REFLECTIONS OF THE AUTHORS

Sukemune

In 1949, there was a major reform of the Japanese system of higher education. But prior to that date, "learning" at the university level meant listening to lectures and writing down verbatim the professor's every word. I remember when I was an undergraduate in the 1940s that my instructors would read directly from their notes, which in some cases were the identical notes they had taken when they were undergraduates. We called such instruction "note lectures". Some instructors would actually pause sometimes and tell their students, "O.K., begin writing a new paragraph [line]!" Students would leave the lecture room with their hands quivering from taking notes so rapidly and without interruption. Some exceptional professors would interject their own opinions between lecture paragraphs, which was very valuable for students. Under such conditions, asking a question was a great annoyance because it interrupted a professor who was feverishly trying to get through his lecture, and it also distracted one's classmates from their notetaking. Therefore, question asking or help seeking during class was not prohibited, but it was suppressed.

After the Pacific War many U.S. scholars came to teach in Japan on the Fulbright program. Rather than giving note lectures, these instructors welcomed our questions, and I recall that many students were stunned and left speechless by this opportunity. We guessed that their new classroom techniques must be related to democracy, which was, of course, unfamiliar in wartime Japanese classrooms. When I was abroad at Ohio University as an exchange student in 1957 to 1958, most of my professors left about one third of the class time for student questions and comments. If students were silent the professors would either ask us questions or elicit questions through a dialogue. I hear that this style is common even today, whereas in Japan, the college classroom atmosphere today is at least partly a remnant of the note lecture method of my own college days.

Shwalb

My experiences with help seeking and helping behavior in Japan are far fewer, shorter term, and less direct than my co-author's experiences. Now, 24 years after my first stay in Japan as a student at Waseda University, I am as impressed as ever with the fact that Japanese people are the same human beings as are people in the United States, and that human characteristics far outweigh cultural variations in thought and behavior. Yet, I am still struck by some basic cultural differences in interpersonal relationships.

The aspects of Japanese behavior and thinking that first impressed me (before I became a psychologist) were the strong cooperative spirit and sensitivity toward the feelings of others, although I do not want to exaggerate these tendencies. These basic psychological patterns are socialized both in the family and at school. And, it is clear to me that something fundamentally different occurs in the socialization of cooperation and sensitivity, comparing family and educational experiences in Japan with those in the United States.

Both U.S. and Japanese people are individuals and are socialized to fit into adult working society. Yet, although the values outlined in the first section of this chapter are common to both U.S. and Japanese societies, they differ in degree of emphasis. For instance, it is relatively more important for persons in the United States to be able to express their ideas as individuals, to feel that they are not too reliant on others, to achieve as individuals, and to be competitive. In Japan, it is relatively more desirable and natural to depend on others, to be cooperative, to be empathic, to achieve as a group, and to fulfill one's roles to perfection. Variations in all of these tendencies influence students' help-seeking behavior.

In my opinion, U.S. students are more skilled at asking questions than are Japanese students, but I find it amusing when Japanese students idealize American classroom communication as perfect and smooth, with free flow of ideas between students and teachers. There is nothing more difficult for many U.S. professors than to lead class discussions, and it is not rare that U.S. undergraduates complain about their instructors' inability to answer or elicit questions. But question asking is a relatively larger weak point for Japanese students.

Based on my experiences as a student, teacher, researcher, and parent in Japan and the United States, I believe that Japanese primary and secondary school education is more organized and predictable. The Japanese people have a national curriculum that is systematic and sequential through high school. And, Japanese teachers are provided with more than a set curriculum; in many instances, their teaching methods are also prescribed in government-issued manuals. The experience, personality, and talents of individual Japanese teachers make a tremendous difference in the classroom, as in any culture. But it strikes me in observing classes across cultures at the Japanese teachers have relatively more control over the learning situation. Students may be unruly in Japan and a lesson plan may fail, but it will not be for lack of effort or planning.

Primary and secondary school instruction have important effect on college education for three reasons. First, students enter the college classroom after 12 years of socialization in a school system where teachers have almost total control over classroom dynamics and communication. They have been trained how, when and about what to ask questions. Second, college professors have undergone the same socialization as did their students, which perpetuates their role expectations. Third, after 12 years of school life in which their teachers deliver a standard content with unambiguous educational goals, college students encounter college teachers who are free to teach whatever they want. Teachers and students face this freedom together with shared uncertainty. Students have the freedom to ask questions but do not know how, and professors have the freedom to engage in a dialogue with students but do not know how. To cope with this incapacity, most teachers and students play it safe and revert to the familiar: one-way communication.

I conclude with another personal observation, based on my four years as a college teacher in Japan. Because they have such a strong regard for order (or fear of disorder), professors frequently chastise their students for chattering during lecture. Such whispering, which is called *shigo* or private-talk, was such an annoyance that it was included on the student rating form at my college in Aichi Prefecture ("How well does the instructor control chattering?"). Students have told me that *shigo* begins with whispering about class material but soon goes into personal matters. In addition, I have observed many lecturers who, in one breath, warn a class to be silent, and in the next breath, criticize students for being passive or not asking questions. I think that students are unable to change gears smoothly from enforced silence to active participation, especially when they receive this type of double criticism from *sensei*. After being told to be silent (*Damare!* or *Shizuka ni shinasai!*) with the same rough expressions they have heard since preschool, they may not believe the teacher who asks an instant later, "Are there any questions?"

IMPLICATIONS

Implications for Japanese Educators

Faculty in-service programs should be promoted carefully in Japan, with an awareness both of knowledge accumulated on help seeking outside Japan, but also with sensitivity to the special needs of Japanese professors. For instance, Japanese faculty members seldom have had teaching experience prior to hiring by their universities. Teaching seminars should be incorporated into graduate school and teacher training should continue after new faculty are hired by universities (hopefully, teachers will be allowed to ask questions at these sessions!) Faculty who have taught for several years or decades need retraining in teaching methods, including lecturing, which must be redefined as more than note lectures.

Meanwhile, students need to be encouraged before college to freely express their ideas and ask questions. Those already in college need to be re-socialized to a new mentality, which redefines the professor and student roles away from the familiar information-giver and information-recipient. At student freshman orientations, we have seldom observed the "How to Study" or "How to Succeed in College" mini-courses on learning or survival skills, which are popular on U.S. campuses.

The preceding recommendations assume that help seeking, question asking and other such behaviors are desirable for Japanese students. This of course involves a value judgment. Let us not forget the remark of the Brazilian undergraduate earlier: "I must also concede that in the end I learned much more than I expected." We do not advocate changing Japanese educational practices or goals just to match those in the West. Yet, we do suspect that if students could choose an educational model for higher education in Japan, they would want to be free to ask questions, give help, and seek help in the classroom. Why? In the words of one of our 18 year old seminar students, "Because we college students are adults, not children!"

Implications for Western Educators

We recommend that readers use the cultural values described in this chapter as a basis for an assessment of their own cultural values. Such an analysis might make readers more aware of how their own educational practices reflect cultural norms and values. For instance, self-reliance is not universally assumed to be preferable to relying on others. Likewise, it is not a universal educational goal that education should foster the ability to study alone rather than as a team. Many Western educators who teach short-term in Japan are frustrated when they direct questions at individual students. The targeted student will confer with friends about the answer, and after a lengthy delay, finally deliver the group's reply. In such a situation, an exasperated teacher may criticize the student for lack of courage, but the student may simply prefer teamwork to individual recitation. We ask you to reconsider the assumptions made in your culture about help seeking and question asking.

Our discussion of question asking also has implications for instructors working in the area of international education. In classes that include students from many cultures and subcultures, educators should realize that students from different societies are taught to behave differently with regard to help seeking. Sensitivity to multiple perspectives is a necessity for such teachers.

Implications for the Study of Help-Seeking Behavior

It is ironic that so very little data is available concerning help-seeking behavior in Japanese college classrooms, given the value Japanese people place on dependency on others (Doi, 1973). Perhaps help seeking is taken for granted as an issue in Japan because it is considered second nature to rely on others. East/West comparative research on help seeking would therefore be fascinating.

At our 1994 symposium on the topic of "The Problem of Lack of Questioning in the Japanese College Classroom," one member of the audience criticized the panel for failing to clarify the purpose of their research. Do we study help seeking to improve our teaching? Or, do we conduct research to better understand psychological aspects of classroom communication? We wonder whether the distinction between applied vs. theoretical focus is commonly addressed in Western cultures where research on help seeking is more common.

We conclude with a final question for the reader. Do you assume that help seeking and question asking are desirable classroom behaviors? In our view, cross-cultural and collaborative studies are necessary to answer this question with clarity.

ACKNOWLEDGMENTS

We acknowledge Jun Nakazawa, Barbara Shwalb, Tak Uemura, Hiroshi Azuma, Shuji Sugie, and the students and faculty of Koryo Women's College and Mukogawa Women's University. We also thank Debbie and Davy Shwalb for their many insights concerning daily life in Japanese public schools. This chapter is dedicated to the memory of Asako Sukemune (1933–1996).

REFERENCES

Ames, R. (1983). Help seeking and achievement orientation: Perspectives from attribution theory. In B. M. DePaulo, A. Nadler, & J. D. Fisher (Eds.), *New directions in helping: Vol. 2. Help seeking* (pp. 165–186). New York: Academic Press.

Asakawa, K., & Shwalb, D. W. (1985, April). *Empathy and intimacy: An investigation of rural Japanese children.* Paper presented at the biennial meeting of the Society for Research on Child Development, Toronto, Canada.

Azuma, H. (1996). Cross-national research: The Hess/Azuma collaboration. In D. Shwalb & B. Shwalb (Eds.), *Japanese childrearing: Two generations of scholarship* (pp. 220–240). New York: Guilford Press.

DeVos, G. (1973). *Socialization for achievement.* CA: University of California Press.

Doi, T. (1973). *The anatomy of dependence.* Tokyo, Japan: Kodansha International.

Doi, T. (1996). Foreword. In D. Shwalb & B. Shwalb (Eds.), *Japanese childrearing: Two generations of scholarship* (xv–xii). New York: Guilford Press.

Fukuzawa, R. E. (1994). The path to adulthood according to Japanese middle schools. *Journal of Japanese Studies, 20*(1), 61–86.

Hamilton, V. L., Blumenfeld, P., & Miura, K. (1990). *Journal of Cross-Cultural Psychology, 22*(3), 317–346.

Harnisch, D. L. (1993). Supplemental education in Japan—*Juku* schooling and its implication. *Journal of Curriculum Studies, 26*(3), 323–334.

Holloway, S. D. (1988). Concepts of ability and effort in Japan and the United States. *Review of Educational Research, 58*, 327–345.

Ibusuki, R., & Naito, T. (1991). Influence of interpersonal relationships on helping norms among Japanese university students. *Psychological Reports, 68*, 1119–1129.

Inagaki, K., Ohshima-Takane, Y., & Hatano, G. (1978, October). *Shyness and informa-tion seeking in imagined experimental situations*. Paper presented at the 42nd annual convention of the Japanese Psychological Association.

Lebra, T. S. (1976). *Japanese patterns of behavior*. Honolulu: University of Hawaii Press.

Lewis, C. C. (1995). *Educating hearts and minds: Reflections on Japanese preschool and elementary education*. Cambridge, England: Cambridge University Press.

McVeigh, B. (1997). Life in a Japanese Women's College. London: Routledge.

Miyake, N., & Norman, D. A. (1979). To ask a question, one must know enough to know what is not known. *Journal of Verbal Learning & Verbal Behavior, 18*, 357–364.

Muto, T. (, 1994, October). Naze shitsumon wo shinainoka, doh sureba shitsumon wo surunoka [Why don't they ask questions? What can we do to get them to ask questions?]. Paper presented at the annual meeting of the Japanese Association of Educational Psychology (JAEP), Kyoto, Japan.

Mutoh, T., Kubo, Y., & Ohshima, Y. (1980). Gakusei wa naze shitsumon wo shinai no ka? [Why don't students ask questions?]. *Shinrigaku Hyoron, 23*(1), 71–88.

Nagai, M. (1971). *Higher education in Japan: Its takeoff and crash*. Tokyo: University of Tokyo Press.

Nakano, Y. (1994, October). Kurasu ni okeru shitsumon kodo: Nichibei no bunkateki kosatsu [Classroom questioning behavior: A Japan/USA cultural inquiry]. Paper presented at the annual meeting of the Japanese Association of Educational Psychlology, Kyoto, Japan.

Nakazawa, J., & Shwalb, D. W. (1997). Japanese developmental psychology in the 1990s. *Journal of Applied Developmental Psychology, 18*(4), 447–452.

Nelson-Le Gall, S. (1985). Help seeking behavior in learning. *Review of research in education,* (Vol. 12, pp. 55–90). Washington, DC: American Educational Research Association.

Peak, L. (1992). *Learning to go to school in Japan*. Berkeley: University of California Press.

Rohlen, T. (1983). *Japan's high schools*. Berkeley: University of California Press.

Sakamoto, T. (1985). Characteristics of study skills in Japanese pupils. *Evaluation in Education, 9*, 243–251.

Sakamoto, T., Matsuda, T., & Muta, H. (1985). An international comparison of student study skills. In G. d'Ydewalle (Ed.), *Cognition, information processing, and motiva-tion* (pp. 727–750). The Netherlands: Elsevier.

Shwalb, B. J., & Shwalb, D. W. (1985). The development of cooperation and competition in Japanese schools: Two national surveys. *Evaluation in Education, 9*, 285–299.

Shwalb, D. W. (1995). Are there any questions?—A Japan/USA survey on the psychology of classroom communication. *Cross-Culture: The Bulletin of Koryo Women's Col-lege, 13*, 43–57.

Shwalb, D. W., & Shwalb, B. J. (1996). *Japanese childrearing: Two generations of scholarship*. New York: Guilford Press.

Shwalb, D. W., Shwalb, B. J., & Nakazawa, J. (1995). Competitive and cooperative attitudes: A longitudinal survey of Japanese adolescents. *Journal of Early Adoles-cence, 15*(1), 267–290.

Stevenson, H. W., & Stigler, J. W. (1992). *The learning gap*. New York: Summit.

Sugie, S. (1995). Cooperative learning in Japan. *International Journal of Educational Research, 23*, 213–225.

Sukemune, S. (1995). Hattatsu to kyoiku. Honyo no daigakusei no mushitsumon kodo ni kansuru shinrigakuteki kenkyu (dai-ipo) [A study of why Japanese college students do not ask questions in the classroom (part 1)]. *Research Reports, 13*, 1–46. Nishinomiya City, Hyogo, Japan: Mukogawa Women's University, Institute for Edu-cation.

8

Theory and Practice
of Student Questioning

James T. Dillon
University of California at Riverside

Nearly everything about student questioning remains open for reflection, for investigation, and especially for action. Here, I venture into three of these openings.

What is student questioning or question asking? In answering we will see a conception of the process of student questioning, giving us an idea of what we are talking about when we say, "a student asks a question" and when we engage in research and practice of student questions.

How might the principles of student questioning work out in practice? We will see a scheme for the practice of student questioning, proposing a systematic and comprehensive approach to the question of practice.

What good might come from student questioning? We will see a display of the benefits of student questioning, listing all manner of features that are desirable for education and human development.

The good of these benefits, the usefulness of this scheme, and the pertinence of this conception may urge us on to reflect on student questions, to investigate them, and above all, to act on them as we seek to educate our young.

THE PROCESS OF QUESTIONING

What is questioning? Let us venture into the theory of questions far enough to get a notion of student questioning, so that we have an idea of what we are talking about when we aim at practice and research on student questions. Here I propose a conception of the process of

171

questioning, after first examining the matter of definition and then making distinctions among cases of questioning.

Definition

Answering the question, "What is questioning?" appears to be a matter of definition. But that proves not to be the case. No satisfactory definition of questioning or question asking has yet been proposed, even by logicians, philosophers, or linguists. The reason may well be that questioning is not a definable entity. There appears to be no one thing that questioning is, no phenomenon or event existing by itself, with a nature or essence that can be discovered and described.

Let us propose rather, that questioning is a character, or a notion, that we attribute to an event under certain conditions but not under others. Given certain conditions or features, one and the same surface event may or may not be seen as questioning. Extensive, but on the whole, fruitless efforts have been devoted to specifying the few conditions or features that will always, or even most of the time, define an event as questioning or encompass all or most of the events called questioning. None of these definitions works. There are always invalidating exceptions to any definition advanced.

The wonder of it is that, despite the complex conditions and features varying this way and that in any given instance, ordinary speakers of language have no difficulty at all in distinguishing a question when they hear one. That is, they readily distinguish instances of questioning and nonquestioning, and further, they agree on their distinctions. Linguistic researchers have empirically demonstrated this lay ability to tell what a question is (Hinds, 1984; Uldall, 1962). The enduring problem remains that scholars cannot formulate a satisfactory definition of what questioning is.

Distinctions

A range of events fall under the rubric of questioning. Only one class of events is of interest here. The event of interest is question asking in contrast to question putting. The event is "a person asks a question" rather than "an official puts a question to someone for an answer."

Terminology in English cannot articulate these two contrasting sets of questioning events in an agreeably clear way. The first might be couched as "raising a question, wondering, asking," and the second as "putting a question, probing, interrogating." But no terms serve well and felicitously. To depict that questioning event that is of interest here, cases and situations can be cited that together serve to discriminate between "a person asks a question" and "an official puts a question."

The most common and familiar questioning events in our experience are not the event of interest here. Question asking, or "a person asks a question," does not describe a teacher's questions to a student, for example, nor a physician's questions to a patient, a manager's questions to a prospective employee, nor, generally, an adult's questions to a child. Rather, it would describe the case of questions asked by the student, the applicant, the patient, and the child. Cases of "an official puts a question" include the questions put by lawyers to witnesses, opinion pollsters to respondents, interrogators to suspects, investigators to informants, interviewers to interviewees, examiners to candidates, and journalists to celebrities. In all these cases, as well as in those of the teacher, physician, manager, and adult, an official or otherwise situationally superior figure puts questions to a subordinate for an answer. These are indeed cases of questioning, but they are not the event of question asking that is being depicted here. For these other cases of questioning, please see *The Practice of Questioning*, (Dillon, 1990).

As instances of question asking, let us take first the case of the child facing the world, wondering about self, others, and life. A child's questions may readily be taken as a paradigmatic case of question asking. A second paradigm, though in a far more structured situation, is the student's asking questions about a subject being taught or learned. A third paradigm is a situation intermediate in structure (less so than the student's, more so than the child's), the case of a scholar or scientist formulating a question at the onset of some research endeavor; that is, the question that the research study is undertaken to answer. Many more situations of question asking can be cited, but not a great deal of literature or research.

In general, we have little understanding of the event "a person asks a question" by contrast to the volume of research and the panoply of techniques for "an official puts a question." We know far more about the answers that people give to questions put to them for answer than we do about the questions asked by children, students, and scientists, for instance. And, although manuals aplenty will guide any official questioner in how to put questions to clients, next to nothing is available for enhancing the asking of questions by children and scholars. Little enough, in fact, is known about the process whereby a person comes to ask a question. We must therefore conceive of the process.

Conception

The process of questioning describes this event: "a person asks a question." No one knows how the process actually goes. Let us picture it to ourselves in terms broad enough to encompass most of what must be involved.

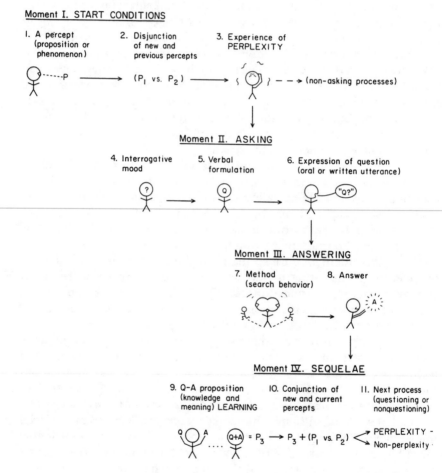

Moment I. START CONDITIONS

1. A percept (proposition or phenomenon) 2. Disjunction of new and previous percepts 3. Experience of PERPLEXITY

$(P_1$ vs. $P_2)$ — — → (non-asking processes)

Moment II. ASKING

4. Interrogative mood 5. Verbal formulation 6. Expression of question (oral or written utterance)

"Q?"

Moment III. ANSWERING

7. Method (search behavior) 8. Answer

Moment IV. SEQUELAE

9. Q-A proposition (knowledge and meaning) LEARNING 10. Conjunction of new and current percepts 11. Next process (questioning or nonquestioning)

$(Q+A) = P_3 \longrightarrow P_3 + (P_1$ vs. $P_2)$ < PERPLEXITY – / Non-perplexity

FIG. 8.1 The process of questioning ("a person asks a question")

We follow the process through four moments from start to finish. One crucial moment is when the person asks the question. Other moments come before and after the asking. The final moment follows on the answering. That is the moment of learning.

Figure 8.1 reproduces the process, showing these moments with their events and movement in a hypothetically smooth way. As we follow along we can think of students going through this process, "a student asks a question." But we do well or even better to bear ourselves uppermost in mind, "I ask."

Perplexity. The main event at the start is the experience of perplexity. That is the precondition of questioning and thus the prerequisite for learning. Questioning still might not follow, nor learning; without perplexity, they cannot follow.

Perplexity is an organismic experience, felt in the body as well as the mind. It shows, too. We display some unease, restlessness, or discomfort when perplexed; a furrowed brow, a scratched head, a purse of the lips; we might bite fingernails and tear out hair. These, and all manner of body language, signal above all to self that over some matter, pressing or fleeting, one is experiencing a degree, minor or great, of doubt, wonderment, ignorance, bafflement, incomprehension, uncertainty, puzzlement—perplexity. Only in that perplexed condition can a question arise.

Perplexity does not occur of itself. It is the main event of the moment but not the first. At the very start, there is some percept, P (Fig. 8.1). We perceive something, a phenomenon or proposition, P. (An account of why we perceive it in the first place, rather than overlook it as we do with thousands of others, lies outside of the depicted process of questioning.)

Next, we introduce P into our scheme of things—other P's in our organized experience. When our scheme does not readily accommodate P, we have a disjunction between the new P1 and selected previous ones, P2. Things do not go together in the complex of propositions describing our knowledge, or things do not go smoothly in the range of phenomena describing our action. For example, we might have a goal and P1 emerges as an obstacle; we might hold an opinion and P1 enters to contradict. The terms encompass any kind of disjunction between any kind of percepts. For instance, the terms seek to encompass various familiar psychological accounts of problematicity, such as cognitive conflict, unachieved goal, and gap.

- *Cognitive conflict* includes Festinger's (1957) cognitive dissonance between beliefs, or knowledge, or values, or opinions; and Berlyne's (1965) conceptual conflict between incompatible symbolic response patterns—beliefs, attitudes, thoughts, ideas.

- *Unachieved goal* includes Duncker's (1945) depiction of an organism that has a goal but does not know how to reach it (ignorance); and Maier's (1970) depiction of an obstacle preventing the organism from reaching the goal (frustration).
- *Gap* includes Bartlett's (1958) view of incomplete information; Wertheimer's (1959) view of incomplete gestalt, wherein S_1 by contrast to S_2 is structurally incomplete; and Goguelin's (1967) view of distance between an unsatisfying situation, S_1, and a satisfying one, S_2.

In the generic terms of Fig. 8.1, the disjunction (P1 vs. P2) describes something that we do not know or understand or cannot do, on any of these accounts. The experience of perplexity ensues, whereupon a question may arise.

Asking.   The main event in this moment is asking a question. But it is the least event of all to follow on perplexity, for, in the majority of cases, a multitude of non-asking events will follow. Rather than go on to ask a question we may, for example, distract ourselves, dismiss or suppress the experience, settle for less, resign ourselves, give up, and so on. (An account of these other strategies lies apart from the depicted process.)

In the case when a question does follow, the process moves from the experience of perplexity through to the expression of a question (Fig. 8.1). First, on the condition of perplexity an interrogative mood arises. Next a question emerges and assumes verbal form in mind. Then the question appears in oral or written utterance to self or others. These events do not proceed of their own, of course, but through our agency and intervention. We get ourselves into an interrogative mood and settle in it; we select a question and formulate it; we utter the question.

The last move is the hardest, and the one least frequently taken. Fully 95% of the questions that we have in mind to ask are never uttered. As before, we may think better of it and follow one of numerous other paths available. These include keeping quiet and giving off that we know and understand. If we speak, our favored strategy is to speak another question than the one we have in mind. For the act of asking can be a formidable one, in classrooms, for instance.

When we do follow through with the process and go on to ask the question that we have formulated in our mind, our act speaks many things other than the question itself. These are called presumptions of questioning. By asking the question, we hold forth our commitment to the genuineness, accuracy, or truth of these presumptions. We aver them as we ask. And, in asking a question of someone, we invite our interlocutor to join us in these—to believe them, and to believe that we believe them. The self that asks asseverates and communicates as follows:

1. *Ignorance*. I am in a state of not-knowing, and I realize that I do not know.
2. *Perplexity*. I am experiencing perplexity (puzzlement, uncertainty, etc.) as a consequence of not-knowing.
3. *Need*. I feel a necessity to know.
4. *Desire*. I aspire to know.
5. *Belief*. I commit myself to the truth of the question. (I believe that its presuppositions are true, its words are as I intend them, etc.)
6. *Faith*. I am confident that the unknown is knowable.
7. *Courage*. I venture to face the unknown and its consequences both within myself and the world.
8. *Will*. I resolve to undertake to know.

These are not trifles to hold forth in a classroom (or elsewhere). Little wonder that we and our students so rarely go on to ask the question that began in our ignorance and perplexity. Yet, the question promises to confer knowledge and understanding, eventuating in learning. That is just the question to ask, in school and out.

Answering. The next moment proceeds in complement to the asking. There are only two events—method and answer.

Method is that which the questioner does to address the question. It is search behavior, systematic or not. For example, students may have recourse to self, searching their knowledge and experience to recall, to deduce or to construct an answer. They may recur to the teacher or to the other students in class, or yet to parents, friends, and other likely outsiders. They may recur to the textbook, the library, or a computerized information system. They may have recourse to observation and experiment or take other action on the world.

Answer is that which is yielded by method and adduced to the question. Anything at all may have the character of answer in complement to the question—actions, things, feelings, information of all sorts—according as will resolve the asking. None of these is answer in itself. Answer is a character that accrues to them as they stand in relation to the question.

Having construed the answer, the questioner conjoins it with the question. Now he enters the moment of learning.

Learning. Learning follows in the final moment. After the answer there are three events (Fig. 8.1). First and foremost, there is now no longer a question that is outstanding or an answer remaining but a new production. This is the proposition that is formed of question plus answer. That is knowledge. As Aristotle first taught us (*Posterior Analytics*, 89b), knowledge consists of question–answer propositions. This proposition further holds meaning and understanding. These inhere in the relation that the questioner construes to hold between the two complements that are made to form the proposition; they can figuratively be located in the hyphen of question–answer.

This question–answer as a proposition represents a new P in our perception. The next event introduces this new percept, P_3, into our scheme of things, a scheme that includes for some moments now our original percept P_1 and previous percepts P_2. We now have a conjunction formed of P_3 as one term, with the other term the earlier disjunction of P_1 versus P_2 (see Fig. 8.1).

With the third and last step, we may find ourselves back at the start. For the last moment fades into the first moment of some new process, whether of nonquestioning or questioning, according to the resolution of the relations obtaining between the conjoined percepts. For example, these may next serve as the presupposition to a further question.

For the moment, we are left with the question–answer proposition that is our knowledge of this matter, and the question–answer relation that is our understanding of it. These, as our possessions, are learning. In that way the process of questioning eventuates in learning.

THE PRACTICE OF STUDENT QUESTIONING

How might the principles of questioning work out in practice? The question of practice remains open. There appears to be no established practice of student questioning, whether in general pedagogy or in particular methods and techniques, and the matter of practice seems little understood, whether by theoretical or empirical investigations. (But see the developing work of van der Meij, 1986, 1994, for a promising exception.)

In this circumstance, Fig. 8.2 proposes a way for us to approach the question of practice systematically and comprehensively. I first present the scheme itself, commenting on its characteristics and possible applications. Then, I examine the actual practices of questioning that are identified in the scheme.

Scheme of Practice

The scheme of practice in Fig. 8.2 situates our efforts in the middle ground between the abstract plateau of general principles and the daily detail of individual techniques. That is by no means to imply that these other two levels—one more general and one more particular—are beyond the reach of our efforts or beneath deserving of special attention. Not so. For our

ASSIGNMENTS ──────── ▶ DISCUSSIONS ─────── ▶ EXAMS ─────── ▶ (Return to Assignments)

1) Study with the question foremost in mind
(e.g., course Q, topic or unit Q, teacher Q, or student Q, see No. 5)

    Develop the answer   Address the question

2) Formulate the question that author/text (or lesson, exercise, lecture . . .) is answering, then formulate the answer

or: Make question-answer outline

    State question-answer as basis for discussion

or: Construct common question-answer outlines

    Identify the major question-answers in the field (or in lesson, text, topic. . .)

or: Classify the question-answers as overview of field

3) Formulate the questions
a) not treated by author/lesson
b) not understood by student
c) remaining in mind afterwards
d) arising next for treatment

    Compare & reformulate the questions

    Identify the unsettled questions in the field (issues for decision, research, practice)

4) Identify 5 questions (+ answers) about striking or useful aspects of the material (e.g., a chapter, a demonstration, a field trip)

    Recite question-answers
S1: Question 1
S2: Answer
S1: Evaluation
S2: Question 2

    Answer the questions
(e.g., a mix of the student's own questions plus other students' questions recited)

5) Write 3 perplexing questions about the subject matter at the very start of course or unit, then pursue one or more questions

(return to (1) Study with the student question in mind)

    Report pursuit of question
Combine in pursuit

    Construct question-answer

FIG. 8.2 The practice of student questioning

179

purposes here, it is a matter of choosing an approach to the question of practice. Techniques are probably best devised at the immediate level of individual circumstance, and reports by happy teachers who devise them surface from time to time in the pedagogical journals and magazines. As for general principles, the pedagogy of student questions is described in Questioning and Teaching (Dillon, 1988a) and selected journal articles, (Dillon, 1986, 1988b).

How might the principles of student questioning work out in a scheme of practice? Fig. 8.2 presents a scheme for our consideration. Were it to be found desirable to do so on the grounds of serving pedagogical purposes in particular classroom or other educational circumstances, the entire scheme could be put into practice. That is not the intention behind presenting the scheme, yet neither is that by any means contrary to intention, as one possible use to make of it. Other uses would include selecting for application certain practices or themes of practice, formulating and substituting more pertinent practices within the framework of the scheme, or constructing a more fruitful scheme that would incorporate general principles and illustrate individual techniques.

The scheme in Fig. 8.2 proposes to identify and to interrelate a range of practices within three successive moments of instruction at five cumulative levels of questioning. The scheme confers educational sense on each individual activity, a sense from the perspectives of both learning and teaching, by locating it within a complex of interrelated activities that take their form from both the instructional moment and the questioning level in which they situate, always by reference to the preceding and the subsequent activities. That is to say, Fig. 8.2 is a scheme of practice: it is not a collection of scattered techniques. The individual activities do not figure therein by some accident but each assumes identity, form, and sense by reason of its positioning within the scheme.

Instructional moments. The three successive instructional moments are assignments, discussions, and exams (Fig. 8.2). Let us not insist on the vocabulary but on the concept. If these words are old-fashioned or hilariously irrelevant to certain circumstances of post modern schooling, let us think instead of a series of instructionally successive activities describing some kind of preparation (assignment), some group lesson (discussion), and an evaluation (exam). The succession continues, as when the exam or other evaluation leads the teacher to form an appreciation of the next instructional step to take, for which all will now begin to prepare (return to assignment).

Activities of questioning. In each moment, there is an activity of questioning. Thus the three activities are themselves interrelated in a succession of questioning that accompanies the succession of instruction. The three questioning activities form a series that makes sense within the instructional series, while each individual activity finds sense by reference not only to the instructional moment in which it occurs, but also the series of questioning activities in which it locates.

Levels of questioning. Finally, all of this activity takes place on five cumulative levels of questioning (Fig. 8.2). At each level, there is a series of three interrelated activities of questioning that accompany the three successive moments of instruction (assignments, discussions, exams). The five levels of questioning distinguish the character of the questioning, which varies from the rather more presented question (Level 1) to the more perplexing and open question discovered by the student (Level 5). In between these levels, the questioning activity involves the student in identifying and formulating questions within the assignment or other preparatory material.

The combination of multiple series of interrelated questioning activities, varying by level of questioning and proceeding through a succession of instructional moments, presents us with an entire program of practice. Were one to be as schematic as Fig. 8.2, as systematic and comprehensive, one could enact the whole scheme. But even if that were to be desirable, it will be found to be impracticable. Most circumstances of schooling do not support the practice of student questioning but actively support its contraries: answering rather than questioning and teacher, rather than student, questions. Yet in many circumstances a given teacher can well and fruitfully practice some part of this scheme, especially if the pieces are not taken apart. For instance, one could

- Pursue a given level of questioning through the three moments of instruction on a given subject matter.
- Base assignments in student questioning activity, starting at any given level and proceeding through to cumulative levels (as, for example, a way of inducing students to engage themselves more intimately with the subject matter).
- Base discussions and exams, on occasion and in part, on student questions.
- Use the activities or the schema itself (viz., Fig. 8.1) to educate children into a habit of questioning.

Several other uses of the scheme may be found desirable, for example

- A template for observing practice.
- A grid for reflecting about questioning, teaching, and learning.
- A framework for devising more pertinent practices.
- A springboard for constructing a more serviceable scheme.

Practices of questioning

To get a sense of the practice of student questions, let us review the activities in Fig. 8.2, briefly reflecting on each of the five levels of questioning as it plays out across the three moments of instruction. What are the practices at each level?

At the first level (Fig. 8.2), the questions are fairly well set and presented to the student. We are already into student questioning but at an incipient level, although far from the more abrupt practices of teacher questioning. Here there is a question already in operation for the course, the unit, the topic, the class, or the assignment. The students can be invited to enter into the question, even to reformulate it or to express their sense of it, in cases in which they have not been invited to participate in its original formulation. The point is to engage students in their questioning activity, by contrast to engaging students in someone else's questioning. The practice at this level involves interrelated activities at each successive moment of instruction.

Assignments. Study with the question foremost in mind. (Fig. 8.2) Don't just read, or stare; keep the question in the forefront of your attention and impose it on the study material. Master it by making it answer your question. (NB: study material is a generic term for items such as reading, video, demonstrations, field trips, or whatever is to be studied).

Discussions. Develop the answer. If, as is likely at this level, all have given their sense of the same question, and if, as suggested, everyone has given his/her sense of the question, then discussion can begin with a statement of the question concurred in. The lesson activity develops the answer. It is nearly always the case that the activity involves an adaptation of the question by reason of the developing answer or the interrogating sense of the students.

Exams. Address the question. This is a more questioning activity than the classic Answer the question. Here, at the first level of student questioning, the student is evaluated by the address to the question, which includes giving a sense of the question, formulating it just so, positioning self with respect to it, and making an approach to it as well as, of course, proposing an answer to it.

Skipping now for sake of contrast to Level 5, we find the questioning activity quite open to the production of the student. The assignment at the start of study is not to answer a question but to produce a question and then pursue it. The recommendation runs, Write three perplexing questions.

- A question is perplexing when it is problematic to the student, when the student does not know the answer and feels a need and a desire to know it.
- The writing helps to locate and to formulate the perplexity.
- Writing three questions helps to enter the mood of questioning and to discover the question that perplexes, typically not among the first three that come to mind.

Next, in the moment of discussion, the student reports the pursuit of the question. Other students may join in with related pursuits, or a few may pursue a question in common. The subsequent exam or evaluation involves constructing the question–answer proposition. We note that the question itself is evaluated or otherwise subject to appreciation, correction, or guidance, not less than the answer and the question–answer relation.

At this point, the cycle of activity on the various levels can be renewed by a return to Level 1 activity, with the significant difference that study now begins with the student's question, Study with the student question foremost in mind. (Fig. 8.1).

Between Levels 1 and 5, the cumulative movement describes an increasing openness of the questioning both in the lesson and in the mind of the student as well as an increasing dynamic of production of the question by the student.

At the second level, students formulate the question that the lesson is answering, then they formulate the answer that the lesson brings to that question. (Note that the lesson may be a reading, a lecture, a demonstration, a video, a field trip, etc.). In discussion, they each state their question–answer as a basis for discussion, proceeding to agree on the questions and then the answers. Imagine the fruitlessness of discussions where everyone is arguing diverse positions, but no one knows the questions to which these apparently diverse positions represent answers. The exam may involve the students in identifying the major question–answers on that topic or in that field.

An alternative series of activity at Level 2 is to make a question–answer outline of the study material. Discussion may then involve the construction of a common question–answer outline, while evaluation may consist of classifying the question–answers as an overview of the topic or field. (What a good way for us to do a review of research, by the way.)

Level 3 also involves formulating the questions but with the significant difference that the student formulates not the question that the author or lesson is answering but the questions *not* treated, along with these related questions of the student:

- Questions not understood by the student.

- Questions that remain in the mind afterwards.
- Questions that arise next for treatment (given the treatment of questions by the material and by the student).

In discussion, students may have all they can do just to compare and to reformulate their questions that, after all, pertain to the lesson they all have in common. They may also join in various questions and happily come to formulate a question that all may then proceed to discuss. The exam at this level bears not on the answers to those questions but the identification of unsettled questions in the field or subject—all manner of questions for civic debate, for individual decision or for joint action, for reflection, for experimentation, for research and so on.

Attention! The fancy vocabulary that we use ought not to mislead us into thinking that only advanced students can engage in these activities. To the contrary, children at the most elementary level can question and discuss perfectly well (please see Dillon, 1994 for these considerations).

At Level 4, just short of raising the perplexing questions of Level 5, students identify questions about five points that strike them in the study material. They will have their own reasons for being struck by these points, and that is part of the pedagogy of questioning at this level. The students also use the material to work out the answers. These are thus questions that are discoverable in the material and that are answerable from the material—no tricks, games, or cosmic implications, but straightforward questions about interesting aspects of the material.

With this questioning activity as preparation, students approach the discussion with the preliminary activity of reciting the question–answers. But it is a student recitation, based on student questions and student evaluations as well as student answers. The details of this process are given in Questioning and Teaching (Dillon, 1988a). Here it is enough to indicate that the students carry the dynamic of the question–answer interaction while the teacher listens, notes, guides, and appreciates the students' question–answers. The exchange follows of its own:

Student 1 asks a question.

Student 2 volunteers an answer.

Student 1 evaluates the answer and comments on the interest of the question.

Student 2 asks the next question.

The exam that follows is based at least in part on the questions of the students, which the teacher will have noted and commented on in class as the process unfolds. Thus, the students who have joined in the questioning of other students will have a set of mutually interesting questions to which they have together formed agreeable answers. These question–answers represent their knowledge of the subject matter. To examine that knowledge, the teacher may engage them in answering a mix of questions, which have been first prepared and then recited, of their own and of their fellows.

Apart from the specifications in Fig. 8.2, we may identify several uses of student questions that are particular to discussion processes.

The first and principal use of student questions in discussion is to establish the question for discussion. The most sensible proceeding is to discuss the question of the class or the group. Therefore, practice would involve the class in identifying and formulating the question to be discussed. A question for discussion expresses the predicament of the group in relation to the subject matter, a predicament arising from its involvement with the subject, and it invites and fairly requires joint inquiry. In general, the question concerns what to think or how to act about the subject matter. Please refer to Using Discussion in Classrooms (Dillon, 1994).

A second use of student questions occurs in the midst of discussion, during the interactions. The practice is to involve the students in raising honest questions about the subject matter as it is conveyed in the contributions of some speaker. There are two cases:

- Raise a question related to the contribution of a previous speaker.
- Formulate a question related to what self as speaker is struggling to think and to say aloud.

Both questions then enter the discussion. A final practice is to involve the students in identifying and formulating the next question. There are two moments:

- At a given phase or turning point of a discussion, what is the question that is now being experienced or that we should now address, given the discussion up to this point?
- Near the end of a discussion, what is the question that remains or that we should take up next (next assignment, next discussion,)?

The class can identify the question together in the final moments, or each student may later bring in a candidate question that has been formulated as an assignment subsequent to the discussion period and preparatory to the next discussion. Then, at the start of the new discussion period, the class may deliberate and reformulate the proposed questions in establishing for itself the question for discussion.

The very practice of involving students in the invention of the discussion question—no matter the subsequent discussion—is of itself an essential education into questioning and discussion.

BENEFITS OF QUESTIONING

What might be some specifically educative benefits of engaging in question-asking activity? On this issue, I venture to propose the longest list defensible of features, aspects, states, processes, and traits that are cognitive, affective, and behavioral in kind. These describe matters that are implicated in questioning such that the act of questioning may be considered to enhance, to produce, to activate, or to exercise them. In that way, they accrue to the person who engages in questioning, representing benefits that are recognizably desirable from the broad viewpoint of human education and development.

Two distinctions help to understand the forthcoming narrative. First, the benefits are not all psychological in kind. Second, the narrative of these benefits is not a review of research.

Much of the discourse in education and human development is psychological, particularly cognitive-psychological, and many of these benefits are couched in psychological terms, even presented in the familiar categories of cognitive, affective, and behavioral. Other categories may serve as well. We should note that the benefits to be presented include important features other than psychological ones, psychological features other than cognitive ones, and cognitive features other than information processing ones. This distinction serves to remind us that question asking cannot rightly be conceived only in terms of cognitive psychological information processing activity. Questioning is not a matter of cognition and information alone, nor does it always involve information.

The presentation of these benefits is speculative and ranging, consisting of commentary and allusive references to research. It is above all not to be read as a review of research, for it is nothing of the kind. The interest here is not on the research but on the identity of likely benefits of questioning. The one or two studies that are cited are neither conclusive nor representative of the research on a given feature. Indeed, they tend to be older studies and, in some cases, they may be the only source that can be cited for that item, whereas for other items, no research at all can be cited. Finally, many references are to sources that are typically not regarded as research, such as psychoanalysis and philosophy.

Let us now have in mind some young students or some senior citizens whom we would deliberately engage in question-asking activity. What educational and developmental benefits might accrue to them from their questioning? Here is a display of likely benefits, ranging among cognitive, affective, and behavioral features.

Cognitive Features

The most obvious cognitive feature enhanced by question asking is *knowledge*. As can readily be imagined, and as depicted in Fig. 8.1, knowledge is implicated throughout the entire process of questioning, from start (presupposition) to finish (question–answer proposition). Our first and best lesson in this respect was taught by Aristotle, who classified the entire domain of knowledge into four questions. He magisterially proposed that the things that we know are as many as the things that we ask, concluding that our knowledge consists in answers to questions (*Posterior Analytics*, 89b). The quality and quantity of a person's knowledge is enhanced by question asking. Those who question more likely know more, or know better.

Other knowledge-like features involved in questioning are metacognitive and autoregulatory processes, and information processing generally. Theoretical and experimental research by Flammer (1981) refers the cognitive psychology of question asking to knowledge structures, inferring, decision making, metacognition, and autoregulation (p. 417). And much more: "Question asking is a way of selecting information; and understanding question asking should help to understand how people regulate their interaction with their material, social, cultural, and mental world" (p. 408). A case in point is prose-processing, of great interest in educational research and practice. A body of experimental research (e.g., Wong, 1985) has amply demonstrated that the student's asking of questions while reading and studying enhances the processing of the prose material read—that is, comprehension and retention.

Construal of meaning is a related but broader feature. Meaning or understanding of a piece of knowledge, in complement to knowing or possessing that item, inheres in the relation that the questioner construes between question and answer. (Knowledge is the question–answer proposition.) For example, work in hermeneutics and literary theory by the philosopher Meyer (1983) demonstrated that interpreting the meaning of a text is a process of questioning. The reader or exegete regards the text as an answer and construes the question to which it stands in relation to the answer; then he questions its character or validity as the answer. This questioning process proceeds through two levels, applying both to the text as a whole and to its individual statements that, together, form a problematic complex. Hence, in general and not alone in reading a book, the formation of meaning and understanding of those things that we know is a function of question asking. Other cognitive features include the familiar trio of intelligence, creativity, and problem solving.

As for intelligence, the prominent psychologist of intelligence, Sternberg, speculated about "a vital half of intelligence—the asking of questions" (1987, p. 11). He proposed that intelligence tests cannot adequately measure intelligence without requiring examinees to ask questions as well as to answer them. A minor study undertaken with secondary students (Lehman, 1972) found a significant, if not large, correlation ($r = .31$) between the questions asked and intelligence, as measured by the Henmon-Nelson Test of Mental Ability.

Creativity, in the form of divergent thinking, has also been associated with question asking. That same study with ninth-grade students (Lehman, 1972) reported a much higher correlation ($r = .60$) for creativity, as measured by the Torrance Tests of Creative Thinking, than for intelligence. A study with college students (Arlin, 1974) also reported a significant association between, on the one hand, the number and quality of questions, and on the other, various Guilford-like measures of divergent thinking—divergent production of semantic systems and figural and symbolic transformations. Also, with Piagetian formal operational thinking! Another study with college students (Glover, 1979) found that creative students, by contrast to less creative ones, according to the Torrance Tests, asked significantly more and significantly more complex or higher-cognitive questions, both while studying and that discussing the assigned course readings. It is interesting that a process which could be regarded as converging on an answer should involve so much divergent thinking; and that tolerance of ambiguity should play a part in a drive to reduce uncertainty. Clearly enough, questioning is not just a matter of seeking information, nor does it eventuate only in knowledge-like things.

Problem solving is related not only to intelligence and creativity, as is well known, but also to question asking. In a study with sixth-grade students in science classes (Blank & Covington, 1965), certain groups of students were trained to ask questions; on a posttest involving problem solving (Science Achievement Test), the questioners solved two thirds of the problems and nonquestioners half of the problems. A minor study with college students (Dillon, 1987) found a significant correlation ($r = .39$) between performance on a question-asking task and a problem-solving task.

Finally, *learning* is a generic cognitive feature that is enhanced by question asking. (We may also consider it as a generic affective and behavioral feature.) Questioning eventuates in learning (Dillon, 1986). As a cognitive feature, learning characterizes the questioner's knowledge and meaning of the subject in the question–answer as cognized. But apart from the product that is learning, the learning process is also enhanced. Learning characterizes the enhancement of knowledge, information processing, understanding and meaning, intelligence, creativity, and problem solving or anything else cognitive that is set for learning and achieved through questioning. Those who question more learn more, in the cognitive domain.

Affective features

By far the most salient feature of the questioner, and one of signal importance to education and human development, is *dynamics*. The dynamics of the questioning person are proactive arousal, by contrast to passivity and reactivity of the nonquestioner and the answerer. The dynamics describe an autonomous agent and independent actor, not dependent and subordinate; purposive and determined, not expectant and resigned. From a psychoanalytic perspective (Olinick, 1957), questioning is an active, assertive, and aggressive act in pursuit of power and mastery; the question is "a searching, acquisitive, prehensile organ of the questioner" (p. 303). Philosophy too reveals this dynamic, for example, in describing questioning as "an intent of mind that works to reveal meaning rather than waiting passively to absorb what may come" (Clark, 1972, p. 35). From an educational as well as developmental perspective, how sad the children seem who sit in classrooms and answer rather than ask questions; and how sad the populace that they thereby grow up to form.

Nearly as salient and equally as impressive are the *moral* or *character dispositions* involved in questioning. These include aspiration to know, commitment to truth, courage to face the unknown, and will to undertake to know. We recall that these number among the presumptions of the act of questioning. Far more than intelligence or other cognitive features, character is the key feature in the venture to inquire. Socrates was intelligent and we may admire him for his thoughts, wits, and methods. But it is his character that was being exercised in his questioning pursuit of right knowing and acting (e.g., *Apology*). This is the essential feature for our attention and application in the study of questioning. It shows us that questioning and its developmental fruits are well within the reach of even the less intelligent among our children and fellows. Courage, venture, and will—not IQ, talent, and giftedness—inform the questioning human and so act to form him or her.

Among other affective features enhanced by questioning are certain motives, attitudes, beliefs, and interests. These figure among the varieties of noncognition that Messick (1979) nicely reviewed with an eye, not to questioning, but to their educational uses and measurement. The character of these features reveals how they might be implicated in the questioning act and further how questioning might enhance them.

Motives are impulses, emotions, or desires that impel to action. Motivation is clearly in force throughout the questioning process and is exercised and strengthened by it. Familiar motives that may be affected are (from Messick's list), achievement or effectance, autonomy, dominance, and understanding, as well as curiosity, which is a type of motivation. Curiosity is an exploratory drive induced by novelty, uncertainty, or insufficient information, and is oriented toward achieving an understanding of the nature and causes of events. Berlyne's concept of epistemic curiosity and his classic studies of children's questioning can be cited here (Berlyne & Frommer, 1966).

Attitudes are feelings plus evaluations of a social object, incorporating a predisposition to behave or an action tendency. Attitudes towards subjects, learning, and self are among those involved in questioning, such as self-concept as a learner. An enhanced self-concept likely flows from the activity of questioning and the learning and confidence that it produces.

Beliefs are convictions or hypotheses about the nature of an object and its relations to other objects. They lead to selectivity in attention, intensification of arousal, and energizing of action tendencies. That is just the case with certain beliefs involved at the start of questioning as well as in the asking of the question. One relevant and familiar belief is locus of control, in which an internal locus regards self as responsible to act and to resolve the perplexing matter encountered. Perhaps a belief in external locus of control leads to no action but either to resignation or to expectancy of answer from some other agent.

Interests are pleasurable feelings accompanying activities undertaken for their own sake. They too entail selective attention to relevant stimuli and an increase in arousal and energy. The factor of self-determined activity is relevant to the questioner's attention and action on some subject or object, and to the general interest that is excited by the pursuit and fruit of the questioning act. Interests are enhanced by questioning in that questioning issues furthers knowledge or other grasp of the interesting object, and because the resulting knowledge, in the form of a question–answer proposition, serves in turn as presupposition to a further question, renewing the pursuit and pleasurable feelings (interests) that accompany it. Those who question more serve more interests and get more interested, continually.

Finally, *learning* is a generic feature describing the questioner's grasp or achievement of the object of pursuit. Here, as an affective feature, learning describes anything of an affective character that is set to be learned and that is achieved through questioning. For instance, many educational objectives are affective rather than cognitive. Affective learning is also enhanced through question asking in the measure that it enhances the person's active dynamics, moral dispositions or character traits, motives, attitudes, beliefs, and interests. Those who question more learn more, in the affective domain.

Behavioral Features

The most salient behavioral feature is the questioner's active reach toward the world. Question asking is not just mentation and emotion, it is also action, interaction, and language.

Action includes the questioner's action on the world as he starts to ask and his search behavior as he starts to answer. These actional features have qualities of system, regulation, method, orientation, strategy, stretching, and achievement. Coping strategies are also involved (listed by Messick, 1979). These are preferred strategies for meeting the adaptive requirements of the environment, especially the social environment. Asking questions enhances not only coping but also adapting and mastering. Nonquestioners remain in quiescence. Those who question more act more, bending the world to their purposes in an active reach for mastery.

Interaction or social features are therefore also involved. They include social competence and interpersonal participation (per Messick, 1979). Clearly these are enhanced by question asking. Questioning also demonstrably serves to initiate and maintain new social relationships (Berger & Kellerman, 1983) to reach out and involve people, as it were, in mutuality of being. Questioning is also address to the Other. It is the first phase of existential inquiry into the person: "the compresence of two searchers, each questing (in dialogue) after the universal characteristics they share, yet each haunted by the utter uniqueness of the other" (Feldstein, 1978, p. 42). More prosaically, questioning is a way of expressing, asserting, and exercising status in the situation and leading or controling the exchange. That is a common finding of sociolinguistic research; and it is a common observation of anthropologists regarding sociocultural factors involved in questioning (e.g., Goody, 1978). Imagine, then, the enhanced social development involved in asking questions in certain situations or of certain figures (e.g., superior or interviewer); or in managing an exchange; or yet in maneuvering through the world to get the object in answer. By contrast, nonquestioners remain alone, stay at home, or, in social situations, assume retiring stances, for example, they answer questions.

Language, quite apart from sociolinguistic aspects, includes the acquisition of language and the expressiveness of self. Expressiveness is an aspect clearly enhanced by asking questions—by the expression of presuppositions, perplexity, and presumptions, for instance, in addition to formulating and uttering the question about all of that. Nonquestioners just keep quiet about it all, not even expressing it to themselves. As for acquisition, research on the questions asked even by two- and three-year-old children reveals the amazing complex of linguistic, conceptual, and pragmatic factors that are learned—the syntactic function of wh words, the syntax and semantics of verbs, and the contingency relations in discourse (Bloom, Merkin, & Wootten, 1982). Question asking enhances linguistic development.

Finally, learning is enhanced by asking questions. Learning is a generic feature characterizing the acquisition of any behavioral feature implicated in questioning—actional, social, or linguistic features. Those who question more learn more, in the behavioral domain.

CONCLUSION

Every time a student asks a question, a mind opens to learning. This is the perfect opening for teaching to enter and for learning to follow in answer. Yet nothing can come from student questions if no room is made for them in school and other educational contexts. And, sad to say, children everywhere are schooled to become masters at answering questions and to remain novices at asking questions.

Nothing much can be done about this anti-questioning and curiously anti-educative circumstance in general. But a great deal can be done about it in particular. We can favor student questioning in our own educational circumstance, whether as theorist, researcher, practitioner, or parent. Student questioning remains a field wide open for our reflection, our investigation, and our action.

REFERENCES

Arlin, C. P. (1974). *Problem finding: The relation between cognitive process variables and problem finding performance.* Unpublished doctoral dissertation, University of Chicago.

Bartlett, F. (1958). *Thinking.* London: Allen & Unwin.

Berger, C., & Kellerman, K. (1983). To ask or not to ask. In R. Bostrom (Ed.), *Communication yearbook* (Vol. 7, pp. 342–368). Beverly Hills, CA: Sage.

Berlyne, D. (1965). *Structure and direction in thinking.* New York: Wiley.

Berlyne, D., & Frommer, F. (1966). Some determinants of the incidence and content of children's questions. *Child Development, 37,* 177–189.

Blank, S., & Covington, M. (1965). Inducing children to ask questions in solving problems. *Journal of Educational Research, 59*, 21–27.

Bloom, L., Merkin, S. & Wootten, J. (1992). Wh-questions: Linguistic factors that contribute to the sequence of acquisition. *Child Development, 53*, 1084–1092.

Clark, M. (1972). *Perplexity and knowledge: An inquiry into the structures of questioning.* The Hague, The Netherlands: Nijhoff.

Dillon, J. T. (1986). Student questions and individual learning. *Educational Theory, 36*, 333–341.

Dillon, J. T. (1987). Levels of problem finding vs. problem solving. *Questioning Exchange, 2*, 105–115.

Dillon, J. T. (1988a). *Questioning and teaching: A manual of practice.* New York: Teachers College.

Dillon, J. T. (1988b). The remedial status of student questioning. *Journal of Curriculum Studies, 20*, 197–210.

Dillon, J. T. (1990). *The practice of questioning.* London: Routledge.

Dillon, J. T. (1994). *Using discussion in classrooms.* Buckingham, England: Open University Press.

Duncker, K. (1945). On problem-solving. *Psychological Monographs, 58* (Whole No. 270).

Feldstein, L. (1978). *Homo quaerens: The seeker and the sought.* New York: Fordham.

Festinger, L. (1957). *A theory of cognitive dissonance.* Evanston, IL: Row Peterson.

Flammer, A. (1981). Towards a theory of question asking; and, predicting what questions people ask. *Psychological Research, 43*, 407–420, 421–429.

Glover, J. (1979). Levels of questions asked in interview and reading sessions by creative and relatively noncreative college students. *Journal of Genetic Psychology, 135*, 103–108.

Goguelin, P. (1967). *Le penser efficace: Vol. 2, la probl•mation.* Paris: Soci•t• •dition enseignement sup•rieur.

Goody, E. (1978). Towards a theory of questions. In E. Goody (Ed.), *Questions and politeness: Strategies in social interaction* (pp. 17–43). Cambridge, England: Cambridge University Press.

Hinds, J. (1984). Japanese. In W. Chisholm (Ed.), *Interrogativity: A colloquium on the grammar, typology, and pragmatics of questions in seven diverse languages* (pp. 145–188). Amsterdam: Benjamins.

Lehman, R. (1972). The effects of creativity and intelligence on pupils' questions in science. *Science Education, 56*, 103–121.

Maier, N. R. F. (1970). *Problem solving and creativity.* Belmont, CA: Brooks/Cole.

Messick, S. (1979). Potential uses of noncognitive measurement in education. *Journal of Educational Psychology, 71*, 281–292.

Meyer, M. (1983). *Meaning and reading: A philosophical essay on language and literature.* Amsterdam: Benjamins.

Olinick, S. (1957). Questioning and pain, truth and negation. *Journal of the American Psychoanalytic Association, 5*, 302–324.

Sternberg, R. (1987). Questioning and intelligence. *Questioning Exchange, 1*, 11–14.

Uldall, E. (1962). Ambiguity: Question or statement? or "Are you asking me or telling me?" *Janua Linguarum 10*, Series Maior, 779–783.

van der Meij, H. (1986). *Questioning: A study on the questioning behavior of elementary school children.* The Hague, The Netherlands: Stitching voor Onderzoek van her Onderwijs.

van der Meij, H. (1994). Student questioning: A componential analysis. *Learning and Individual Differences, 6*, 137–161.

Wertheimer, M. (1959). *Productive thinking.* New York: Harper & Row.

Wong, B. (1985). Self-questioning instructional research. *Review of Educational Research, 55*, 227–268.

The Great Divide Between Teacher and Student Questioning

Hans van der Meij
University of Twente

> Since questions are the most important intellectual tool we have, is it not incredible that the art and science of question-asking is not systematically taught? —*Postman (1988, p. 26)*

Socrates is famous for leading the youth by his questioning. An example of his approach is shown in the following excerpt from the Lysis dialogue (from the translation of Hamilton & Cairns, 1987). Menexenus, the friend of Lysis, has just asserted that he knows what friendship means.

Socrates: ... to appeal to you as connoisseur of friendship. Answer me this. As soon as man loves another, which of the two becomes the friend: the lover of the loved, or the loved of the lover? Or does it make no difference?

Menexenus: None that I can see.

Socrates: Are then both friends, if only one loves?

Menexenus: I think so.

Socrates: Indeed! And is it not possible that the one who loves is not loved in return by the one he loves?

Menexenus: It is.

Socrates: Nay, is it not possible for him even to be hated, as lovers often imagine?

Menexenus: Quite true.

Socrates: Well, in such a case as this, which of the two is the friend of the other? Or is neither the friend of the other, unless both love each other?

Menexenus: The latter certainly seems to be the case.

Socrates: If so, we now think differently before. Then it appeared that if one loved, both were friends, but now, neither are friends unless both love.

Menexenus: Yes, I'm afraid we have contradicted ourselves.

SOCRATES MODELS QUESTIONING

His probing questions in the dialogue arouse perplexity, revealing the boy's ignorance. The Lysis dialogue ends with Socrates stating that, because the boy is a friend of Lysis, he should know friendship. Socrates thus gives hope for the future, but he leaves this knowable unknown open. He does not impose his own definition or point of view.

In the Lysis dialogue, as well as many others, Socrates' objective is not to resolve difficulties, but to get the youth to think. In the 2,400 years that have evolved since, this objective has remained crucially important in education. One of the ways to achieve this is to have both teachers and students engage in the right kind of questioning.

TEACHER QUESTIONING VERSUS
STUDENT QUESTIONING

Recently, the second edition of the International Encyclopedia of Education appeared. The book was an ambitious undertaking, seeking "to embrace all relevant studies and research in the field of education" (Husén & Postlethwaite, 1994, p. xii). With contributions from 1,380 experts from more than 65 countries, 1,266 chapters with 6,821 pages were created to cover all aspects of education.

All aspects? Well. Not all. There is no chapter on student questioning. Student questioning is mentioned only in passing, and, by and large, so is help seeking. Educators thus do not seem to share Postman's view that student questioning is an important topic for educators. In contrast, educators attach great importance to teacher questioning. Some even consider this to be one of the most distinguish-ing characteristics of teaching.

The number of published studies on student and teacher questioning is telling. Research on student questioning is published infrequently. Between 5 and 10 publications on student questioning appear annually. Generally, only a few of these papers examine the main processes involved in questioning. They analyze genuine information seeking, describing how perplexity arises, how it transforms into question asking, and how students process answers. The majority of papers on student questioning falls into one of the following categories: help-seek-ing studies and intervention studies. Help-seeking studies examine, for example, facilitative and inhibitive conditions to asking for assistance in school. Intervention studies aim to improve student questioning by giving some kind of training. For example, students may be given a list of question stems (e.g., "How would you use … ?", "Explain why … ?", "What's a new example of … ?") to help them generate (more) questions during prose processing.

In contrast, research on teacher questioning abounds. Gall and Ar-tero-Boname (1994) estimated that, from 1982 onward, over 100 re-search reports and professional papers on teacher questioning were published annually. Main topics concern the kinds of questions teachers ask (e.g., lower or higher order questions); contextual factors such as grade level; teacher characteristics and student characteristics; helping students answer questions; and training teachers in questioning skills.

Teacher questions do not just feature strongly in research, they also dominate the questioning that goes on in school. Teachers engage in questioning much more frequently than do students. If one considers both the oral questions and the written ones asked in recitation, seat work, and quizzes, teacher questions consume a huge proportion, possibly varying between 25% and 50% of classroom time.

This chapter focuses on how teacher questioning relates to student questioning, an issue that has not been given much attention (West & Pearson, 1994). The majority of studies on teacher questioning examine the relationship with students' academic achievement (e.g., scores on a retention test). The relations between teacher questioning and student questioning are thus not exactly clear. The point of departure is a componential model of student questioning (van der Meij, 1994). This model depicts questioning from start to finish—from the onset of per-plexity until the learning that may result. Contributions of teacher questioning to the main processes in, and products of, student ques-tioning are discussed.

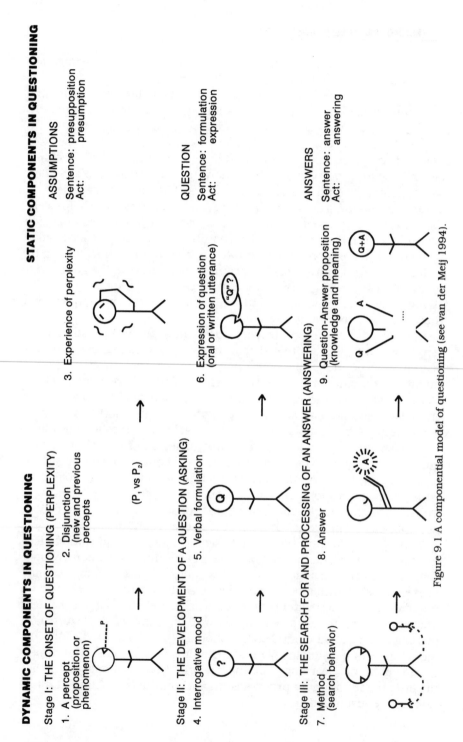

Figure 9.1 A componental model of questioning (see van der Meij 1994).

THE MAIN PROCESSES IN AND PRODUCTS
OF STUDENT QUESTIONING

Questioning knows three main moments or stages (Fig. 9.1). The first moment, the onset of questioning, may be a state of surprise, novelty, conflict, and the like. It is characterized as perplexity. Perplexity occurs when the student notes a discrepancy between a known fact and some new information. The second moment is that of question posing. It occurs when the student has succeeded in transforming the perplexity into a verbal expression. The third moment is that of the search for and processing of an answer. It occurs when the student engages in search behavior. If the search leads to an answer, and that answer is connected to the question, it leads to a new proposition the student holds to be true.

The left part of Fig. 9.1 shows, for each moment or stage, the dynamic aspects, the main processes, in questioning. The right part of Fig. 9.1 displays the static aspects, the main components per stage. These components fall into a sentence and an act. The sentences represent the logical part. They reveal the content that is communicated in questioning. The acts represent the pragmatic part. They reveal the motivational and social-communicative aspects involved (Dillon, 1990; van der Meij, 1994).

Stage 1: The Onset of Questioning

A student can become perplexed simply by thinking about a topic. Questioning can be triggered by thought processes for which there are no apparent cues from the outside. For example, the student may, in reflection, relate certain known facts to one another and discover that they are in contradiction, or such reflections may bring into question the certainty of knowing some fact. In cases such as these, questioning is said to be triggered internally, to originate within the student. This kind of questioning is a vital process in self regulated learning in which students must, among others, frequently question (check) their own under-standing without being prompted by teacher or textbook questions.

Perplexity can also be triggered by external cues, by events or phenom-ena in the environment of the questioner (e.g., Berlyne, 1960, 1965; Chinn & Brewer, 1993; Markman, 1979). For example, a text can trigger perplexity by presenting surprising or conflicting facts. Another impor-tant external condition for the onset of questioning concerns the ques-tions teachers ask in interactions with students. The next example suggests that a joint effort of textbook content and teacher questioning may be needed to achieve perplexity.

Children from third, fifth, and sixth grade were presented a story containing an explicit contradiction (Markman, 1979). One story with such a contradiction was about how ants find their way back home. It ran as follows:

> ... Sometimes they go very, very far from their nest to find food.... To help them find their way home, ants have a special way of leaving an invisible trail. Everywhere they go, they put out an invisible chemical from their bodies. This chemical has a special odor. Another thing about ants is they do not have a nose. Ants never get lost. (Markman, 1979, p. 646)

After reading this story, the children were asked to give suggestions for improving the comprehensibility of the story. Between 40% and 50% of the children failed to question the experimenter about the contradiction. No age difference was found, sixth-grade students were just as likely not to be perplexed as third grade students. The students who failed to notice the inconsistency were probed for understanding in the following way:

Experimenter: How do ants get back?

Third Grader: They leave an invisible path

Experimenter: What kind of path?

Third Grader: It has an odor.

Experimenter: Did everything make sense?

Third Grader: Yes.

Experimenter: What do you need in order to smell?

Third Grader: A nose.

Experimenter: Do ants have noses?

Third Grader: No.

Experimenter: Can ants smell?

Third Grader: Yes.

Experimenter: How do ants smell without noses?

Third Grader: That's a tough one!

Just as in Socrates' dialogue with Menexenus, the inquiry is carefully staged to achieve an optimal effect, starting with one or more statements about something known in advance or taken to be true until proven otherwise. In this case, the statements are the facts presented in the story. The explicit contradiction provides an objective reason for questioning. When the child does not question the contradiction, that is, when the child is not perplexed, the experimenter begins a questioning dialogue whose main purpose is to arouse perplexity.

To help the student realize that something in the story is wrong, the questioner builds up a case in which each question and answer establishes an important fact (e.g., ants have no nose). Each interaction serves to settle just one new fact, which may just be a reminder or a check of the students' memory. In addition, the questions are asked in a sequence such that each question represents a crucial chain in the line of reasoning that leads to perplexity: ants far away from their nest—path with odor—path finding by smelling the odor—use nose—no nose.

The careful staging of the questions is vital for building the case. The students must give thought to only those facts that are relevant. So, just as in the dialogue of Socrates and Menexenus, the questions leave room for no other responses than student answers. And even these are constrained by the closed questions asked in the dialogue. In short, in questioning dialogues such as these, students are taken by the hand. The questions and answers settle basic facts. When these facts are considered in combination they lead to perplexity (i.e., the discovery of the contradiction).

Presuppositions. The presuppositions are all the propositions entailed by the question. Every question contains presuppositions. For example, two presuppositions to the question "Does the Queen of the Netherlands have red hair?" are (1) there is a Queen of the Netherlands, and (2) the Queen is a person, animal, or thing with hair as an attribute. To really understand the question, one must get to know its most critical presupposition(s), the one(s) to which the questioner is committed.

Special attention is needed for the truthfulness or validity of the presuppositions (Dillon, 1990). When a student asks a question whose presuppositions the teacher knows to be false, the teacher should not answer the question. Instead, the teacher should address the presuppositions, possibly questioning the student about these.

The cooperativity principle on which this rests is so common that film makers use it to create humor. One such humorous situation, for example, occurs when Inspector Clouseau (Peter Sellers) meets a dog when he enters a hotel. While bending down to caress the dog, he asks the attending manager "Does your dog bite?" The response is negative. And so Clouseau continues his action and, of course, gets bitten. Angry, he turns to the manager saying "I thought you said your dog doesn't bite," whereupon he receives the answer "That's not my dog." People easily assume cooperativity. The dog biting scene is funny because the falsity of the main presupposition is not obvious beforehand. More generally, the example illustrates that it can be quite useful to question the main presupposition(s) held by the questioner.

Presumptions.   The presumptions relate to the personal motives and beliefs of the questioner and to the social-communicative aspects of questioning. They include, among others, certain conditions the questioner holds to be true. The primary presumption in questioning is that the questioner believes in the truthfulness or validity of the presuppositions. In addition, Dillon (1986, 1990) suggested that a person asking a genuine information seeking question holds the following attitudes: ignorance, perplexity, need, desire, commitment, belief, faith, courage, and will (Flammer, 1986; van der Meij, 1986, 1987).

Most teacher questions tend not to arise from a genuine need to know. For example, to support reading for understanding, most textbooks give adjunct questions to texts whose answers are not, at heart, of interest to the teacher. Teachers want to know whether students know, or can find out, the answers to these questions. Doblaev (1984) showed that reading for understanding does not necessarily have to evolve around these known-answer type questions. Teachers and students can engage in a joint venture in which genuine information seeking takes place, and, simultaneously, the students also build up their reading skills.

Doblaev's approach centers around the notion of the hidden questions in a text. What these questions might be can best be explained with an example. Suppose that you read the following two sentences: By the end of the nineteenth century, the United Kingdom was no longer the major industrialized country in the world. Nevertheless, the United Kingdom did become the world's banker. The hidden question or problem here is "What explains the fact that the United Kingdom became the world's banker while it lost its first place among industrialized countries?"

Discovering the hidden questions and answers is a very complex process. It usually requires the reader to relate two lines or more of text to one another. Hidden questions are genuine information seeking questions. The questioner is really interested in their answers. Children and teachers tend not to ask these hidden questions spontaneously. They must be trained intensively before they can ask them (Doblaev, 1984).

In the help-seeking literature, a distinction is made between instrumental and dependency oriented help seeking (Nelson-Le Gall 1985; Newman, 1991). These acts are often discussed as if they originate from two mutually exclusive motifs; students ask for help to learn how to solve a problem, or they ask for help to have others solve their problem for them. This is, in my view, not an adequate description of the personal motifs and beliefs (presumptions) of student questions.

Students' requests are likely to stem from more than just a single motif (e.g., a genuine need for information), and both dependence and independence may be involved.

My students and I once conducted an experiment in an attempt to catch a glimpse of the multiple motifs underlying student questioning (van der Meij, Meer, & Ponte, 1989). We did this by trying to prove that students regularly ask pseudo information seeking questions—questions that look like real questions, but that do not stem from a need to know. We started the research by observing a number of regular spelling lessons in six elementary school classrooms. In all these classrooms, the spelling lessons were highly individualized; each child received a personal worksheet with spelling problems. During the lessons, we registered what questions students asked and how often they posed questions to the teacher. In addition, we analyzed the completed worksheets to obtain an exact view of the students' mastery of certain spelling problems. In the experimental spelling lesson, everything was the same (e.g., the regular teacher was present) except for the worksheets. Each student was given a worksheet with problems that the student had already mastered nearly to perfection (more than 95% correct).

The changed worksheets significantly affected the number of questions asked. For these known problems, we had expected a (small) decline. The students, however, asked twice as many questions as they normally did. The framing of the students' questions was the same as in the regular lessons. That is, most questions seemed to signal a genuine need for help. The conclusion we drew from this experiment was that the students were using information seeking questions as "maid of all work." Within a school setting, these are the kinds of questions to which teachers nearly always favorably respond. It is an acceptable question to ask, and it arises from multiple motifs (e.g., increase certainty of knowing, get teacher attention, or handle a novel situation).

Stage 2: The Development of a Question

In this stage, the student must come to grips with what perplexes and make that perplexity more tangible. The student must articulate and express the problem or perplexity. Whereas this articulation may take place almost simultaneously with perplexity, this is not necessarily the case. In fact, it is quite likely that the transition from perplexity to the formulation and expression of a question is a most difficult process.

The difference between being perplexed and framing or formulating a question is what distinguishes problem finding from problem formulation. In problem finding, the student must be perplexed by something and decide to give it more thought (e.g., not to discard the problem as insignificant or insoluble). Thereafter, the student enters the stage of problem formulation in which it should become clear what question(s) the student holds and how these can be expressed so that they work well (e.g., others should be able to understand them). Success in problem formulation, therefore, is a necessary condition for starting a creative attack to the problem (Dillon, 1982; Getzels, 1982, 1988).

Prior knowledge and general verbal ability strongly affect this phase of questioning (van der Meij, 1990a, 1990b; van der Meij & Dillon, 1994). For example, we found that fifth-grade students with low verbal ability frequently failed in formulating questions (van der Meij & Dillon, 1994). In the experiment, students had to find the meaning of a word. They could ask questions for this purpose, and question formulation was supported by question stems (e.g., "Does it have anything to do with ... ?"). Students with low verbal ability frequently were aware of their ignorance, but were found to be incapable of asking the right question.

There seemed to be two problems. One problem had to do with finding something to ask, with framing the question in the first place. The students frequently made false starts; they would first indicate their intention to ask a question after which they began expressing the question's stem. Then they would hesitate for several seconds, and, after apparently failing to find something to ask, they would go back on their first decision and decide not to ask anything at all.

The other problem had to do with the content of students' questions. In general, these questions were not very discriminative (e.g., "Does imitate have something to do with doing something?"), or they added little to what was already given (e.g., "Has estimation something to do with estimate?"). In contrast, students with high verbal ability more often came up with their own thoughts about the target words and formulated sharper questions (e.g., "Has estimation something to do with making a guess?").

In school, students may have to overcome strong inhibitions to posing questions (Karabenick & Sharma, 1994; van der Meij, 1988). But after having decided to ask for help, it tends to become easy for students who may be given too much support in formulation. Teachers frequently take over the process of framing the questions from the student. During seat work, for example, students often can get by with very simple signals for help. Teachers, pressed for time, usually elaborate the problem or question for the student. The following example is illustrative:

Student: I don't know how to do this (points to "10% of $ 250 = ").

Teacher: What don't you understand?

Student: Well ... eh ... I don't know.

Teacher: OK. What do you do first?

Student: ... (silence)

Teacher: We start with 1%. What's 1%?

Student: One hundredth.

Teacher: All right! Now, let's see what's 1% of 250?

Student: Twenty-five.

Teacher: No. That's one tenth. You need one hundredth, remember?

Student: Oh, yes. Eh ... two fifty.

Teacher: ...

The student signals a need for help by approaching the teacher's desk and by roughly pointing at the problem. From thereon, except for a feeble attempt to have the student formulate the question, the teacher is in charge and remains in charge.

The dialogue, which probably represents a fair proportion of the student-initiated interactions during seat work, shows that the teacher does not wait for the student to express a question properly. The teacher takes control and frames the question. There is a weak attempt to get the student to better formulate the request for help—"What don't you understand?", but the teacher does not wait long enough for the framing to happen. From thereon, the initiative remains tightly in the hands of the teacher. It is not even relinquished after the student signals comprehension—when the student said twenty-five he jumped ahead to the right answer. The teacher follows a personal agenda, which is to deal systematically with all the steps in the method that leads to the right solution.

In a reflective discourse, the teachers' questioning serves an opposite role, namely, to help students articulate questions (van Zee & Minstrell, 1997a, 1997b). Such a discourse might begin with the teacher introducing a physical event, after which students are to predict what happens. Typically, students give divergent responses that form the starting point for the discourse. In the discourse, the teachers' questions focus on the reasons for the students' predictions, fostering their thinking by asking for a confirmation of comprehension, a repetition of an argument, an elaboration, a clarification, and so on. Basically, the teacher follows the students' lead in the discourse, the premise being that students already know a great deal about the physical world and that it is the teachers' task to examine their current ways of thinking and to further stimulate that thinking.

Teacher neutrality is a critical factor in a reflective discourse. In order to have the discourse evolve around the students' own ideas, the teacher abstains from evaluating responses. By remaining neutral, the teacher creates an intellectually stimulating atmosphere in which the exploration of ideas is really valued as such. It prevents the discourse from becoming a fishing enterprise; it prevents students from becoming engaged more by what they think the teacher wants to hear than by what they want to get to know.

A parallel development can be found in attempts to improve peer interactions to enhance knowledge construction. For example, King (1991, 1994) found that students, working in pairs, would engage in fruitful discussions over some subject matter only if supported by question stems such as "Why is ... important?", "What would happen if, ... " and "What's a new example of ...?" The guided cooperative questioning, as the approach was called, was superior to less guided and unguided questioning (e.g., in one condition students' questioning was supported only by signal words such as why, what, and how). The generic, thought-provoking questions help students engage in thought processes such as comparing, contrasting, defining, explaining, justifying, and inferencing which, in turn, mediate learning.

Formulation. In formulation, the questioner invents the logical or conceptual units of the question and relates these units to one another. In simple terms, the person must find the right words and structure for the question (Allen, 1987; Dillon, 1990). This is the stage for studies into the what of people's questions.

Armstrong (1986, 1993) presented an intriguing approach to linking teacher questioning and student questioning in her Inquiry in Art method. The method evolves around student questioning, which is described as a set of thinking behaviors that are "common to most persons producing art" (p. 37). These behaviors are setting a direction, discovery, visually analyzing, classifying, personalizing, hypothesizing, reordering, synthesizing, and evaluating.

In planning Inquiry in Art questions, teachers are given suggestions for posing questions that help students find the critical concepts and questions. For example, to support students' personalization, teachers are prompted to ask questions such as "How do you like to view things?" and "What do you like most about the inside of the clock?"; and to support reordering, teachers could ask "How could the insides of shapes vary?", "How can the amount of overlap vary?", and "What could you do to vary your shapes so that they fit with the interpretation you want?"

Inquiry in Art teaches teachers to ask higher order questions that fit the students' moment in inquiry. The questions help provide focus to the students' thought processes; together, teacher and student frame the important questions. Teachers do not engage in this kind of questioning spontaneously. Inquiry in Art must be taught (Armstrong, 1993).

What is asked may not always be the real question in mind. In a classic paper on questioning in libraries, Taylor (1968) stated that "It is an obvious truism to every librarian ... that inquirers seldom ask at first for what they want" (p.185). Taylor sees questions as the result of four consecutive processes of questioning: (1) the actual but unexpressed need for information, (2) the conscious, within-brain description of the need, (3) the formal statement of the need, and (4) the question presented to the librarian. In this last stage, questions of users are compromised by, among other things, a need to accommodate the librarian or certain preconceived ideas of the possible answer. Taylor, therefore, suggests that librarian and questioner enter a negotiating (question–answer) dialogue in which the two work back from the expressed question to the formal one, perhaps even to the conscious one, to get to the core of the real question. One of the results of this process is to alter the questioners' a priori picture of what is expected.

Expression. This term refers to the act of putting the question into words. Questions vary widely with regard to how they are expressed and which characteristics of the questioner they reveal. In many classrooms, however, questioning is bound to rules students must obey, rules that often work as strong inhibitions to question posing. It is, therefore, not surprising that many students appear to be afraid to pose the questions they have in mind. The last move in this stage, the expression of the question, may thus be the most difficult to take. "Fully 95% of the questions that we have in mind to ask we never go on to utter. As before, we may think the better of it and follow one of the numerous other paths available. These include keeping quiet and giving off that we know and understand" (Dillon, 1988, p. 20). The factors that cause questions to be dissolved or their expression blocked vary. Personal but also social-normative factors are operative (Corno, 1993; van der Meij, 1988).

Inhibitions to pose questions exist at all levels of schooling, universities not excepted (e.g., Karabenick, 1994; Karabenick & Sharma, 1994). For example, in a study of antecedent conditions to student questioning in university classrooms, West and Pearson (1994) found that student questions were asked most frequently after an explicit teacher request. One fifth of all student questions were posed after the teacher had explicitly asked students whether they had any questions or comments about what was discussed (e.g., "Do you have any questions?"). Interestingly, Nielsen (1988) considered precisely this kind of teacher question "the least effective method of checking for understanding" (p.

94). Presumably, the author meant its effects on directing students' thoughts, rather than its social or contextual effects.

Removing the social, or contextual, inhibitions to ask is, at least initially, probably the most important stimulus for student questioning. It creates a favorable atmosphere for the expression (and birth) of student questions. Indeed, in studies that aim to stimulate students to ask more questions of their teachers, the reported effects may primarily be due to a better social climate than to more focused thought processes or better monitoring by the students.

Good suggested that there is an interaction between what students ask and how teachers respond (Good, Slavings, Harel, & Emerson, 1987; Good, Slavings, & Mason, 1988). When students formulate their questions well, teachers are more likely to react positively, which, in turn, reinforces further student questioning, leading to a favorable atmosphere for student questioning. In contrast, when students do not express their questions very well, teachers may structure their classroom to avoid problems. That is, when students ask vague questions, when they pose questions at the wrong time, or for the wrong purpose (e.g., to avoid listening), teachers may react by imposing restrictive rules (Good et al., 1988).

Stage 3: Answering

Answering consists of a search for information, the finding of an answer, and its processing. Clearly, there are many ways of obtaining an answer. A questioner may find an answer through direct retrieval in memory or by inferring one (Reder, 1987). Most of the research on student questioning does not deal with these internal processes, however, but concentrates on the processes involved in finding answers to one's questions by consulting other sources, personal and nonpersonal.

There is a growing interest in search behavior and all other steps in answering. A fair body of literature in this area comes from research on reading to locate, whose main aim is to depict search literacy, which is the motivation, knowledge, and skills people need for gaining access to information and for processing that information. An influential model on search literacy is that of Guthrie. It details distinct processes such as the selection of an appropriate navigating aid (e.g., index or table of contents), of the appropriate page and section, of extracting the right information from the right section, and of the coupling or integration of questions and answers (e.g., Byrnes & Guthrie, 1992; Dreher & Guthrie, 1990; Symons & Pressley, 1993). Some of these processes are mentioned in the model of answering presented in Fig. 9.1.

Nearly all research on reading to locate departs from a given problem or question; the focus is on what it takes to find information.

For example, students, mostly from college level, may be given the task of searching an introductory psychology textbook for to find an answer to a question such as "What four factors account for why people like each other?" (Dreher & Brown, 1993). The findings generally indicate that the students' performance is far from optimal. Dreher and Brown, for example, found that 47% of the college level students could not locate information to questions such as described.

One vital process in answering is the coupling of question and answer. A student should always consider whether the response or retrieved information is a sufficient answer to the question asked. Elementary school students do not always spontaneously evaluate reactions in light of their initial question. Kobasigawa (1983) suggested that there is a developmental trend for doing so. For example, he found that 60% of the fourth-grade students did not find anything wrong with the answer "Black bears are the smallest bears of North America" to the question "How heavy are black bears?" Eighth-grade students, in contrast, were significantly more skilled at noting that something was amiss. Only 15% of these students failed to note that the question was not sufficiently answered. This suggests that fourth-grade students are less sensitive than eighth-grade students to the need to evaluate collected information in light of their questions.

Kobasigawa (1983) examined how students judged questions and answers posed by others. In several experiments, evaluation and processing of students' own questions were examined (e.g., van der Meij, 1986, 1990a, 1990b; van der Meij & Dillon, 1994). Some of these studies note that students can be harmed by the answers they receive; but, perhaps being harmed is too strong a word for someone who changes a very fragile opinion for another fragile opinion. All studies indicate unequivocally that students often do not profit optimally from the answers they receive to their questions. In one experiment, for example, fifth-grade students were invited to ask yes–no questions to find the cause of a car accident. More than once students were found to ask two or more unnecessary questions on the same topic (i.e., type of cause). For example, a student would first ask "Did the driver cause the accident?", receive a "No" response, and then ask another, lower-level question bearing on the same matter (e.g., "Was the driver not careful?"). In this, and other, studies it is not exactly clear what may have caused the difficulty. Is it that students find it hard to abandon a preconceived idea even to the point that they sometimes cling to it even in the face of disconfirming evidence? Is it that students sometimes do not realize the strategic qualities of their own questions? Is it too difficult to infer that an answer that generally excludes the driver as the cause of an accident also means that a specific behavior of that person did not cause the accident? Or, is it that students fail to connect question and answer?

Answer. A cooperative respondent replies with a response that is relevant, informative, comprehensible, and true (Grice, 1975). What counts as an answer can be determined only by the questioner, however. Only the questioner can decide whether the question has been answered. In addition, it should also result in what Dillon calls learning.

The result of an inquiry may not be a full or definite answer, and yet it may have that effect on the student. Students may decide to stop their inquiry when they feel they have enough information or when they feel they know the answer. This was shown in an experiment in which we found a fairly high frequency of discontinued inquiries (van der Meij & Dillon, 1994). In such inquiries, students would stop their inquiry before having asked a question on the correct alternative. For example, a student might ask one or two questions to eliminate two of the five possible meanings of a word. Then, the student would stop questioning and tell the experimenter what the target word meant.

The students' verbal ability strongly affected their success in inferring the right answer. Students with a medium to high verbal ability arrived at the correct answer for 40% of the discontinued inquiries, whereas students with a low verbal ability hardly ever succeeded. Another important factor was task difficulty. Students were more likely to discontinue their inquiry when they were given an easy word than when they had to find out the meaning of a difficult word.

Answering. With the possible exception of Dillon's work, little is known about answering student questions. Answering these questions is a different matter than responding to a question per se, because the respondent should also take pedagogical issues into consideration (e.g., Dillon, 1986, 1988, 1991). Among other things, the teacher might want to respond so that the student's inquiry is sustained and take the possibility of stimulating independence into consideration. How, then, should student questions be answered, and how well are they being answered?

According to Dillon (1988, 1991), the last thing to do is to answer a student question. Teachers, he suggests, should sustain the asking "even if the question concerns 1066 and all that" (Dillon, 1988, p. 30). Dillon advances five general ways to sustain the asking: (1) reinforce and reward the experience of perplexity and expression of inquiry, (2) help the student and classmates to devise a method to address the question, (3) find out the question that the student has in mind to ask, (4) examine together the grounds of the question, and (5) appreciate the student's state of knowledge revealed by the question. Only at a later time may the teacher find it appropriate to answer the question. Dillon's suggestions have some similarities with what is proposed in reflective discourse and in what Scardamalia and Bereiter (1991, 1992, 1993) suggested for an environment in which cooperative knowledge building is central.

When teachers ask questions and students respond, teachers, of course, think of whether their questions have been answered. If it is not, they may wonder whether to ask for a clarification, whether to ask the same or another student, whether to rephrase or repeat the question, and so on. The most striking characteristic feature of such exchanges, however, is the teachers' evaluation of the student response. This has been illustrated most clearly by Mehan (1979) who presented two nearly identical exchanges, of which the latter is typical of a teacher–student, question-answer-evaluation, dialogue:

Speaker: What time is it, Denise?

Denise: Two thirty.

Speaker: Thank you, Denise

Speaker: What time is it, Denise?

Denise: Two thirty.

Speaker: Very good, Denise

The modeling effects of such teacher behavior (i.e., evaluation of known-answer questions) can easily be underestimated, as my students and I once experienced. Fifth to sixth grade students were observed while asking questions of fellow students and evaluating their answers in a classroom discussion about a text. In these discussions, two children acted as discussion leaders. Before the discussion, they worked in the documentation center choosing the text that was to be read and preparing the questions they would ask (van der Meij, 1993).

Two months of observations showed that the students mainly asked text-explicit, low level questions about their texts (e.g., "What's the name of Iviks' father?"). After discussing this finding with the teacher it was decided to try to stimulate the students into asking real questions, questions whose answer could not be found in the text. This led to the introduction of opinion and experience questions (e.g., "Do you like to hunt?", and "Have you ever been arrested?"). The teacher explained these question types and also gave the students some hints for raising such questions and for handling responses. The children immediately caught on to the idea enthusiastically (compare Nicholls, Nelson, & Gleaves, 1995). Raising opinion and experience questions was easy, but the barriers to handling the responses in a nonevaluative way were very hard to overcome. Invariably, the students stopped all discussions short by evaluating the answers, as shown in the dialogue below:

Paul: "Do you like a famine?".

Miriam: (emphatically) "No."

Paul: "Good answer."

Paul: "Where does Ivik live?"

No discussion. The opinion question just turned into another known-answer question.

TEACHERS AS ROLE MODELS

The development of questioning skills is part of most teacher training programs. The approach used for training tends to be called the Socratic or inquiry method. Most of these trainings are at best pseudo-Socratic, however. The Socratic method is "undoubtedly the most misunderstood, yet widely attempted questioning scheme in most classrooms" (Bean, 1985, p. 337). This is illustrated well in one Dutch textbook for teacher training. The textbook uses the famous dialogue between Socrates and Meno's slave boy, which is shown later in this section, to teach its readers how to ask questions. The book does not inform its readers of three vital facts.

First, the reader is not told that this is the only dialogue in which Socrates explicitly shows his method. Had the textbook also given some other dialogues, the reader would have been in a better position to appreciate the more refined notions of the Socratic method—readers can compare the Menexenus (Lysis) dialogue with the slave boy (Meno) dialogue to see the added depth.

Second, the textbook omits the first part of the dialogue in which Socrates arouses the boy's perplexity. He has succeeded in making the boy confused and ignorant. The perplexity provides an important starting point for the boys' active participation in the dialogue. For the reader, it adds direction. The textbook now leaves the reader wondering where Socrates' questions are supposed to lead.

Third, the reader is never told that Socrates held dialogues on topics such as friendship, piety, temperance, beauty, courage, and the like. Nor is the reader told that Socrates may have deliberately chosen a mathematical problem for displaying his method because it permits a definite answer. (Recall that the Menexenus dialogue ends in perplexity.) In short, at best, teachers are learning some of the techniques or skills of asking questions.

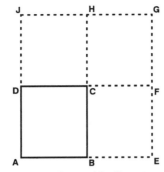

Figure 9.2 The square drawn in the sand by Socrates

Socrates: Tell me, boy, is not ABCD our square of four feet? You understand?

Boy: Yes.

Socrates: Now we can add another equal to it like BCEF?

Boy: Yes.

Socrates: And a third here, CEGH, equal to each of the others?

Boy: Yes.

Socrates: And then we can fill in DCHJ in the corner?

Boy: Yes.

Socrates: Then here we have four equal squares?

Boy: Yes.

Socrates: And how many times the size of the first square is the whole?

Boy: Four times.

Socrates: And we want one double the size. You remember?

Boy: Yes.

Socrates: Now does this line going from corner to corner cut each of these squares in half?

Boy: Yes.

Socrates: And these are four equal lines enclosing the area BEHD?

Boy: They are.

Socrates: Now think. How big is this area?

Boy: I don't understand.

Socrates: Here are four squares. Has not each line cut off the inner half of each of them?

Boy: Yes.

Socrates: And how many such halves are there in this figure BEHD?

Boy: Four.

Socrates: And how many in ABCD?

Boy: Two.

Socrates: And what is the relation of four to two?

Boy: Double.

Socrates: How big is this figure then?

Boy: Eight feet.

Socrates: On what base?

Boy: This one.

Socrates: The line which goes from corner to corner of the square of four feet?

Boy: Yes.

Socrates: The technical name for it is 'diagonal'; so if we use that name, it is your personal opinion that the square on the diagonal of the original square is double its area.

Boy: That is so, Socrates. (Cairns & Hamilton, 1989)

What may be the outcome of this dialogue for the student, for the boy? Does he now know that the square on the diagonal of an original square is double its area? Does he now know how to solve similar problems of calculating the surface? Does he now know how to inquire after the nature of things? John Holt, one of the best observers of classroom life, gives the following answer: "We must not fool ourselves into thinking that guiding children to answers by carefully chosen leading questions is in any respect different from just telling them the answers in the first place.... The only answer that really stick in a child's mind is the answer to a question that he asked or might ask of himself." (Holt, 1965, p. 122).

Traditionally, teacher questioning is full of low level questions. For example, Barba and Cardinale (1991) reported that 91% of the 642 teacher questions they registered during science classroom interactions were of a low level (e.g., factual). Surely, if nine out of ten teacher questions are low level questions, it comes as no surprise that students too are learning to value asking such questions themselves (Alexander, Jetton, Kulikowich, & Woehler, 1994). Asking more higher order questions will make teacher questioning a better model for student questioning. It may help students acquire the knowledge of how to ask better questions. But the heart of the matter will still be lacking and difficult to obtain. In questioning, displayed so wonderfully by Socrates, everything centers around the attitude, the will, the desire of wanting to know. Thereafter, the practice should follow. Students should be given the opportunity to develop their skills in questioning. This will, among other things, mean less teacher questioning.

CONCLUSION

In most schools, the teacher's traditional role as one who transmits knowledge is shifting toward being a discussion leader, a coach, and a conversational partner. The chapter has given some insights, but not yet a detailed agenda, for how these new roles affect teacher questioning. Such an agenda should, however, not be considered all by itself. Changing the teacher's role and contribution to student questioning is likely to succeed only if considered along with other changes in the students' learning environment.

There are many trade-offs to consider here. Collins (1996) sketched the trade-offs for three main areas. The first area concerns learning goals; it has to do with what students should learn. One of the critical issues is when students should aim for memorization and when they should seek understanding. In some conditions it is, for example, not adaptive to ask questions to seek understanding. The second area concerns learning contexts. Trade-offs in this area include deciding when it is desirable to have students engage in active or passive learning, when to aim for incidental learning or direct learning, and whether to design for efficient or natural learning. The third area concerns the sequencing in the learning activities. These may include trade-offs between structured and exploratory learning, between grounded and abstract learning, and between simple and complex learning.

Perhaps, now that computers have made available at our fingertips an incredible amount of information waiting and constructivist learning gains ground, this is the time for revising both the learning environment and the teacher's questioning behavior in service of better student questioning.

REFERENCES

Alexander, P. A. , Jetton, T. L. , Kulikowich, J. M., & Woehler, C. A. (1994). Contrasting instructional and structural importance: The seductive effect of teacher questions. *Journal of Reading Behavior, 26,* 19–45.

Allen, J. (1987). *Natural language understanding.* Menlo Park, CA: Benjamin Cummings.

Armstrong, C. L. (1986). Stages of inquiry in producing art: Model, rationale and application to a teacher questioning strategy. *Studies in Art Education: A Journal of Issues and Research in Art Education, 28,* 37–48.

Armstrong, C. L. (1993). Effect of training in an art production: Questioning method on teacher questioning and student responses. *Studies in Art Education: A Journal of Issues and Research in Art Education, 34,* 209–212.

Barba, R., & Cardinale, L. (1991). Are females invisible students? An investigation of teacher–student questioning interactions. *School Science and Mathematics, 91,* 306–310.

Bean, T. W. (1985). Classroom questioning strategies: Directions for applied research. In A. C. Graesser & J. B. Black (Eds.), *The psychology of questions* (pp. 335–358). Hillsdale, NJ: Lawrence Erlbaum Associates.

Berlyne, D. E. (1960). *Conflict arousal and curiosity.* New York: McGraw-Hill.

Berlyne, D. E. (1965). *Structure and direction in thinking.* New York: Wiley.

Byrnes, J. P., & Guthrie, J. T. (1992). Prior conceptual knowledge and textbook search. *Contemporary Educational Psychology, 17,* 8–29.

Cairns, H., & Hamilton, E. *The collected dialogues of Plato* (1987, Trans.) Princeton, NJ: Princeton University Press.

Chinn, C. A., & Brewer, W. F. (1993). The role of anomalous data in knowledge acquisition: A theoretical framework and implications for science instruction. *Review of Educational Research, 63,* 1–49.

Collins, A. (1996). Design issues for learning environments. In S. Vosniadou, E. de Corte, R. Glaser, & H. Mandl (Eds.), *International perspectives on the design of technology supported learning environments* (pp. 347–361). Mahwah, NJ: Lawrence Erlbaum Associates.

Corno, L. (1993). The best-laid plans: Modern conceptions of volition and educational research. *Educational Researcher, 22,* 14–22.

Dillon, J. T. (1982). Problem finding and solving. *Journal of Creative Behavior, 16,* 97–111.

Dillon, J. T. (1986). Questioning. In O. Hargie (Ed.), *A handbook of communication skills* (pp. 95–127). London: Croom Helm.

Dillon, J. T. (1988). *Questioning and teaching: A manual of practice.* New York: Teachers College.

Dillon, J. T. (1990). *The practice of questioning.* New York: Routledge.

Dillon, J. T. (1991). Questioning the use of questions. *Journal of Educational Psychology, 83,* 163–164.

Doblaev, L. P. (1984). *Studieteksten lezen en begrijpen* [Reading and understanding study texts]. Apeldoorn, the Netherlands: Van Walraven. (Original work published 1982)

Dreher, M. J., & Brown, R. F. (1993). Planning prompts and indexed terms in textbook search tasks. *Journal of Educational Psychology, 85,* 662–669.

Dreher, M. J., & Guthrie, J. T. (1990). Cognitive processes in textbook chapter search tasks. *Reading Research Quarterly, 25,* 323–339.

Flammer, A. (1986, May). *Asking a question: Which one—if any?* Paper presented at the meeting of the Memphis Conference on Question Generation, Memphis, TN.

Gall, M. D., & Artero-Boname, M. T. (1994). Questioning strategies. In T. Husén & T. N. Postlethwaite (Eds.), *The international encyclopedia of education,* (2nd ed. pp. 4875–4882). Oxford, England: Pergamon.

Getzels, J. W. (1982). The problem of the problem. In R. Hogarth (Ed.), *New directions for methodology of social and behavioral science: Question framing and response consistency* (pp. 37–49). San Francisco: Jossey-Bass.

Getzels, J. W. (1988). Problem finding and creative thought. *Questioning Exchange, 2,* 95–103.

Good, T. L., Slavings, R. L., Harel, K., & Emerson, K. (1987). Student passivity: A study of question asking in K–12 classrooms. *Sociology of Education, 60,* 181–199

Good, T. L. , Slavings, R. L., & Mason, D. A. (1988). Learning to ask questions: Grade and school effects. *Teaching and Teacher Education, 4,* 363–378.

Grice, H. P. (1975). Logic and conversation. In P. Cole & J. L. Morgan (Eds.), *Syntax and semantics* (Vol. 3, pp. 41–59). New York: Academic Press.

Holt, J. (1965). *How children fail.* London: Pitman.

Husén, T., & Postlethwaite, T. N. (Eds.) (1994). *The international encyclopedia of education* (2nd ed.). Oxford, England: Pergamon.

Karabenick, S. A. (1994). Relation of perceived teacher support of student questioning to students' beliefs about teacher attributions for questioning and perceived classroom learning environment. *Learning and Individual Differences, 6,* 187–204.

Karabenick, S. A., & Sharma, R. (1994). Perceived teacher support of student questioning in the college classroom: Its relation to student characteristics and role in the classroom questioning process. *Journal of Educational Psychology, 86,* 90–103.

King, A. (1991). Effects of training in strategic questioning on children's problem-solving performance. *Journal of Educational Psychology, 83,* 307–317.

King, A. (1994). Autonomy and question asking: The role of personal control in guided student-generated questioning. *Learning and Individual Differences, 6,* 163–185.

Kobasigawa, A. (1983). Children's retrieval skills for school learning. *The Alberta Journal of Educational Research, 29,* 259–271.

Markman, E. M. (1979). Realizing that you don't understand: Elementary school children's awareness of inconsistencies. *Child Development, 50,* 643–655.

Mehan, H. (1979). "What time is it, Denise?": Asking known-information questions in classroom discourse. *Theory into Practice, 28,* 285–294.

Nelson-Le Gall, S. (1985). Help-seeking behavior in learning. In E. W. Gordon (Ed.), *Review of research in education* (Vol. 12, pp. 55–90). Washington, DC: American Educational Research Association.

Newman, R. S. (1991). Goals and self-regulated learning: What motivates children to seek academic help? In M. L. Maehr & P. R. Pintrich (Eds.), *Advances in motivation and achievement: Vol. 7. Goals and self-regulatory processes* (pp. 123–146). Greenwich, CT: JAI.

Nicholls, J., Nelson, J. R., & Gleaves, K. (1995). Learning "facts" versus learning that most questions have many answers: Student evaluations of contrasting curricula. *Journal of Educational Psychology, 87,* 253–260.

Nielsen, R. S. (1988) Improving teacher questioning. *Illinois School Research and Development, 24,* 94–101.

Postman, N. (1988). *Conscientious objections: Stirring up trouble about language, technology, and education.* New York: Vintage Books.

Reder, L. M. (1987). Strategy selection in question answering. *Cognitive Psychology, 19,* 90–138.

Scardamalia, M., & Bereiter, C. (1991). Higher levels of agency for children in knowledge building: A challenge for the design of new knowledge media. *The Journal of the Learning Sciences, 1,* 7–68.

Scardamalia, M., & Bereiter, C. (1992). Text-based and knowledge-based questioning by children. *Cognition and Instruction, 9,* 177–199.

Scardamalia, M., & Bereiter, C. (1993). Technologies for knowledge-building discourse. *Communications of the ACM, 36,* 37–41.

Symons, S., & Pressley, M. (1993). Prior knowledge affects text search success and extraction of information. *Reading Research Quarterly, 28,* 250–261.

Taylor, R. S. (1968). Question-negotiation and information seeking in libraries. *College & Research Libraries, 29,* 178–194.

van der Meij, H. (1986). *Questioning: A study on the questioning behavior of elementary school children.* The Hague, The Netherlands: Stichting voor Onderzoek van het Onderwijs.

van der Meij, H. (1987). Assumptions of information-seeking questions. *Questioning Exchange, 1,* 111–117.

van der Meij, H. (1988). Constraints on question-asking in classrooms. *Journal of Educational Psychology, 3,* 401–405.

van der Meij, H. (1990a). Effects of prior knowledge on question asking. *Zeitschrift für Pädagogische Psychologie, 4,* 87–96.

van der Meij, H. (1990b). Question asking: To know that you don't know is not enough. *Journal of Educational Psychology, 82,* 505–512.

van der Meij, H. (1993). What's the title? A case study of questioning in reading. *Journal of Research in Reading, 16,* 46–56.

van der Meij, H. (1994). Student questioning: A componential analysis. *Learning and Individual Differences, 6,* 137–161.

van der Meij, H., & Dillon, J. T. (1994). Adaptive student questioning and students' verbal ability. *Journal of Experimental Education, 62,* 277–290.

van der Meij, H., Meer, M., & Ponte, M. (1989). Vragen stellen op de LOM-school [Questioning in special education]. *Nederlands Tijdschrift voor Opvoeding, Vorming en Onderwijs, 5,* 279–287.

van Zee, E. H., & Minstrell, J. (1997a) Using questioning to guide student thinking. *The Journal of the Learning Sciences, 6,* 2, 227–269.

van Zee, E. H., & Minstrell, J. (1997b). Reflective discourse: Developing shared understanding in a physics classroom. *International Journal of Science Education, 19,* 2, 209–228.

West, R., & Pearson, J. C. (1994). Antecedent and consequent conditions of student questioning: an analysis of classroom discourse across the university. *Communication Education, 43,* 299–311.

Help Seeking in the Information Age

Jane A. Keefer
West Chester University

Stuart A. Karabenick
Eastern Michigan University

Technology's impact on learning and teaching is increasingly attributable to the exponential growth of computer-mediated communication and the availability of information. The ability to use a few
commands or hypertext selections to access a wide variety of
databases or contact other individuals can dramatically affect both
how and what students learn. Although the consequences of information technology and communication for learning and educational
institutions are the subject of continual discussion and debate (e.g.,
Cognition and Technology Group at Vanderbilt, 1996; Jonassen,
1996), their impact on the incidence and form of help seeking has
not been systematically examined. We undertake this analysis by
drawing on research in education, library science and information
systems, and communications. We begin by describing the changing
information environment, the help-seeking process, and how the
characteristics of computer-mediated communication (CMC) environments affect that process. Examined next is how the assistance
that libraries provide has adapted to technological change and
parallels are drawn between the processes of help seeking and
information search. We conclude by discussing the implications of
changing information technologies for information service professionals, classrooms, and teachers and raise the issue of whether
increasingly sophisticated artificial assistance may force us to reconsider the definition of help seeking as necessarily including social
agency (i.e., human intervention).

THE INFORMATION ENVIRONMENT

Just how much has the information environment grown? If information is taken to be the general encoding of human meaning as expressed first orally, then by written and printed languages, and now further encoded into a variety of machine readable formats, then an examination of commercial production is a reasonable index of growth. Although scholars may not agree on when the Information Age was born (Schement & Curtis, 1995) it is clear that the 1960s was the decade that signaled a major production shift. As shown in Fig. 10.1, in 1960, the total U.S. book title production was slightly over 15,000 volumes. By 1970, this figure had more than doubled to 36,000 titles (Hokkanen, 1981). No other twentieth century decade comes close to this rate of expansion. U.S. publishing output has increased by more than an order of magnitude since 1900, moving from an initial output of some 2,000 titles to 56,000 in 1987, with the latest figures showing the publication of nearly 50,000 titles in 1993. A parallel expansion in scientific publishing is also evident. Using the chemical research literature as an example, from 1907 to 1996 the number of papers abstracted annually by the American Chemical Society's Chemical Abstracts Service (CAS) jumped from nearly 8,000 to close to 580,000. Overall the cumulative total of all types of CAS abstracts grew from close to 12,000 in 1907 to some 16.9 million in 1996 (Chemical Abstract Service, 1997).

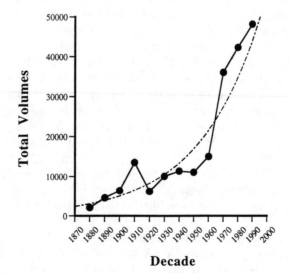

Decade

FIG. 10.1 Total U.S. Book Production. Based on data from Hokkanen (1981) and Grannis (1992).

The search for a specific piece of information in this huge and ever growing haystack can be daunting indeed. In the 1990s, the Internet and the World Wide Web (Web) hypertext transfer protocol (HTTP) produced a similar explosive expansion, as electronic mass storage costs have decreased and the telecommunications infrastructure required to support the expanded traffic has increased. In a very brief time, graphics-based Internet systems have been transformed from a primarily scholarly research medium to a general public, commercial, media-oriented, and advertising subsidized system. Commercial search services are now ubiquitous, with claims for the number of Web pages indexed ranging from 20 to 80 million (Anon., 1997; Falk, 1997). Despite some serious limitations, libraries of all kinds are starting to use the Web for ready reference (Koutnik, 1997). It is also easier to communicate with others about that information. The Internet erases spatial and temporal boundaries, and soon most of the developed (and even developing) world will have global access, with the number of permanently connected host computers almost doubling in one year (from 14.7 million to 26 million).

In order to more completely understand the new environment in which help seeking will increasingly occur, it is useful to review the evolution of information systems as structures that employ information management technology. These technologies, rooted in manual methodologies associated with the development of libraries and card catalogs in the nineteenth century, have been amplified considerably. At every stage of this development, the increase in information has been the mother of invention, spawning new technologies to manage and provide access to the larger knowledge base. These new technologies, in turn, encouraged the generation of even greater amounts of information to be organized, stored, and retrieved. Accompanying these enhancements are new interfaces that function as intermediaries between system users and the stored information.

Although developed to facilitate access to information, early interfaces were not designed from the user's point of view. Thus, it is not surprising that the development of information intermediary tools has been paralleled by an increase in the need for information mediators, such as librarians, technical information professionals, and information brokers, whose function is to assist users in overcoming barriers to access. It is important to distinguish between mediators, who guide and assist information seekers in the use of information systems, and intermediators, which are the interfaces and tools of information access (Kuhlthau, 1993). Although both can provide assistance in obtaining information, human mediators are considered the sources we approach when seeking help in information intensive environments. Because information mediators are important sources of assistance, their characteristics and relationships to those seeking information are critical.

Attempts to quantify and define information have been undertaken within a number of disciplines, including physics (Brillouin, 1963), biology (Wicken, 1987; Young, 1987), psychology (Cutting, 1987), and psychiatry (Bateson, 1972). Practical and useful mathematical formulations of information are generally concerned with the symbolic encoding and decoding of messages from one system or medium to another (Shannon & Weaver, 1964; Rapoport, 1953). Concepts such as channels, noise, messages, redundancy, senders, and receivers form the basis of our modern telecommunications infrastructure. Efforts to transfer such concepts to the level of human communication have, however, been much less successful. Although it is easy enough to generate statistics about information activities, such as books circulated, accuracy of answers to reference questions, and audience ratings, these say little about the meanings communicated or the uses made of the information (Dervin, 1976).

For this and other reasons, the consideration of information as inherently embedded in human situations, goals, and processes is now the theme and focus of much research in a number of areas (Dervin & Nilan, 1986). Although we speak of information as existing in documents, books, and now computers, in actuality this is a convenient shorthand for information as the encoding of human meaning stored in these various documents and texts. Furthermore, this meaning is socially constructed out of the shared experience of human beings as they inherit and adapt to their immediate sociocultural environment (Keefer, 1994). An important issue for information management is the conflict between information as process versus content.

Generally, as information systems evolve beyond the individual and personal sphere, their organization necessarily responds to the human need for control and access. Prior to the development of the computer, the technologies of access were relatively stable. They consisted primarily of classification systems and indexing methodologies, including such basic techniques as cross-referencing (a precursor of hypertext), keyword concordances, and field-assigned indexing (e.g., authors, titles, subjects, and citation). These basic information management techniques remain central to much of our modern digitized systems, but they are now amplified by many orders of magnitude via computer processing. Additionally, computers have facilitated the synergistic development of these techniques in combinations not previously possible. Later, we describe the development of information archiving and retrieval, including developments of the Web that provide near instantaneous access to information without regard to location. As we will see, a central theme is the shift in focus from systems to users and its relevance for the help-seeking process.

Information Seeking and Help Seeking

Before proceeding further, however, it is useful to draw some important distinctions between information seeking and help seeking, terms that are often used interchangeably, especially by those in the library and information sciences (e.g., Kuhlthau, 1993). In Dervin's (1992) sensemaking approach to information seeking, for example (to be discussed in detail later), information is anything that helps people progress toward their goals. Because other individuals could provide that assistance, help seeking would be subsumed under Dervin's definition. Examples would be obtaining information from a reference librarian or asking another student for assistance in locating an article for a term paper. Dervin's definition may be overinclusive, however, because not all information seeking involves seeking help. Using a library computer to determine whether the book is available, for example, may constitute seeking information, but it does not involve seeking help. Nor of course is information a necessary component of all help seeking, such as asking someone else to check out a library book. Thus, even though help seeking frequently has an informational component, and information seeking often requires assistance, it would be inappropriate to consider them synonymous. In fact, we see later the utility of contrasting these two processes.

THE HELP-SEEKING PROCESS

Several heuristic models have been used to describe the help-seeking process (Gross & McMullen, 1983; Nelson-Le Gall, Gumerman, & Scott-Jones, 1983; Newman, 1994; van der Meij, 1986) as involving a series of decisions that, in many respects, mirror decision models of help giving (Latané & Darley, 1970). Although persons may not be mindful of all phases of the process or experience them in the order specified by the models, the sequence of steps described is probably typical. The precipitating event in help-seeking episodes is thought to occur when people judge they have inadequate resources to complete a task (Rosen, 1983). This may be a function of insufficient information, the perceived inability to understand material (i.e., inadequate declarative knowledge), not knowing the steps necessary to complete an assignment (i.e., inadequate procedural knowledge), or the results of evaluations, such as poor grades on exams or assignments. When judged inadequacy exceeds some threshold (Newman, 1994; Rosen,

1983), and dependent on patterns of causal attributions (Ames, 1983; Weiner, 1985), seeking help may be considered an option to continued persistence or abandoning the task.

Once problems are acknowledged, the relative benefits and costs of seeking or not seeking help become critical (DePaulo, Nadler, & Fisher, 1983; Spacapan & Oskamp, 1992). In addition to the effort and time required to obtain help, considerable research has focused on the need to reciprocate and indebtedness to the help provider (Greenberg & Westcott, 1983), overcoming culturally prescribed individualism (van der Meij, 1986), public disclosure and embarrassment (Karabenick & Knapp, 1988b; Shapiro, 1983), and most generally, threat to self-esteem (Fisher, Nadler, & Whitcher-Alagna, 1982; Karabenick & Knapp, 1991; Nadler & Fisher, 1986). There is considerable evidence, for example, that the perceived threat to self-esteem from seeking help is inversely related to college students' intentions to seek help (Karabenick & Knapp, 1991), to the amount of help sought during an academic term (Karabenick & Knapp, 1991; Knapp & Karabenick, 1988b), and to the likelihood of asking questions in class (Karabenick & Sharma, 1994).

Some of the relative costs and benefits of help seeking are linked to types of helping resources, differentiated primarily according to the degree of formality. Informal (e.g., classmates, friends, family) compared to formal resources (e.g., teachers, study skills personnel) are generally not as threatening, are more available, and require less time and effort to access. However, they may not have the required expertise and, except for communal relationships (Clark, 1983), are more likely to induce indebtedness, the need to reciprocate, and inferiority (Fisher, Nadler, & Whitcher-Alagna, 1982). Whereas younger children may prefer help from teachers (formal source) rather than peers (Nelson-Le Gall & Gumerman, 1984; Newman & Goldin, 1990), studies indicate a general preference for help from informal sources (Knapp & Karabenick, 1988b; Spacapan & Oskamp, 1992). And how learners approach and negotiate the process depends on help-seeking goals (executive vs. instrumental; Nelson-Le Gall, 1981), degree of self-regulation (Newman, 1994), and learning goals (e.g., ego, mastery; Arbreton, this volume; Ryan & Pintrich, this volume) that are present.

COMPUTER-MEDIATED COMMUNICATION

As did voice communication before it, computer mediation has increased the potential for frequent interaction among individuals. The most common types of CMC are one to one (e-mail), one to many (e.g., bulletin boards, e-mail distribution lists), and many to many (e.g., computer conferencing systems, listservs) as well as more customized applications such as computer supported cooperative work and group decision support systems. Each type of CMC functions somewhat differently, but all involve conversations using text (although increasingly accompanied by graphics and sound) among individuals or groups that are mediated by a computer interface. The sheer amount of communication and the characteristics that distinguish CMC from face-to-face communication, video conferencing, and telephone conversations (including voice mail), have important implications for both the likelihood and the type of help seeking that occurs in learning contexts. With the advent of the Internet and e-mail during the late 1970s and early 1980s, researchers began to examine how these characteristics affected such variables as the types and rates of participation in discussions and effects on social roles (e.g., Harasim, 1986, 1993; Heydinger, 1978; Hiltz & Turoff, 1978; Kerr & Hiltz, 1982; Romiszowski & Mason, 1996; Williams, 1977), and that research continues (e.g., Hiltz, 1990). Although these studies did not examined help seeking per se, they offered evidence to suggest what those effects might be.

Social Status Cues

Among the most important characteristics of CMC is the absence of contextual and non-verbal cues that provide most of the information that is present, even unavoidable, in face-to-face interactions (Baron, 1984; Baym, 1995; Chesboro & Bonsall, 1989; Keisler, Siegel, & McGuire, 1984; Mehrabian, 1981; Walther & Burgoon, 1992). Unless supplied by the interactant, absent are cues to such social categories as sex, age, race, physical attractiveness, and the myriad others (e.g., style of dress) that are used to infer beliefs, attitudes, and dispositions and that convey much of the emotional tone of face-to-face conversations. Even when such discretionary information is provided, its lower salience in CMC is likely to reduce its social impact (Fiske, 1980; Latané, 1981). The lack of manifest social status cues has considerable consequences, especially in task-related discussions in hierarchical group structures (Keisler, Siegel, & McGuire, 1984). As status differences diminish, there tends to be greater participation (e.g., Barnes & Greller, 1994; McComb, 1994) by lower status group members, such as women and minorities who might be hesitant to contribute in certain face-to-face interactions (Baron, 1984). The evidence thus suggests that in CMC environments, more information is communicated, and it is more evenly distributed.

Anonymity

CMC also provides interactants with relative degrees of anonymity, which is virtually complete with the use of pseudonyms (or handles), although it decreases with such identifiers as computer IDs. As would be expected, communicants are less inhibited with complete anonymity, and is evidenced even when identifiers are present. The general experience is that the CMC interface creates greater psychological distance and a measure of protection that would seem unwarranted, even when actual names accompany messages (Myers, 1987; Reid, 1991).

Archiving, Forwarding, and Publishing

In what can be considered the obverse of anonymity, archiving, forwarding, and publishing CMC material create conditions that would be expected to increase inhibition. However, despite the fact that one's communications are potentially available to entire communities, from small groups and classroom peers to many hundreds and thousands in the case of large listservs and newsgroups, people seem willing to convey very personal information, seemingly oblivious to these possibilities. Once again, this appears attributable to the lack of proximal cues that make such contingencies salient.

Timing

The temporal characteristics of CMC can also be disinhibiting. In contrast to face-to-face communication, most CMC is asynchronous, with varying time intervals (from minutes to days) between messages. Although to a lesser degree, such temporal safe havens are even present in synchronous (chat) systems given the leeway afforded by the requirement that messages be converted to text. Delays that would not be tolerated in ordinary conversations or discussions are woven into the fabric of the medium, freeing communicants to reflect, compose, and edit their remarks before publishing them.

Community, Cues, and Identity

In contrast to the specter that CMC environments would increase societal distancing and formalism, there is often substantial cohesion among participants in the thousands of online communities that arise from shared interests and the social networks that form in task-oriented groups (Jones, 1995). Baym (1995), for example, describes the conditions that affect how such communities develop in ways that make them more comfortable. Included are the invented social cues to convey common expressions (such as the ubiquitous smiley face, or acronyms such as ROFL (for rolling on the floor with laughter; see Danet & Rosenberg, 1992), and the emergence of experimentation with alternate social identities and self-disclosure (Myers, 1987; Reid, 1991).

Implications for Help Seeking

We can summarize the effects of CMC as increasing the potential for people to initiate and to maintain communicative relationships under conditions that engender informality and decreased threat. Although not inevitable (e.g., Spears & Lea, 1994), the consequences of reduced threat include more self-disclosure and egalitarian information flow. From what is known about the pivotal role played by threat, it follows that CMC environments should be very conducive to help seeking, especially under highly evaluative conditions and for persons more threatened by public admissions that help is needed (Karabenick, 1987; Karabenick & Knapp, 1988a; 1991).

In addition to the general reduction in threat, CMC may even affect the comprehension monitoring process (Markman, 1985) by increasing the frequency of episodes of noncomprehension. By creating more communication channels for discussion (e.g., in class computer conferences), for example, learners may be more likely to become aware that others (co-learners) have questions about material they are attempting to comprehend, as suggested by evidence that becoming aware that others have questions raises doubts about one's own level of understanding (Glaser & Bassok, 1989; Karabenick, 1996). Because of the richer communications environment, therefore, there is a greater likelihood that learners will determine that they are inadequate and need help. Combined with lower levels of threat, CMC should therefore increase the frequency of requests for assistance. And, iteratively, the increased likelihood of help seeking under those conditions may affect norms so as to destigmatize such requests. Members of listservs and newsgroups, for example, are notorious for encouraging and responding to questions and requests for information and help, which constitutes much of the traffic in large CMC communities.

Four additional factors may contribute to more prevalent help seeking. First, because the status relationships in CMC tend to be more egalitarian, communicants are likely to be perceived as more informal, which, as noted earlier, are preferred to formal sources (e.g., Knapp & Karabenick, 1988b). Second, requests for assistance in most CMC environments are directed at multiple targets rather than individuals, which reduces the perceived burden that the help seeker imposes on any one group member (division of social impact; see Latané, 1981). Third, help seeking is likely to be more successful, and even of higher quality, because there tends to be more potential sources of assistance in CMC environments. Finally, using CMC generally reduces the effort that people often cite as the reason for not seeking help (Karabenick & Knapp, 1991).

In summary, CMC social environments should facilitate help seeking (as well as help giving) because of the reduced threat that is created by increased psychological distance, forgiving temporal communication requirements, and the lower salience of status. Students using CMC, for example, are more likely to contact their instructors—leaving an e-mail message is more convenient than arranging an office visit, and students are likely to perceive that responding asynchronously is not as burdensome for instructors, which renders the exchange less inequitable. These and other advantages of CMC for instruction were discovered soon after its introduction (Welsch, 1982). For example, "students could ask questions without publicly embarrassing themselves" (G. Phillips & Santoro, 1989, pp. 159–160). CMC creates a comparably receptive context for communicating with mediators (e.g., reference personnel) by those seeking information, which we now turn to beginning with the role of libraries and library systems.

KNOWLEDGE INTERMEDIATION SYSTEMS

Libraries

Although we now think of information systems as necessarily computer based, libraries, and especially academic libraries, have always served as their predigital equivalent. Indeed, for centuries libraries have functioned as repositories of the cumulative store of human knowledge. In educational settings, this sense of the library as a knowledge commons is particularly appropriate as teachers and learners alike search and re-search this knowledge store to accomplish learning and scholarly tasks (Plum, 1994). Libraries and other print-based information systems typically contain two kinds of information. The first, called content or primary, refers to the information in texts and articles, whereas the second type, termed pointer or secondary, points to, or is an index for, the content information. Systematically organized pointer information thus functions as an information intermediation system. Historically, as library collections expanded, these intermediation technologies developed in two ways. Archivally, new storage media such as microfilm were developed, and organizationally, finding tools expanded both in size and complexity.

As classification schemes were researched and developed, indexing became a professional activity carried out by specialists, and handbooks and data collections began to be published in increasing variety and size, ranging from multivolume data systems to directories, dictionaries, and bibliographies for every conceivable subject area. Initially, library users and information seekers were expected to learn how to use these finding aids on their own. However, as library collections grew and the tools themselves became more complex, the need for human mediation became apparent. In response, the now familiar reference desk staffed by librarians became an integral part of all types of libraries. The demand for reference, first publicly articulated more than a century ago by Green (1876), can be taken as one indicator of the beginnings of the modern information society. As described by Green, and later articulated by Rothstein (1961), the library reference function provides patrons (or in more modern terminology, users or clients) with three basic types of service—guidance, information, and instruction—each of which can be construed as providing assistance.

Guidance. Guidance services generally are concerned with advice about the kind of information to be sought. Public libraries have a long history of reader advisory services that recommend genres, as well as specific titles. A similar function is provided by academic libraries within the context of term paper counseling sessions. Such functions require direct knowledge of the items being recommended, and many best of type books are published to meet this need. As library holdings have shifted to electronic formats, the distinction between instruction and guidance has blurred because recommendations can point to either primary or secondary sources and digital resources may require assistance and instruction in their use. From the perspective of help seeking goals, therefore, reference guidance services can serve both executive and instrumental functions.

Information. Information services are generally involved with providing some known item data or well defined specific information in response to queries. These range from the delivery of entire documents to providing missing details of bibliographic citations. Broadly construed, these services may include both facts and secondary information, such as the results of database searches, selective dissemination of information (SDI), annotated bibliographies, and summary research reports. In every case, the person seeking assistance does not participate directly in the information search but instead delegates the search. Information is received in the same way that help may be received in response to an executive request for assistance. Most ready reference services by telephone, and now e-mail, fall into this category, which is discussed further in the section on electronic reference.

Instruction. Instructional services are especially prominent in educational settings where the use of academic and school libraries is an integral part of students' learning assignments. Such services aim to provide users with the knowledge required to find information on their own with little or no assistance, and thus can be contrasted with information delivery services described earlier. Hence, instructional services are functional for instrumental (adaptive and self-regulatory) rather than executive help-seeking goals. Acquiring these skills is considered essential for scholars and researchers in a discipline or subject area. Instruction may be delivered in one-on-one or group settings, and the outcome, often called information literacy, may include learning how to use libraries efficiently, understanding how to develop searching strategies at both specific and general levels, and developing a practical knowledge of specific information finding tools (Bopp, 1995). Referred to as bibliographic instruction (BI) in academic libraries, the format is typically a single lecture delivered by librarians either in the classroom or on site, but can also include formal courses for credit.

Because BI can be viewed primarily as an instrumental, adaptive strategy, studies have examined whether it successfully reduces users' subsequent need to ask for help. Most, but not all, evaluations do indicate that users have some improved ability to maneuver success-fully within the library's informational terrain without assistance. The degree to which this is true depends on whether BI includes conceptual and real world assignments that provide hands-on practice, something that the predominant instruction vehicle, a single lecture, cannot easily accomplish. Some librarians have proposed, therefore, that BI, at least in abbreviated form, be abandoned because, for the most part, it fails to fulfill its primary instrumental function of producing independent users (Eadie, 1990).

Whatever its value in reducing the subsequent need for assistance, BI might also function to encourage help seeking as a strategy for successful information seeking (Mann, 1993). That is because BI sessions often include content and experiences that can affect the decision to seek needed help. Even if conveyed during a single BI session, assurance that both asking for help and anxiety are not uncommon experiences when searching for information, especially at early stages of the process, should lead to more effective search behavior, which includes asking for help when needed (Keefer, 1993; Mellon, 1988).

One-on-one instruction or consultation is at the heart of what has become known generally as the reference interview, and considerable discussion has been generated as to the appropriate interpersonal and communication skills that will produce the best results for information seekers (Bunge, 1984; Doyle-Wilch & Miller, 1992). As noted by Taylor (1968), Mellon (1987), and others, users for a variety of reasons may not express their full information needs initially when seeking help.

Instead, patrons may express their need in terms of what they believe the system has to offer (Mann, 1993), or ask a broad test question to determine the ability of a mediator to provide assistance (Dewdney & Ross, 1994). Dervin and Dewdney (1986) and others have discussed techniques for enhancing communication skills of this primary mediating service. Several researchers have documented that important factors in a successful reference transaction are patron satisfaction and a mediator's ability to determine their users' information needs (Blackwell, 1995; Durrance, 1989; Dyson, 1992). Such results clearly have implications for the development of computer-mediated reference services and help seeking in the information search process.

Reference and CMC

As suggested earlier, the characteristics of CMC offer important advantages for the effective use of reference services, and several forms of CMC are now being integrated into the reference process. Privacy, the convenience of being able to ask and answer questions without regard to time or place, and the informal character of e-mail and other forms of CMC can alleviate difficulties for library users. This is especially true for those with limited information seeking skills. CMC expands the pool of resources available to information seekers even further by providing reference librarians themselves with additional resources of their own. From the beginning, librarians have created and participated in information-oriented listservs that function as forums for answering difficult patron questions. Ranging from general reference listservs, such as STUMPERS-L, to subject-specific information-oriented forums, these discussions are most effective at providing specialized information and general guidance assistance (Ladner & Tillman, 1993). This serves both the executive and instrumental help-seeking goals of professionals who provide assistance to others.

A second form of computer-mediated reference is the use of e-mail for patron inquiries. Academic libraries now routinely provide a means for e-mail reference questions on Web pages that describe services with direct links to networked resources. Because most Web pages are open to anyone at any time and students may connect through nonacademic Internet services, the inquirer's relation to the library can be difficult to ascertain. However, a survey of e-mail factual type reference questions (Bushallow-Wilbur, DeVinney, & Whitcomb, 1996) noted that faculty and graduate students accounted for more than two thirds of the users and that most usage was from offices during the day. Furthermore, consistent with the discussion of CMC earlier, more than half of the respondents listed e-mail as their preferred means of asking ready reference-type questions.

When the queries involve how to conduct database searches or more topically oriented requests for help, the need for question negotiation combined with the asynchronous nature of e-mail can be problematic. Abels (1996), for example, discussed these issues with respect to a project that used library science students as mediators. She noted that because of the time lag between replies, clarification of queries could involve many messages and extend over weeks. Without a systematic strategy, therefore, many of the interviews failed to produce the desired results for the client. Using a series of logically organized questions and fill-in-the-blanks forms similar to those used for written reference requests improved client satisfaction; some problems remained, however, due to the delays in feedback to patrons.

Computer Supported Cooperative Training (CSCT) environments may offer a solution to the need for real time feedback. Swigger and Hartness (1996) described such a computer system for information retrieval, where groups can converse in real time while using structured forms and search tools. Novice online search mediators, who were consulted by students seeking information for a term paper, were judged more effective in producing usable citations than were face-to-face pairs. The structured environment of the CSCT pairs appear to have stimulated the novice mediators to engage in more question negotiation, in effect teaching them how to conduct a reference interview.

How Much Help To Give?

Throughout the evolution of library reference services, there has been a tension between information delivery and information empowerment (White, 1992). At the one extreme, there is the philosophy of full and complete delivery of information to patrons. In this case, the library functions as the intermediary agent for users who depend on the library to execute their request for assistance. According to this perspective, librarians function as executive helping agents, performing a job or acting as information brokers who deliver specific information on request. At the other extreme is the philosophy of the self-reliant user who will have no need for help of any kind. Within this latter tradition, two complementary approaches are advocated. First, because there will always be new users, the librarian's main mediating function is to provide assistance that develops greater self-regulation; that is, the primary function of reference must include a strong instructional component (Lewis, 1995). The second view, moving further back in the information chain, champions the development of computerized intermediation tools that are sufficiently user friendly (Marchionini, 1995) so as not to require help. Similarly, within the context of physical libraries, the prevention of questions is advocated by instituting a systematic program to analyze and correct library failures, in essence, improving the physical library interface (Rettig, 1992).

INFORMATION SCIENCE: FROM DOCUMENT MANAGEMENT TO INFORMATION SEARCHING

The information environment in which help is often required is reflected in the emergence and development of information science (IS). Prior to the appearance of computer technology, research on information was concerned with document management and control, and the technology was focused on the efficient storage and retrieval of nonprint media such as microfilm. A vision of what was to come was articulated by Bush (1996) in his now famous article that described a primitive hypertext system that would manage what he and others were beginning to recognize as the coming postwar information explosion. Bush's original concepts became the basis for later work by Nelson (1988), who coined the term hypertext, along with others who developed modern hypertext information systems (Simpson, Renear, Mylonas, & van Dam, 1996).

From the first, it was obvious that computers could provide help by relieving much of the burden of manual searching in print indexes for articles and books. Thus, the newly created discipline of IS began to develop and design computerized versions of index and abstracting tools that formed the basis of information intermediation systems. Like all new technologies, these early databases imitated the older print indexes and were organized using the well-established bibliographic categories of author, title, journal or source title, subject headings, call number, and so forth. Although these early first generation information retrieval systems (IRS) could search vast stores of data, it was still necessary for seekers of information to have a knowledge of the pre-established subject terms and to understand the filing order of the various categorical indexes. Thus, these systems generally required human mediators at both the query and computer level to process users' requests. To address this problem, several key concepts, especially keyword searching and Boolean operators (e.g., AND, NOT, OR) were introduced with the intent of reducing the need for human assistance in information retrieval. Although these concepts enhanced the effectiveness of modern IRS, they also required users to understand new concepts and to explicitly formulate their information needs in ways quite different from print search tools. Human mediation was often required either in executive or instrumental form.

Early IRS research identified two basic types of information retrieval failure. The system either returned too many off-topic hits or
failed to retrieve all the relevant records. Using the mathematically
defined concepts of precision and recall to describe these phenomena,
researchers began to investigate factors leading to improvements in
these variables. This research, using both artificial and actual IRS
(Swets, 1969), indicated a trade-off between the two values, in contrast
to the desired ideal of high precision and recall. Although these two
concepts are convenient mathematical relations to evaluate the effectiveness of IRS, their values ultimately depend on what users subjec-
tively judge as relevant or useful (Neill, 1987; Swanson, 1986). Many
system-oriented ways to overcome or compensate for this subjectivity
were tried, with little or no improvement.

The greatest improvements came from user relevance feedback
studies (Salton, 1985) and, ultimately, researchers turned to detailed
studies of human–computer interactions from the user's perspective
rather than the system's. Using concepts from cognitive psychology
and analyzing user-mediator transcripts, Belkin (1980) proposed a
more process-oriented understanding of the information system–user interaction. His model focused on the user's initial inability
to articulate fully their information needs, as detailed by professional
mediators in their interviews with clients seeking information from
online databases. This basic problem, described earlier in the library
world by Taylor (1968) in his question negotiation model, is that, if
users knew exactly what information they needed, there would be no
need to ask for it. Belkin's approach, which defined a new paradigm
within the computer-based IRS community, was the first to explicitly
consider the cognitive component of information seeking.

INFORMATION RETRIEVAL
AND THE INFORMATION SEARCH PROCESS

Since the 1970s, there has been a flurry of user-centered studies
designed to improve the functioning of computer-based intermediary
information retrieval tools (Sugar, 1995). Two basic approaches to
understanding the nature of user–system interactions have evolved.
The first approach, emanating from the computer-oriented IRS area,
focuses on describing and understanding user conversations with
both human and machine mediators, whereas the second examines
the information seeking process as experienced and described by
individuals. Both approaches employ naturalistic, qualitative methods supplemented by laboratory-based quantitative experiments.

Computer Help: The Human–Computer Interaction(HCI) and Information Science

From the very beginning of their development, software and artificial systems have generated a need for assistance in their use. Because early software was primarily text based and command driven, HCI research focused on creating natural language help systems, so that users could ask for help without having to remember arcane commands. A useful method for understanding the context of natural language help systems is the Wizard of Oz (WOZ) technique, wherein a human, who is remotely connected to the user's computer, simulates a natural language help system. In such studies, the WOZ has limited or no knowledge about what appears on the user's screen and may provide natural language replies either in a directive form or as responses taken from text contained in the software help system. Thus far, most WOZ studies have shown that natural language help systems are only marginally better than a fully searchable text-based help system. Borenstein (1986) found that with respect to querying a database of information on command, natural language questions had little advantage over the user's direct use of the same database, whereas a face-to-face tutor was more than 2 1/2 times faster than either approach. A discourse analysis of dialogs using a WOZ technique revealed similar difficulties. Half of the time more than a single exchange was required to produce a successful user outcome, thus indicating the importance of question negotiation and a thorough understanding of the user's context (Pilkington, 1992).

In a similar study by Hill (1993) on providing help for statistical software, users were found to follow prescriptive advice efficiently and effectively only slightly more than half the time due primarily to presumptions on the part of the WOZ as to the user's prior knowledge about the system. Thus, for complex systems with many possible choices, the literal answering of questions is apparently not sufficient for effective assistance. Other non information-retrieval man–machine studies (Suchman, 1987) have also confirmed the essential problem of displaying information or help in the typically limited context that most automated systems currently provide. In many ways, these results illustrate Belkin's anomalous state of knowledge model of information seeking, wherein the seeker may not know enough to ask the right question of a mediator or intermediary system (see also van der Meij, 1990). One basic tactic that humans use when confronted with the need to clarify their information need is to obtain enough feedback to allow them to scan or browse.

Although early retrieval systems had almost no provision for this, it was quickly realized that the feedback provided by browsing was very important, and most modern databases have displays that provide for the rapid scanning of titles. For users seeking to elucidate their information needs, browsing helps to quickly determine the proper terminology to use in searching a database, as well as suggesting other possible topics of interest. As noted by Marchionini (1995), browsing has become more important with the migration to computerized information search, and he described and reviewed the research and designs that have been developed in numerous areas to support browsing, as well as more analytically oriented search strategies. Whatever its limitations, however, computer help has the advantage of being able to provide a safe environment in which people can pursue information seeking. Karabenick and Knapp (1988a) found, for example, that the privacy afforded by computer help resulted in twice as many requests for assistance compared to when help was available from another individual.

The Information Seeking Process (ISP)

Communications research has a long history of involvement with information, and much early work was concerned with its quantification (Shannon & Weaver, 1964). Such an approach fit with the prevailing concept of information as something contained in messages sent and received over channels. This mechanical model worked well at the microscopic level but was unable to effectively model everyday human action and speech. In particular, it was incapable of explaining human information needs. According to Dervin (1983), and consistent with other studies (e.g., Knapp & Karabenick, 1988b), most people are uninterested in, or are unwilling to use, formal information sources, preferring informal sources instead. Yet formal information channels presumably contain superior and more noise free information.

In contrast to the mechanical information or systems approach are the models that attempt to capture information seeking as a process best viewed from the user's perspective. Dervin's (1983) sense making model, outlined in Table 10.1 along with other models to be discussed, was one of the first to propose that information is a user construct. Examining information seeking in many different areas of society, including library use, she noted that information seekers spoke of their search in terms of their own situated need and of information as a gap or barrier that, when overcome, would allow them to proceed with their life. Seeking information was the process by which they made sense of some uncertainty or difficulty.

Another approach that embraces the concept of information as process rather than content is Taylor's question negotiation model (1968),

TABLE 10.1
Models of the Information Seeking Process

	Model			
Stage	Kuhlthau	Belkin	Dervin	Taylor
	ISP	ASK	Sense-making	Question Negotiation
Initial	Initiation	New problem, & situation, Questions, Experiential need	Situations	Visceral need
	Selection			Conscious need
	Exploration		Gaps	
Middle	Formulation	Defined problem, Well-understood situation, Commands, Informative need		Formal need
	Collection		Uses	Compromised need
Final	Presentation			

developed to explain why academic library users often have difficulty articulating their information needs. He described the four stages that users progress through and described the reference interview as a process of question negotiation between the seeker and the librarian. Building on both Taylor's and Dervin's models, Kuhlthau (1988) proposed a six-stage ISP that students presumably advance through as they work on gathering information for assigned term papers. For each of the stages, she obtained data on students' thoughts, feelings, and actions, using student journals, interviews, and surveys. As with other models, the initial stages include considerable feelings of uncertainty and anxiety, which decrease in the later stages of the search process.

Kuhlthau's ISP model, which, for the first time, explicitly included affective as well as cognitive components of the search process, provides an important link to help-seeking models. She notes that new students are reluctant to ask for help in using the library even though, as discussed by Keefer and Karabenick (1993), the need for help is built into the ISP at every stage. Furthermore, as noted by Keefer (1993) and Mellon (1986), anxiety can interfere with students' cognitive abilities as they attempt to negotiate the unfamiliar terrain of the library, which, in turn, will lead to an increased need for assistance. Clearly, in educational settings, there is a built-in need to provide students with a strong sense of the importance of help seeking as a mature strategy for learning and for libraries to create a variety of congenial settings for that purpose (Keefer & Karabenick, 1993; Valentine, 1993; Hatchard & Toy, 1986).

Following Kuhlthau, other researchers have begun to study the explicit role of affect in the search process. In a study documenting the questions posed by novice online searchers, affective questions outnumbered cognitive and sensori-motor questions two to one (Nahl & Tenopir, 1996). They discussed the implications of these results for the design of online database searching interfaces and help systems, noting that many of the affect-related questions involved seeking confirmation of the correctness of a proposed action. Such questions, generated by users' unfamiliarity with online searching, are already being built into some systems through dialog, asking users to confirm actions that may have unintended consequences. But there is much more that can be done once it is understood how the affective domain can impact the information and help seeking processes.

Help Seeking and the ISP

As suggested earlier, there is considerable overlap between models of the ISP and the help seeking process (HSP). The lack of knowledge, combined with the need to search for information, can engender the HSP, part of which includes the ISP. And portions of the ISP may involve the HSP. What bears examination for information providers are procedures that hinder learners' progression through the ISP. Some of the more troublesome aspects of the ISP and their relation to the HSP are examined. Both the HSP and the ISP start with an initial uncertainty or gap that seekers experience as a block. The fact that new students may have a naive view of the current knowledge terrain and the modern library's increasing reliance on electronic information retrieval resources does little to dispel this view. The apparent ease of use and simplicity of computer databases may mislead students into erroneous conclusions as to both the nature and quantity of information available on a topic. Anxiety over both too much and not enough information can occur, as well as the unsettled feeling students have with their first glimpse of knowing they don't know something (Belkin, 1980).

Once this uncertainty is acknowledged, an information seeker must attempt to understand the source of the problem, either as internally or externally generated. At this stage, it is very easy for students to rationalize failures to locate items as due to the library's poor collecting practices, rather than as a mismatch in searching terminology (see Ames, 1983). Blaming the system is a common way of dealing with the anxiety and frustration that is part and parcel of information seeking in libraries, and numerous techniques have been developed by reference librarians to help defuse angry or annoyed clients (Rubin, 1990). Similarly, information mediators may decide to actively seek out users in an effort to prevent this aspect of the HSP from happening (Mendelson, 1994).

Alternatively, users may respond to failure in the search process by internal (often stable) attributions. They understand that the difficulty may be due to their own lack of knowledge about the specific details of information finding tools. At this stage in the HSP, they may conclude that help would or would not be useful. In the latter case, after multiple failures in the search process, students may conclude they are too dumb to learn how to use the library. Social comparisons to others in the library who are perceived as more successful may reinforce this inference. Students with low self-esteem are particularly vulnerable to the many potential knowledge gaps that the library search process can generate (Karabenick & Knapp, 1991). Each failure then acts to reinforce further their explanation for failure and discourages them from asking for help. If they do ask for help, questions are often of a superficial nature rather than addressing the more complex aspects of their difficulties. Offers of assistance that focus on the help aspect of the situation may be rejected, because students have already determined they are inadequate. However, inquiries that are framed more narrowly in terms of the library's failure are less emotionally loaded and may be used to start a dialog.

At this stage of the HSP, students may decide that getting help with their searching would be an appropriate strategy, but for a variety of reasons they may still refrain from doing so. They may feel that asking for help is equivalent to admitting failure or losing a competition (Valentine, 1993). Here, again, if questions are asked they may be phrased to disguise a lack of knowledge of basic searching routines. Furthermore, mediators themselves can sometimes aggravate seekers' vulnerability to perceptions of loss of status by their own unconscious or overt judgments as to when it is appropriate to seek help and when it isn't.

As noted earlier, the public aspect of libraries can interfere with novice users' abilities to get the help they need. Students with low self-esteem, in particular, may feel embarrassed to ask for assistance in public. In response to this and other aspects of the reference process, many academic libraries have developed two-tiered systems for help seekers. The first tier, remaining in the public area, focuses on routine questions and is generally staffed by graduate students and paraprofessionals, whereas the second tier provides a more private consultation area where reference librarians can discuss clients' information needs in depth.

Studies indicate that users like both the privacy and the chance to explore their information search more fully (Massey-Burzio, 1992). On the other hand, at the public information desk, some students may feel even more threatened by having to ask their peers for help, and they may not always understand the two-tiered nature of the system.

Traditionally, libraries and other information intensive organizations have focused internally on the organizational and content aspects of their systems. Similarly, computerized information systems originally concentrated on enhancing the retrieval or system aspect of information databases. As mature technologies, however, both now are focusing more on user-centered research. Both human–computer interface designers and traditional information search mediators are concerned with creating user friendly environments (including CMC and the Web) that empower users in all aspects of the ISP (e.g., Westbrook & DeDecker, 1993). A knowledge of the help-seeking process is a powerful tool in the process of developing such systems.

In an empirical integration of the help-seeking and information-seeking processes, Bailey (1997) examined the perceived help required, that obtained, and from whom by undergratuates given assignments that required significant library research. Consistent with earlier studies (Karabenick & Knapp, 1988b), most students indicated needing some help with their assignments, which, as predicted by Kuhlthau, occurred either as students attempted to focus their topic or to find relevant information. More than half of the time, help was sought from informal sources (other students, relatives); about half the time, from professors; but most often, from library personnel. Of the students who did not ask for help from their professors, one-fourth were reluctant to admit their ignorance ("should have known how to do it myself"). Only 7% of the students cited this reason for not approaching library personnel. The large proportion of students who turned to informal sources is revealing and raises concerns about the quality of assistance received. As concluded by Bailey, if corroborated by subsequent research, especially more qualitative long-term (e.g., diary) studies, greater attention should be directed towards ensuring the effectiveness of informal as well as formal assistance.

IMPLICATIONS FOR INFORMATION
MEDIATION AND INSTRUCTION

What are the implications of help seeking in information- and communications-rich environments for the practice of information mediation and instruction? As discussed earlier, there has always been a tension between information delivery and literacy approaches to mediation in information seeking. From the information delivery perspective, the purpose of mediation is analogous to providing executive assistance. This view is based on the premise that the information seeker knows what is needed and that what is needed exists. The query may range from simple factual data to a fully annotated bibliography, but the mediator is asked to carry out an executive type of request. Early electronic retrieval systems based on this model of information retrieval initially seemed successful. Problems were recognized later, however, and, over time their design and development has become more user-centered, as library and communication studies began to focus on the user's context rather than the system's. By contrast, the user-centered perspective recognizes the ambiguities inherent in information seeking, viewing the process as a search for meaning (Kulthau, 1995) rather than a search for specific source material. According to this view, the information professional's role consists of providing information literacy that fosters subsequent independent functioning rather than specific facts.

Although the virtual library with its immense storage capacities, enhanced searching capabilities, and intelligent feedback abilities may reduce the need for direct executive-type human assistance, it is unlikely that the need for information literacy will disappear. Rather, the desire to browse and clarify, link and connect, and judge and recognize relevant information in the context of the ISP is likely to remain (Marchionini, 1995). It also seems that some guidance will continue to be required, given the frequent interface and other changes in the information access environment. Responding to such changes, one librarian (James-Catalano, 1996) noted that her colleagues were "used to collections revolving around a central core and forget that the whole point of the Internet is not to be centralized" (p. 28). Even in this new environment, she continued,

> librarians have skills essential to doing research, whether on the Internet or in a more traditional library. We know how to evaluate information and how to group resources into similar subjects. We can point researchers in the right direction and make intuitive leaps. Information seekers often don't know how to phrase their requests. Librarians help to narrow the query and provide a more focused collection of materials to read through. In a world where time is money, librarians can save both. (p. 28)

Evidence also suggests the continued importance of guidance, as well as help seeking, even with intelligently enhanced search systems. In one study (Stewart, 1993), coaches averaged more than 200 comments covering such issues as the appropriate database, topic focusing, synonym alternatives, and reviewing of search results during sessions designed to familiarize students with an online search system. In addition, results indicated that students valued help, especially assistance that involved explanations, asking an average of 31 questions during the session. Consistent with an instrumental, autonomous, self-regulatory perspective, they viewed the help they received as a step toward independence and thought that too much help was preferable to too little. Reference mediators, therefore, remain essential in the information search process.

Similarly, although not yet fully realized or equitably distributed (Doctor, 1992), increased access to information and CMC from classrooms and school media centers has important implications for help seeking in instructional contexts. Connectivity is transforming the stand-alone use of intelligent technologies into networked configurations where learners can profit by their immersion in larger social communities. In those communities, ideas can be more readily shared and questions posed and responded to (Brophy, 1996; Scardamalia & Bereiter, 1994; Scott, Cole, & Engel, 1992). And there are multiple zones of proximal development for strategic help seeking (Henderson & Cunningham, 1994; Murfin, 1994) to complement those proposed for stand-alone systems (e.g., Salomon, Globerson, & Guterman, 1989; Schofield, 1995). In contrast to many early computer applications (e.g., drill and practice), these developments are accelerating the trend toward learning environments that are more active, self-regulatory, mastery driven, project-oriented, and cooperative (e.g., Barr & Tagg, 1995; Maehr & Midgley, 1991; Schunk & Zimmerman, 1994; Slavin, 1996).

For reasons discussed earlier, CMC can play an especially important role by creating less threatening conditions that increase the likelihood that learners will seek assistance. Decreased concern over status, greater anonymity, and the easing of temporal demands can translate into more frequent help seeking by students from their instructors, from the broader Internet audience, and from their peers. Although characteristics of CMC environments are likely to facilitate help seeking in educational settings, that consequence is not inevitable (Spears & Lea, 1994). Therefore, as recommended in other settings, teachers are counseled to avoid CMC goal structures and incentive systems that undermine these advantages. In general, that would mean systematic attempts to instill mastery-oriented goals and cooperative incentive systems, to find effective strategies to obtain and share information, and to minimize a climate of punitive surveillance (such as that practiced in certain industry settings) or competition that could not only nullify the benefits of CMC but create an even less hospitable learning environment than without it.

As this review indicates, describing and understanding the effects of technology on help seeking and information seeking in the Information Age is a multidisciplinary effort, involving the fields of library and information services, social, cognitive, and educational psychology; and information science. An excellent example of information-centered multidisciplinarity can be found in Harris and Dewdney's (1994) work in the social services arena. By drawing on several fields, they were able to elucidate the help-seeking process of victims of spousal abuse by focusing on the barriers they faced in acquiring needed information. Many elements of the process are similar to, and illustrate the problems faced by, those in learning contexts.

It should be recognized that the present analysis is based on the current state of information systems and technology and foreseeable trends in an ever changing technological landscape. Although predictions about the future are perilous, for both teachers and information professionals, a better understanding of both help seeking and the information search process should provide a more complete perspective on how new technological systems are likely to affect learning environments (e.g., Karabenick, 1990; Keefer & Karabenick, 1993; Schofield, 1995) and how best to adapt their practices to those changes. What we can say for certain is that technology will continue to affect the conditions under which help seeking will take place. This would be especially important for post-secondary settings that are experiencing rapid growth in the number of distance learning programs and commercial electronic degrees (e.g., Noam, 1996; V. Phillips, 1996). For example, synchronous communication (e.g., video conferencing) is likely to become more ubiquitous. It would be somewhat ironic if such advances counter some of the advantages of asynchronous environments.

We also need to consider the way that learners construe the use of increasingly sophisticated information system and communications technologies. At present, most major software applications and information providers routinely include extensive help systems, ranging from online versions of print documentation to full-scale tutorials. These systems are in their infancy, and evidence suggests they can function only in certain limited domains (Richardson, 1995) or act as generic helping systems in library and information settings (see also Lauer, Peacock, & Graesser, 1992). In addition, despite the label help, these technologies are typically seen as self-help tools in much the same manner as print reference material. However, that could change as mature, automated decision aids and expert systems focus on meeting needs that include both specialized knowledge and heuristic assistive processes.

Important for the present discussion, these systems' cognitive capacities, natural language communication interfaces, and knowledge of a user's past behavior may render them more humanlike and social. As proto-social agents, the likelihood and type of help sought from artificial sources would seem to depend not only on their capacity to supply needed information but also on how learners are affected by the social meanings attached to their behavior, which are a function of person (e.g., self-efficacy) and situation characteristics (e.g., teacher promoted learning goals, task-ego relevance). As a consequence, it would be important that designers of artificial assistive systems (as well as teachers and information providers) understand the determinants of help seeking to avoid those social elements that may inhibit their effective use. It also suggests that we reconsider the definition of help seeking as obtaining assistance from social agents to include the possibility that these agents may be artificial. How persons view seeking and receiving help from artificial systems and respond to them would be an important direction for future research.

We close with an example of the impact of information systems and computer-mediated communication on help seeking, learning, and teaching, which arrived quite serendipitously when one of us received the following e-mail message as this chapter was in its final stages of preparation. It seemed altogether fitting to reprint it here.

To: psy_karabeni@online.emich.edu

From: Usuario de Biblioteca Kennedy@qro1.telmex.net.mx

My name is Elias Vera 4th grade student. I am doing a science project on how sound affect plants. I need a magazine for the project. Can you help me?

The request was forwarded to a reference librarian.

REFERENCES

Abels, E. G. (1996). The e-mail reference interview. *RQ, 35,* 345–358.

Ames, R. (1983). Help seeking and achievement orientation: Perspectives from attribution theory. In B. M. DePaulo, A. Nadler, & J. D. Fisher (Eds.), *New directions in helping: Vol. 2. Help seeking* (pp. 165–186). New York: Academic Press.

Anon. (1997). Internet/web growth exponential as usual. *Searcher, 5,* 54–55.

Bailey, E. C., Jr. (1997). *Help-seeking behavior in the research process of college students* [Electronic document]. Available on-line: http://www.ala.org/acrl/papertm/d35.html.

Barnes, S., & Greller, L. M. (1994). Computer-mediated communication in the organization. *Communication Education, 43,* 129–142.

Baron, N. S. (1984). Computer mediated communication as a force in language change. *Visible Language, 18,* 118–141.

Barr, R. B., & Tagg, J. (1995). From teaching to learning: A new paradigm for undergraduate education. *Change, Vol. 27* (November/December), 13–25.

Bateson, G. (1972). Form, substance, and difference. In *G. Bateson (Ed)., Steps to an ecology of the mind* (pp. 448–465). San Francisco: Chandler.

Baym, N. K. (1995). The emergence of community in computer-mediated communication. In S. G. Jones (Ed.), *Cybersociety: Computer-mediated communication and community* (pp. 138–163). Thousand Oaks, CA: Sage.

Belkin, N. J. (1980). Anomalous states of knowledge as a basis for information retrieval. *Canadian Journal of Information Science, 5*, 133–143.

Belkin, N. J., Marchetti, P. G., & Cool, C. (1993). BRAQUE: Design of an interface to support user interaction in information retrieval. *Information Processing and Management, 29*, 325–344.

Blackwell, C. A. (1995). A good installation guide increases user satisfaction and reduces support costs. *Journal of the Society for Technical Communication, 42*, 56–60.

Blandy, S. G., & Libutti, P. O. (1995). As the cursor blinks: Electronic scholarship and undergraduates in the library. *Library Trends, 44*, 279–305.

Bopp, R. E. (1995). *Reference and information services: An introduction.* Englewood, CO: Libraries Unlimited.

Borenstein, N. S. (1986). Is English a natural language? In K. Hopper & I. A. Newman (Eds.), *Foundations for human–computer communication* (pp. 60–72). Amsterdam: Elsevier.

Brillouin, L. (1963). *Science and Information Theory.* New York: Academic Press.

Brophy, S. (1996, April). *Computer support of inquiry skills in science: A pilot study.* Paper presented at the annual meeting of the American Educational Research Association, New York, NY.

Bunge, C. A. (1984). Interpersonal dimensions of the reference interview: An historical review of the literature. *Drexel Library Quarterly 20*, 4–23.

Bush, V. (1996). As we may think. *Interactions, 3*, 35–46 (Reprinted from *Atlantic Monthly*, July, 1945).

Bushallow-Wilbur, L., DeVinney, G., & Whitcomb, F. (1996). Electronic mail reference service: A study. *RQ, 35*, 359–371.

Chemical Abstracts Service. *CAS Statistical Summary, 1907-1996 [Electronic File].* (1997). Available on-line: http://www.cas.org/EO/CAS.summ.pdf.

Chesboro, J. W., & Bonsall, D. G. (1989). *Computer-mediated communication.* Tuscaloosa: University of Alabama Press.

Clark, M. S. (1983). Reactions to aid in communal and exchange relationships. In B. M. DePaulo, A. Nadler, & J. D. Fisher (Eds.), *New directions in helping: Vol. 2. Help seeking* (pp. 205–229). New York: Academic Press.

Cognition and Technology Group at Vanderbilt. (1996). Looking at technology in context: A framework for understanding technology and education research. In D. C. Berliner & R. C. Calfee (Eds.), *Handbook of educational psychology* (pp. 807–840). New York: Macmillan.

Cutting, J. E. (1987). Perception and information. *Annual Review of Psychology, 38*, 61–90.

Danet, B., & Rosenberg, L. (1992, October). *Smiley icons: Keyboard kitsch or new communication code?* Paper presented at the annual meeting of the American Folklore Society, Jacksonville, FL.

DePaulo, B. M., Nadler, A., & Fisher, J. D. (Eds.). (1983). *New directions in helping: Vol. 2. Help seeking.* New York: Academic Press.

Dervin, B. (1976). Strategies for dealing with human information needs: Information or communication? *Journal of Broadcasting, 20*, 324–333.

Dervin, B. (1983). Information as a user construct: The relevance of perceived information needs to synthesis and interpretation. In S. A. Ward and L. J. Reed (Eds.), *Knowledge Structure and Use* (pp. 155–183). Philadelphia, PA: Temple University Press.

Dervin, B. (1992). From the mind's eye of the user: The sense-making qualitative-quantitative methodology. In J. D. Glazier & R. R. Powell (Eds.), *Qualitative research in information management* (pp. 61–84). Englewood, CO: Libraries Unlimited.

Dervin, B., & Dewdney, P. (1986). Neutral questioning: A new approach to the reference interview. *RQ, 25*, 506–513.

Dervin, B., & Nilan, M. (1986). Information needs and uses. *Annual Review of Information Science and Technology, 21*, 3–33.

Dewdney, P., & Ross, C. S. (1994). *Flying a light aircraft: Reference service evaluation from a user's viewpoint. RQ 34*, 217–230.

Doctor, R. D. (1992). Social equity and information technologies: Moving toward information democracy. *Annual Review of Information Science and Technology, 27*, 42–55.

Doyle-Wilch, B., & Miller, M. I. (1992). Mediation and schemata theory in meaningful learning: The academic librarian's role in the educational process. *Reference Librarian, 37*, 121–127.

Durrance, J. (1989). Reference success: Does the 55 percent rule tell the whole story. *Library Journal, 114*, 31–36.

Dyson, L. S. (1992). Improving reference services: A Maryland training program brings positive results. *Public Libraries, 31*, 284–289.

Eadie, T. (1990). Immodest proposals: User instruction for students does not work. *Library Journal, 117*, 42–44.

Falk, H. (1997). World Wide Web search and retrieval. *The Electronic Library, 15*(1), 49–52.

Fisher, J. D., Nadler, A., & Whitcher-Alagna, S. (1982). Recipient reactions to aid. *Psychological Bulletin, 91*, 27–54.

Fiske, S. T. (1980). Attention and weight in person perception: The impact of negative and extreme behavior. *Journal of Personality and Social Psychology, 38*, 889–906.

Glaser, R., & Bassok, M. (1989). Learning theory and the study of instruction. *Annual Review of Psychology, 40*, 631–666.

Grannis, C. B. (1992). Book title output and average prices: 1991 preliminary figures. In *The Bowker Annual, (37th ed.)*. (pp. 502–507). New Providence, NJ: R. R. Bowker.

Green, S. S. (1876). Personal relations between librarians and readers. *Library Journal, 1*, 74–81.

Greenberg, M. S., & Westcott, D. R. (1983). Indebtedness as a mediator of reaction to aid. In J. D. Fisher, A. Nadler, & B. M. DePaulo (Eds.), *New directions in helping: Vol. 1. Recipient reactions to aid* (pp. 85–112). New York: Academic Press.

Gross, A. A., & McMullen, P. A. (1983). Models of the help seeking process. In B. M. DePaulo, A. Nadler, & J. D. Fisher (Eds.), *New directions in helping: Vol. 2. Help seeking* (pp. 45–70). New York: Academic Press.

Harasim, L. (1986, April). *Computer learning networks: Educational applications of computer conferencing.* Paper presented at the annual meeting of the American Educational Research Association, San Francisco, CA.

Harasim, L. (1993). Collaborating in cyberspace: Using computer conferencing as a group learning environment. *Interactive Environments, 3*, 119–130.

Harris, R. M., & Dewdney, P. (1994). *Barriers to information: How formal help systems fail battered women.* Westport, CT: Greenwood.

Hatchard, D. B., & Toy, P. (1986). Psychological barriers between library users and library staff. *Australian Academic and Research Libraries 17*, 63–69.

Henderson, R. W., & Cunningham, L. (1994). Creating interactive sociocultural environments for self-regulated learning. In D. H. Schunk & B. J. Zimmerman (Eds.), *Self-regulation of learning and performance: Issues and educational applications* (pp. 255–282). Hillsdale, NJ: Lawrence Erlbaum Associates.

Heydinger, R. B. (1978, October). *Computer conferencing: Its use as a pedagogical tool.* Paper presented at the meeting of the World Future Society Education Conference, Houston, TX.

Hill, W. C. (1993). A Wizard of Oz of advice giving and following. *Human Computer Interaction, 8*, 57–81.

Hiltz, S. R. (1990). Evaluating the virtual classroom. In L. M. Harrasim (Ed.), *Online education: Perspectives on a new environment* (pp. 133–183). New York: Praeger.

Hiltz, S. R., & Turoff, M. (1978). *The network nation: Human communication via computer*. Reading, MA: Addison-Wesley.

Hokkanen, D. B. (1981). U.S. book title output: A one hundred-year overview. In *Bowker annual of library & book trade information* (pp. 324–329). New York: R. R. Bowker.

James-Catalano, C. N. (1996). Look to the librarians. *Internet World*, (August), 28–30.

Jonassen, D. H. (Ed.). (1996). *Handbook of research for educational communications and technology*. New York: Macmillan.

Jones, S. G. (Ed.). (1995). *Cybersociety: Computer-mediated communication and community*. Thousand Oaks, CA: Sage.

Karabenick, S. A. (1987, April). *Computer conferencing: Its impact on academic help seeking*. Paper presented at the Symposium on Computer Conferencing and Allied Technologies, University of Guelph, Guelph, Ontario.

Karabenick, S. A. (1990). When students need help. *Journal of Professional Studies, 13*, 41–56.

Karabenick, S. A. (1996). Social influences on metacognition: Effects of co-learner questioning on comprehension monitoring. *Journal of Educational Psychology, 88*, 689–703.

Karabenick, S. A., & Knapp, J. R. (1988a). Effects of computer privacy on help-seeking. *Journal of Applied Social Psychology, 18*, 461–472.

Karabenick, S. A., & Knapp, J. R. (1988b). Help seeking and the need for academic assistance. *Journal of Educational Psychology, 80*, 406–408.

Karabenick, S. A., & Knapp, J. R. (1991). Relationship of academic help seeking to the use of learning strategies and other instrumental achievement in college students. *Journal of Educational Psychology, 83*, 221–230.

Karabenick, S. A., & Sharma, R. (1994). Perceived teacher support of student questioning in college classrooms: Its relation to student characteristics and role in the classroom questioning process. *Journal of Educational Psychology, 86*, 90–103.

Keefer, J. A. (1993). The hungry rats syndrome: Library anxiety, information literacy, and the academic reference process. *RQ, 32*, 333–339.

Keefer, J. A. (1994, October). *The hungry rats syndrome revisited: A holistic approach to the information seeking process*. Paper presented at the SUNY Buffalo Symposium on Information Anxiety, Buffalo, NY.

Keefer, J. A., & Karabenick, S. A. (1993). Help-seeking and the library reference/instruction setting: A social-psychological perspective. In L. Shirato (Ed.), *What is good instruction now?* (pp. 63–71). Ann Arbor, MI: Pierian Press.

Keisler, S., Siegel, J., & McGuire, T. W. (1984). Social psychological aspects of computer-mediated communication. *American Psychologist, 39*, 1123–1134.

Kerr, E. B., & Hiltz, S. R. (1982). *Computer-mediated communication systems: Status and evaluation*. New York: Academic Press.

Knapp, J. R., & Karabenick, S. A. (1988). Incidence of formal and informal academic help seeking in higher education. *Journal of College Student Development, 29*, 223–227.

Koutnik, C. (1997). The World Wide Web is here: Is the end of printed reference sources near? *RQ, 36*, 422–429.

Kuhlthau, C. C. (1988). Developing a model of the library search process. *RQ, 28*, 232–242.

Kuhlthau, C. C. (1993). *Seeking meaning: A process approach to library and information services*. Norwood, NJ: Ablex.

Ladner, S. J., & Tillman, H. N. (1993). Using the Internet for reference. *Online, 17*, 45–51.

Latané, B. (1981). The psychology of social impact. *American Psychologist, 36*, 343–356.

Latané, B., & Darley, J. M. (1970). *The unresponsive bystander: Why doesn't he help?* New York: Appleton-Century-Crofts.

Lauer, T. W., Peacock, E., & Graesser, A. C. (1992). *Questions and information systems*. Hillsdale, NJ: Lawrence Erlbaum Associates.

Lewis, D. W. (1995). Traditional reference is dead, now let's move on to the important questions. *Journal of Academic Librarianship, Vol. 21*(1), 10–14.

Maehr, M., & Midgley, C. (1991). Enhancing student motivation: A schoolwide approach. *Educational Psychologist, 26*, 399–428.

Mann, T. (1993). *Library research models.* New York: Oxford University Press.

Marchionini, G. (1995). *Information seeking in electronic environments.* Cambridge, England: Cambridge University Press.

Markman, E. M. (1985). Comprehension monitoring: Developmental and educational issues. In S. F. Chipman, J. W. Segal, & R. Glaser (Eds.), *Thinking and learning skills* (Vol. 2, pp. 275–291). Hillsdale, NJ: Lawrence Erlbaum Associates.

Massey-Burzio, V. (1992). Reference encounters of a different kind: A symposium. *Journal of Academic Librarianship 18*, 276–282.

McComb, M. (1994). Benefits of computer-mediated communication in college courses. *Communication Education, 43*, 159–170.

Mehrabian, A. (1981). *Silent messages: Implicit communication of emotions and attitudes* (2nd ed.). Belmont, CA: Wadsworth.

Mellon, C. A. (1986). Library anxiety: A grounded theory and its development. *College and Research Libraries 47*, 160–165.

Mellon, C. A. (1987). *Bibliographic instruction: The second generation.* Englewood, CO: Libraries Unlimited.

Mellon, C. A. (1988). Attitudes: The forgotten dimension in library instruction. *Library Journal, 114*, 137–139.

Mendelson, J. (1994). Human help at OPAC terminals is user friendly: A preliminary study. *RQ, 34*, 173–90.

Murfin, B. (1994). Constructing a MEZOPED (multiple electronic zone of proximal development). *Journal of Computers in Mathematics and Science Teaching, 13*, 405–413.

Myers, D. (1987). Anonymity is part of the magic: Individual manipulation of computer-mediated communication contexts. *Quantitative Sociology, 19*, 251–266.

Nadler, A., & Fisher, J. D. (1986). The role of threat to self-esteem and perceived control in recipient reactions to aid: Theory development and empirical validation. In L. Berkowitz (Ed.), *Advances in experimental social psychology*, (Vol. 19, pp. 81–123). New York: Academic Press.

Nahl, D. & Tenopir, C. (1996). Affective and cognitive searching behavior of novice end-users of a full text database. *Journal of the American Society for Information Science 47*, 276–286.

Neill, S. D. (1987). The dilemma of the subjective in information organization and retrieval. *Journal of Documentation 43*, 193–209.

Nelson, T. H. (1988). Managing immense storage. *Byte*, (January), Vol. 13(1), 225–237.

Nelson-Le Gall, S. (1981). Help-seeking: An understudied problem-solving skill in children. *Developmental Review, 1*, 224–246.

Nelson-Le Gall, S., & Gumerman, R. (1984). Children's perceptions of helpers and helper motivation. *Journal of Applied Developmental Psychology, 5*, 1–12.

Nelson-Le Gall, S., Gumerman, R., & Scott-Jones, D. (1983). Instrumental help seeking and everyday problem-solving. In B. M. DePaulo, A. Nadler, & J. D. Fisher (Eds.), *New directions in helping: Vol. 2. Help seeking* (pp. 265–283). New York: Academic Press.

Newman, R. S. (1994). Adaptive help seeking: A strategy of self-regulated learning. In D. H. Schunk & B. J. Zimmerman (Eds.), *Self-regulation of learning and performance: Issues and educational applications* (pp. 283–301). Hillsdale, NJ: Lawrence Erlbaum Associates.

Newman, R. S., & Goldin, L. (1990). Children's reluctance to seek help with schoolwork. *Journal of Educational Psychology, 82*, 92–100.

Noam, E. (1996). On the future of the university. *EDUCOM Review*, (July/August), 38–41.

Phillips, G. M., & Santoro, G. M. (1989). Teaching group communication via computer-mediated communication. *Communication Education, 38*, 151–161.

Phillips, V. (1996). Earn a masters, virtually. *Internet World*, (September), 67–70.

Pilkington, R. M. (1992). Question-answering for intelligent on-line help: The process of intelligent responding. *Cognitive Science, 14*, 455–89.

Plum, T. (1994). Academic libraries and the rituals of knowledge. *RQ, 33*, 496–508.

Rapoport, A. (1953). What is information? *ETC: A Review of General Semantics, 10*, 5–12.

Reid, E. M. (1991) *Electropolis: Communication and community on Internet relay chat* [Electronic document].Available on-line: http://www.irc.org.au/neutrino/electrop.html.

Rettig, J. (1992). Self determining information seekers. *RQ, 32*, 158–163.

Richardson, J. V. Jr., (1995). *Knowledge-based systems for general reference work.* New York: Academic Press:.

Romiszowski, A. J., & Mason, R. (1996). Computer-mediated communication. In D. H. Jonassen (Ed.), *Handbook of research for educational communications and technology* (pp. 438–456). New York: Macmillan.

Rosen, S. (1983). Perceived inadequacy and help-seeking. In B. M. DePaulo, A. Nadler, & J. D. Fisher (Eds.), *New directions in helping: Vol. 2. Help seeking* (pp. 73–107). New York: Academic Press.

Rothstein, S. (1961). Reference service: The new dimension in librarianship. *College and Research Libraries, 22*, 11–18.

Rubin, R. J. (1990). Anger in the library: Defusing angry patrons at the reference desk (and elsewhere). *Reference Librarian, 31*, 39–51.

Salomon, G., Globerson, T., & Guterman, E. (1989). The computer as a zone of proximal development: Internalizing reading-related metacognitions from a reading partner. *Journal of Educational Psychology, 81*, 620–627.

Salton, G. (1985). Advanced feedback methods in information retrieval. *Journal of the American Society for Information Science, 36*, 200–210.

Scardamalia, M., & Bereiter, C. (1994). Computer support for knowledge-building communities. *Journal of the Learning Sciences, 3*, 265–283.

Schement, J. R., & Curtis, T. (1995). *Tendencies and tensions of the information age.* New Brunswick, NJ: Transaction Publishers.

Schofield, J. W. (1995). *Computers and classroom culture.* New York: Cambridge University Press.

Schunk, D. H., & Zimmerman, B. J. (1994). *Self-regulation of learning and performance: Issues and educational applications.* Hillsdale, NJ: Lawrence Erlbaum Associates.

Scott, T., Cole, M., & Engel, M. (1992). Computers and education: A cultural constructivist perspective. In G. Grant (Ed.), *Review of research in education* (Vol. 18, pp. 191–251). Washington, DC: American Educational Research Association.

Shannon, C. E., & Weaver, W. (1964). *The mathematical theory of communication.* Urbana: University of Illinois Press.

Shapiro, E. G. (1983). Embarrassment and help-seeking. In B. M. DePaulo, A. Nadler, & J. D. Fisher (Eds.), *New directions in helping: Vol. 2. Help-seeking* (pp. 143–163). New York: Academic Press.

Simpson, R., Renear, A., Mylonas, E., & van Dam, A. (1996). Fifty (50) years after "As We May Think": The Brown/MIT Vannevar Bush symposium. *Interactions (IEEE), 3*, 47–51.

Slavin, R. E. (1996). Research on cooperative learning and achievement: What we know, what we need to know. *Contemporary Educational Psychology, 21*, 43–69.

Spacapan, S., & Oskamp, S. (1992). *Helping and being helped: Naturalistic studies.* Newbury Park, CA: Sage.

Spears, R., & Lea, M. (1994). Panacea or panopticon?: The hidden power in computer-mediated communication. *Communication Research, 21*, 427–459.

Stewart, L. (1993). Helping students during on-line searches: An evaluation. *Journal of Academic Librarianship, 18*, 347–351.

Suchman, L. A. (1987). *Plans and situated actions: The problem of human–machine communication.* Cambridge, England: Cambridge University Press.

Sugar, W. (1995). User centered perspective of information retrieval research and analysis methods. *Annual Review of Information Science and Technology, 30,* 77–109.

Swanson, D. R. (1986). Subjective versus objective relevance in bibliographic retrieval systems. *Library Quarterly, 56,* 389–398.

Swets, J. A. (1969). Effectiveness of information retrieval methods. *American Documentation, 20,* 72–89.

Swigger, K. M., & Hartness, K. (1996). Cooperation and on-line searching via a computer-supported cooperative problem solving enviornment. *Journal of the American Society for Information Science, 47,* 370–379.

Taylor, R. S. (1968). Question-negotiation and information seeking in libraries. *College and Research Libraries, 29,* 178–94.

Valentine, B. (1993). Undergraduate research behavior: Using focus groups to generate theory. *Journal of Academic Librarianship 19,* 300–304.

van der Meij, H. (1986). *Questioning: A study on the questioning behavior of elementary school children.* The Hague, The Netherlands: Stichting voor Onderzoek van her Onderwijs.

van der Meij, H. (1990). Question asking: To know that you do not know is not enough. *Journal of Educational Psychology, 82,* 505–512.

Walther, J. B., & Burgoon, J. K. (1992). Relational communication in computer-mediated interaction. *Human Communication, 19,* 50–88.

Weiner, B. (1985). An attributional theory of achievement motivation and emotion. *Psychological Review, 92,* 548–573.

Welsch, L. A. (1982). Using electronic mail as a teaching tool. *Communications of the ACM, 23,* 105–108.

Westbrook, L. & DeDecker, S. (1993). Supporting user needs and skills to minimize library anxiety: Considerations for academic libraries. *Reference Librarian, 40,* 43–50.

White, H. S. (1992). The reference librarian as information intermediary: The correct approach is the one that today's client needs today. *Reference Librarian, 37,* 23–35.

Wicken, J. S. (1987). *Evolution, thermodynamics, and information.* New York: Oxford University Press.

Williams, E. (1977). Experimental comparisons of face-to-face and mediated communication: A review. *Psychological Bulletin, 84,* 963–976.

Young, P. (1987). *The nature of information.* New York: Praeger.

Author Index

Subject Index

A

Ability, beliefs on, 40, 43–45, 54–55
  socialization of, 46
Ability-focused context, 101
Ability grouping, and goal orientation, 130
Ability level, and help seeking, 123–124
  in Japan, 163
Achievement motivation. *See* Goal orientation
Action control theory, help seeking in, 2
Adaptive help seeking, 3–4, 13–37.
      See also Autonomous help seeking; Instrumental help seeking; Negotiating help seeking
  cognitive strategy perspective on, 14–17
  sequence in, 14–15
  social interaction and, 16–31
  traditional view of, 13–14
Affective features, of questioning, 188–190
African-American students
  motivation among, 50
  socialization of, 49–50
  and help seeking, 49–54
Age. *See* School level
Anonymity, in CMC, 225–226
  and help seeking, 236
Answer, 177, 210
  evaluation of, 209
    by teacher, 211

Answering, 177, 208–212
Anxious-ambivalent style, 71–72
Aristotle, 178, 187
Asian cultures. *See also* Japanese education
  goal orientation in, 47–48
Asking, 172–173, 176–177. *See also* Questioning
Assignments, as instructional moments, 180, 182
Attachment theory, 19, 71–73
Attitudes, questioning and, 190
Attributions
  and help seeking, 84–86
  and information seeking process, 238–239
Authority, and goal orientation, 129–130
Autonomous help seeking, 5, 61–93.
      See also Adaptive help seeking; Instrumental help seeking; Negotiating help seeking
  attributions and, 86
  cognitive processes and, 78–86
  definition of, 63–64
  dependent personality and, 70
  and helper selection, 66
  promotion of, 76–78
Autonomy, in Japanese education, 144
Avoidance
  of help seeking. *See* Help seeking, avoidance of
  of questioning, motives for, 154*t*–155*t*, 156–160
Avoidant style, 71–72